Essential Articles 15

Complete Issues

articles · opinions · statistics · contacts

Get instant online access to this book by logging on to:
www.completeissues.co.uk

Username: _____

Password: _____

See page 2 for details of **Complete Issues** ⟶

The book

The articles you will find in this volume have been chosen because they are relevant, interesting and well written. They include:

- **thought-provoking discussion pieces**
- **opposing viewpoints**
- **personal accounts**
- **informed insights**

We looked at thousands of articles from a wide variety of newspapers, magazines and online journals. You'll find material from little known sources as well as from well respected national media – all selected with the needs of UK users firmly in mind.

The Essential Articles book is an attractive item on any library shelf. Its bright, magazine-style format entices readers to browse and enjoy while learning about current issues and dilemmas, making even difficult issues approachable.

Online - Complete Issues

Essential Articles also comes to you online. Using the Complete Issues website **www.completeissues.co.uk** you can view individual pages on screen, download, print, use on whiteboards, edit to suit your needs. It makes the book even more flexible and useful.

As well as being able to access all the articles in both PDF and editable formats, there are additional references and links. Your purchase of the book entitles you to use this on one computer. You can find your access codes on your covering letter or by contacting us. You can also buy an unlimited site licence to make the service and the material available to **all** students and staff at **all** times, even from home.

We have included a checklist poster of major topics or key words in the current Essential Articles and Fact File for you to display. You can record your log-in details on this and on the front page of this book to make access to the online service quick and easy.

Our major publications, Essential Articles, Fact File and Key Organisations, work beautifully together in the Complete Issues Website – a complete source of opinions, facts, figures and further research.

Users can search and browse individual books or all books together, past and present editions. You can instantly produce a package of relevant articles statistics and relevant websites just by entering a topic.

If you do not yet have the other publications in the Complete Issues Package you can sample the service and upgrade here: **www.completeissues.co.uk**

Unique features

UP-TO-DATE: A new edition is published every year.

RELEVANT: To the UK and its education system and to advanced learners of English.

ORGANISED: Articles are grouped by theme, cross referenced, indexed and linked on the page to closely related pieces and statistics. Our online searches will find even more!

STIMULATING: Each article has an accompanying group of questions to raise awareness of the issues.

ATTRACTIVE: Full colour and eye-catching with appealingly designed pages and great photos.

EASY TO USE: You don't have to worry about copyright issues as we've cleared these. Because you have both the book and online access you can use Essential Articles in different ways with different groups and in different locations. You can simultaneously use it in the library, in the classroom and at home.

FLEXIBLE: You can make paper copies, use a whiteboard or a computer. Different groups or individuals can be using different parts of the book at the same time. Editable text makes it even more adaptable.

BOOSTS LIBRARY USE: The posters provided free with each volume list the topics in Essential Articles and its sister publication Fact File and make it very easy to find the issues you are looking for. You can put one of your free posters in the library/LRC and one elsewhere – in the staff room, in a corridor, in a subject area. If you would like more copies of the poster just let us know.

SAFE: Although we have included controversial, hard-hitting articles and tackled difficult subjects, you can be confident that students are not going to encounter inappropriate material that an internet search might generate.

ADDITIONAL BENEFITS: Subscribers to Essential Articles and Fact File are entitled to 10% discount on all our other products. They also receive occasional free posters to help promote library use and reading in general.

Contents

> 66 The status, and perhaps age and skin colour, of our "hidden" drug users means they are not a target – unlike, say black, inner-city youth 99
> Page 36

Photo: YouTube

> 66 Do you realise what this looks like, given your appearance? asked the officer... 99
> Page 16

Photo: Featureflash / Shutterstock.com

Contents

66 I've become used to people wondering who my parents are when I'm with them 99
Page 58

66 Many of the most highly polluting countries are resisting taking further action, until after 2020 99
Page 54

Photo: Featureflash / Shutterstock.com

66 If a rich man wants to help the poor, he should pay his taxes, not dole out money at a whim 99
Page 78

IT'S A DRESS NOT A YES

Photo: Padmayogini / Shutterstock.com

Contents

> *Is power over food really a power or is it a weakness? You thought you were in control, but look at you now*
> Page 110

> *Doctors routinely help people facing death, such as my Gran, to end their own lives. That this is rarely publicly acknowledged gives a false impression*
> Page 122

Contents

66 Take away the cameras and you have a pack of men chasing a woman 99 Page 130

66 These men see a vulnerability, a need for affection and they meet it. They pretend to care in order to control and abuse 99 Page 152

Contents

Photo: Featureflash / Shutterstock.com

❝ At his lowest ebb, self-medicated on alcohol, there was a haunted look in Flintoff's eyes
page 169 ❞

Photo: SCOTT HEPPELL/AP/Press Association Image

❝ The fact that in a democratic country a religious extremist is able to frighten people into calling off a meeting is shocking ❞
page 158

Photo: Zzvet / Shutterstock.com

> 66 It would be impossible for Australians not to have an uneasy relationship with race, with national identity and with immigration 99
> page 187

Photo: Regien Paassen / Shutterstock.com

Britain & its citizens

Race, resentment and the white working classes

The Government worries about 'the squeezed middle', but less so about 'the pinched bottom'

Christine Patterson

SOME ISSUES:

Do you think that resentment exists between people of different nationalities?

Do you think these resentments get worse at times of poverty and financial struggle?

Why?

See also:
"My tram experience" is shocking – but should it be cause for arrest? p14

www.completeissues.co.uk

If this is entertainment, count me out. If this shaky footage, shot on a smartphone, and posted, among the kittens on a slide, and dogs chasing deer, and Russian newscasters making unexpected gestures, on YouTube, and watched, within 24 hours, by more than two million people, is someone's idea of a really good laugh, then I'm not at all sure what isn't.

The footage is of a woman on a tram. She's clutching a blonde boy on her lap. And what she's doing isn't singing, or dancing, or saying something charming, something which might give you a nice little pick-me-up if you happened

The woman told her fellow passengers 'get back to where you came from', which must have surprised all the ones who, in getting on the tram to Wimbledon, were trying to do just that

to find your mouse clicking away from the sales figures you were meant to be collating, but shouting. "What has this country come to?" she screams, at a carriage full of surprised-looking people. "With loads of black people and a load of fucking Polish... None of you," she adds, "are fucking English."

The woman, who actually tells her fellow passengers to "get back to where you came from", which must have surprised all the ones who, in getting on the tram to Wimbledon, were trying to do just that, has now been arrested for making racist comments. But her outburst hit the news on a day when a report suggested that "white working-class communities" are fed up.

Large sections of the white working classes, according to a new report from the Rowntree Foundation, feel that, when it comes to things like the allocation of social housing, they are "last in line". They think that "political correctness" leads to "beneficial treatment" of people who aren't white. They think minority groups get "preferential support and funding", for community organisations they can't access. They think, in other words, that they don't "get a fair deal".

The report, which is written by an academic, which you can certainly tell by the language, "discusses white working-class perspectives on community cohesion". The people interviewed were, apparently, not too clear what "community cohesion" was. It's not clear whether they were quizzed on "stakeholders", "key policy drivers" or "grassroots intervention", and also found wanting. But it is clear that their voices, from social economic groups that policy

makers say are "in the top 20 per cent of the Index of Multiple Deprivation", aren't often heard, not even in academic studies like this. "Studies of the white working-class", says its author, perhaps a bit unfortunately, "have paled into insignificance compared to those on minority groups."

And so, it seems, have certain strands of community funding. Alongside the millions poured into "initiatives" to tackle Muslim extremism in the wake of 9/11, and 7/7, and the funding for Asian women's centres, and mosques, and council-funded festivals (often for things like Diwali and Eid, but rarely for things like Advent, or Easter) the report mentions only little dribbles of public funds for community projects likely to be used by local residents who were white. It mentions, for example, £80,000 given to Camden Council for a project called "Connecting Communities". This, according to the author, was "primarily used to undertake outreach work with white working-class communities such as talking to white men in local pubs".

It isn't naughty to claim benefits you've been entitled to, and it isn't racist to worry about immigration, though it is racist to yell abuse at people that refers to the colour of their skin.

If I were on my fourth pint of Foster's in The Dog and Duck, I'm not sure how pleased I'd be to be approached by someone with a clipboard. I think I might want to ask whether they'd like their Chilean merlot in the revamped (if now a little pricey) Rose and Crown to be interrupted by someone asking them about their "community". And about how well they got on with their Bangladeshi neighbours, and their Somali neighbours, and their West African neighbours. And if they wanted me to organise a festival so that they could meet them.

I think I might be tempted to say that I was perfectly happy to talk to Bangladeshis, and Somalis, and West Africans, if they spoke English, and wanted to talk to me. And that I didn't mind my child being one of only a handful in the school who were white, but that it was a bit weird to grow up in an area where most of the people were like you, and suddenly find that most of them followed a different religion, and had different values, and spoke a different language. But I think I'd say that what I was really worried about was money, and homes, and jobs.

The people in the report who feel "let down" by the authorities are right. They have been "let down" by people who encouraged immigration, and who changed the allocation of social housing from one that gave priority to local people to one that gave priority to need. No one set out to make their lives more difficult, but they did. It isn't middle-class "communities" that are disrupted by mass immigration. It isn't their homes, and their low-wage labour, that are under threat. Middle-class people, in middle-class jobs, don't have to compete with people who have saved for years to cross a continent, and who are determined to make their effort pay.

The people in the report have also been let down by people who decided to make it a more sensible idea, in economic terms, not to work than to work. If you're legally entitled to a bigger income if you don't work than you'd get if you did, and claim the benefits that will give you that bigger income, that doesn't make you stupid, it makes you clever. It may not be a great idea in all kinds of other ways, not least the cost to the taxpayer, but it seems a bit unfair to blame people for doing what the Government encouraged them to do.

This Government, of course, is different. It has decided that it isn't fair, or a good idea, or affordable, to keep paying so many people not to work. It has decided that it isn't fair that people who don't work sometimes live in bigger houses than people who do. It has decided to change the benefits system to make sure they can't any more. It has talked about these people as if they were "scroungers". It has sometimes talked about these people as if they were scum.

It isn't fair that people who don't work sometimes have more money, and bigger houses, than people who do. It also isn't fair that when, due to changes in the welfare system, they're forced back into the jobs market, they're competing against a workforce who will always have an extra edge. And in a world where that flow of workers with the extra edge continues, in spite of the Government's rhetoric, to grow.

This Government is very worried about the "squeezed middle". It seems a bit less worried about what we might call, if it didn't sound so rude, the "pinched bottom". It seems to like carrots for the middle, and sticks for the bottom. It seems to think that it has been naughty, and must be punished.

It isn't naughty to claim benefits you've been entitled to, and it isn't racist to worry about immigration, though it is racist to yell abuse at people that refers to the colour of their skin. But if the white working classes are feeling worried about the future, maybe that's because it's looking extremely grim.

The Independent, 30 November 2011

"MY TRAM EXPERIENCE" IS SHOCKING – BUT SHOULD IT BE CAUSE FOR ARREST?

The views of the woman on the Croydon tram may be repugnant, but laws that criminalise hate speech usually backfire
Sunny Hundal

SOME ISSUES:

Do you think free speech is important?

Are there any occasions when freedom of speech should be taken away?

What is the difference between free speech and abusive language?

Should abusive language be outlawed?

See also:
Race, resentment and the white working classes, p11
The Stephen Lawrence Legacy, p136

www.completeissues.co.uk

The video of the woman ranting against black and Polish people ("What has this country come to? ... with loads of black people and load of fucking Polish") on the Croydon to Wimbledon tram has caused quite a stir, generating quite a storm on social media and swiftly leading to an arrest. But I have to say it strikes me as one of the less shocking videos I've seen in my lifetime. Compared to footage of guys filming themselves attacking "pakis" on the tube, the storm over this video (which contains explicit comments some viewers may find offensive) looks no worse than an argument over whether X Factor tweeters should be publicly flogged or not.

In fact, it reminded me a little of the brilliant sketch by Stewart Lee where his nan says: "It's political correctness gawn mad Stew". I can imagine the woman leaving the tram complaining that she couldn't even talk about immigration in her own country.

Still, I was indignant about the incident until I saw the backlash on Twitter. Piers Morgan was calling for the woman to be deported, some asked for her to be locked up, while others said her child should be taken away. And those are only the printable responses.

I hate to write an article defending such a woman but I think calling for her to be arrested and then prosecuted is over the top. I don't think such behaviour is acceptable or have a problem with condemning it. My issue is that calling for the law to get involved is about the worst way to deal with such incidents. And there are several reasons for this.

First, the law has little impact. The Race Relations Act made it illegal for organisations to discriminate but you can count the number of successful prosecutions on your fingers. It works much better in tightly defined instances of outright discrimination rather than hate speech.

What actually changed attitudes against racism was a shift in popular culture pushed by brave people. The people who joined together in solidarity against skinheads (at Cable Street in the 30s and Southall in the 80s) changed attitudes. Rock Against

Racism shifted popular attitudes. Love Music Hate Racism changed attitudes. The Anti-Nazi League did. But trying to push for better social attitudes through the law is a futile task. Popular condemnation and viral piss-takes work far better instead.

Second, you may argue she can already be prosecuted under the Public Order Act for a "breach of the peace" but the law is currently an overbearing ass. It allows the police to make an arrest if someone feels "insulted". The same laws allow them to detain political activists and make arbitrary arrests.

In short, the very law that some people are cheering here can easily be used against them. Do you really want to give police the power to arrest people simply for having an argument?

Third, laws that criminalise hate speech almost always backfire on minorities themselves. A few years ago British Muslim organisations campaigned vigorously for a law against religious hatred, hoping it would stop the BNP from using them as electoral fodder. Labour passed the law but it did little to stop the BNP. Instead, most of the people prosecuted under the law were – you guessed it – Muslims.

There are other examples too. When Sikh playwright Gurpreet Bhatti was criticised by Sikh activists for her play Behzti in Birmingham in 2005, one Sikh group said they were planning to get her charged with racial hatred against Sikhs.

I have no problems with laws against outright discrimination. But when crafted against inciting hatred

The people who joined together in solidarity changed attitudes – Rock Against Racism, Love Music Hate Racism, The Anti-Nazi League did – but trying to push for better social attitudes through the law is a futile task

or "breaching the peace" – they almost always work against minorities and other vulnerable people rather than for them.

And let's be honest, the woman was just sitting there with a child on her lap. She offended people but posed no threat and didn't harm anyone (the person behind her had to be calmed down or it could have turned a lot uglier). It isn't the same as a group of drunken blokes swearing in a train carriage and to criminalise simply being offensive or swearing in public would have half of Britain in jail.

My fourth argument is simply this: I would rather a world where such incidents didn't exists but the world will never

be perfect. I would much prefer such racism to be open and visible because there are still far too many Westminster commentators who think racism is a thing of the past.

There are still far too many reporters on tabloids who think their biased reporting doesn't have an impact. It does, and this woman is a product of the opinions of the rightwing press.

You may ask how I would have responded if I was there. Like the other woman, I would say what I've said for years – I'm English whether racists like it or not. Then I'd go back to pretending to playing games on my phone like most people in that carriage.

The Guardian, 29 November 2011
© Guardian News & Media Ltd 2011

Laws that criminalise hate speech almost always backfire on minorities themselves

"I was mistaken for a suicide bomber..."

..."I noticed a police officer on the other side of the street, crouching down and partly obscured by a tree... He slowly approached me, and I realised he had a gun'"

Goudarz Karimi

I'd been doing the same training walk for several weeks, twice a day, six days a week, on a quiet residential street near where I live in Oxford. I'd chosen it because it had a steep hill, perfect for a good workout and, as always, I was wearing my weighted exercise vest. Black and rectangular, it straps across your chest with pockets for the weights to build muscle. Because I'm used to being around other people with the same interest, it never occurred to me that it might look odd.

In retrospect, I'd had the occasional double take, but my training times are so regular I'd pass the same people every day. Normally I walk up and down the street five times, which takes about an hour. That afternoon I'd been up and down twice, and was just starting down the hill again when I noticed a police officer on the other side of the street, crouching down and partly obscured by a tree. He wasn't dressed in the usual uniform — instead of a standard jacket, he was wearing a bulky vest. This struck me as unusual, but I didn't loiter. As I continued, though, I realised he was pointing at me, and appeared to be saying something.

I had my headphones on — I'm a PhD student at University College, and usually listen to a lecture while training. It was only when I removed them I heard him shouting, "Stop! Stop! Put your hands up in the air!" I couldn't fathom what the problem was but I did as he said, automatically taking one or two steps forward as I raised my hands. "Don't move, don't move!" the officer shouted. He slowly approached me, and I realised he had a gun.

As he drew close, the policeman started examining my vest, and tried to take it off — he couldn't work out how, so I had to lower my arms to help him. Another armed policeman appeared, and started to examine the vest on the ground as his colleague questioned me.

"What are you doing here?" he asked, in a severe tone. "What is this vest?" As I explained my training routine, the other policeman searched me, apparently for hidden weapons. "Do

SOME ISSUES:

Do you think the police were justified to have done what they did?

Would the sight of this man running with his weight pack alarm you?

How would you feel if it were you who were stopped?

Why do you think such suspicion exists?

See also:
'I was questioned over my harmless snapshot'
Essential Articles 13, p156

www.completeissues.co.uk

Photo © INS News

I'd never seen a bomb suit, but I was certain they wouldn't be emblazoned with a "Maxivest" logo.

you realise what this looks like, given your appearance?" asked the officer. "We had a call from someone saying they'd seen a suspicious man. We were told he might be wearing a bomb suit."

This seemed pretty odd to me — I'd never seen a bomb suit, but I was certain they wouldn't be emblazoned with a "Maxivest" logo. I was more surprised by what happened next, though. "We need to do a background check on you," said the policeman. He told me that under the Terrorism Act, they were entitled to take me to the station for further questioning, and that they needed my details to ensure I wasn't already known by intelligence agencies.

Now my bemusement turned to indignation. We'd established I was a student, that the vest was a piece of training equipment and that I was no terrorist — that even if I'd been attempting some kind of prank, I'd have been making a poor job of it. It was only then I realised the possible significance of his earlier remark — "...someone of your appearance..." Although I grew up in the Netherlands, my parents are Iranian — did he mean my Middle Eastern looks made me more suspicious? Never feeling restricted in my freedom of movement before, it was a possibility that genuinely hadn't occurred to me.

After about 20 minutes, I was allowed to go on my way. But I hadn't finished my training, so at the end of the street I turned and walked back

"Do you realise what this looks like, given your appearance?" asked the officer.

again, passing the police car with the officer in it. "You're still walking?" he asked. "Why don't you call it a day?" I explained I wanted to continue with my training, but he ordered me to take off my vest. I pointed out it wouldn't be feasible for me to walk with it in my hands — it weighs 30kg — but he insisted, sharply. Not wishing to provoke him, I agreed to cover the vest with my jacket. I walked away looking ridiculously bulky, and probably more suspicious than I would have otherwise.

I still train twice a day, on the same street, and don't make any attempt to cover up the vest. I'd have appreciated the opportunity to meet with whoever raised the alarm, to explain what I was really doing. It seems everyone I pass knows who I am now, but rather than react with fear and suspicion, people wave and smile.

The Guardian, 11 November 2011
© Guardian News & Media Ltd 2011

Modernising the monarchy? Hardly

In our storybook world, royalty open hospitals with their shiny-haired brides, rather than stomping in muddy wellingtons over democracy.

Laurie Penny

Photo: Featureflash / Shutterstock.com

SOME ISSUES:

What is the purpose of the monarchy?

Can any nation that has a monarchy really be a democracy?

Does having a royal family affect our sense of 'Britishness'?

See also:
Let's hear it for mad monarchy,
Essential Articles 12, p38

www.completeissues.co.uk

The true purpose of the British monarchy, as the late Douglas Adams might have put it, is not to wield power, but to distract attention away from it. We can be curiously coy about the way privilege works in this country: consider, if you will, the horrified reaction to the news that Prince Charles has been allowed to dabble in the affairs of government.

Parliamentary loopholes have meant that the unelected heir to the throne has been granted power of veto over matters that affect the private interests of the Duchy of Cornwall, including road safety, planning and environmental policy. We are shocked by the reminder that the royal family is more than a tinselly relic to bring in the tourists: it actually has political influence and some of its members are uncouth enough to use it.

While all of this has been going on, there has barely been a day when the young

In Britain, we are comfortable with the trappings of power as long as they are phrased in the manner of a fairy tale.

Duke and Duchess of Cornwall have been absent from the front pages. It's as if the loveliness of the Duchess, wafting in designer gowns around various official engagements with her subtly balding beau and the international media in tow, were enough to distract the world from a nation creaking with corruption and civic breakdown.

In Britain, we are comfortable with the trappings of power as long as they are phrased in the manner of a fairy tale. At the end of last month, changes to the royal succession were made, to much fanfare, to ensure that female firstborn will be able to inherit the throne. "Put simply, if the Duke and Duchess of Cambridge were to have a little girl, that girl would one day be our queen," said David Cameron, with all the political gravitas of an episode of Jackanory. This "modernisation", which, like most recently hailed feminist triumphs, makes cosmetic alterations to the existing system while ensuring that nothing of relevance changes, is as clear a message as any that the House of Windsor intends to squat in its position of privilege for many generations to come.

Giving it welly

The real story of power and privilege in Britain is far murkier than the Disney-princess version peddled by the tabloids. In this storybook world, royalty open hospitals with their shiny-haired brides, rather than stomping in muddy, expensive wellingtons over the democratic process.

It is worth noting, in these circumstances, that the word "privilege" actually means "private law". It means that wealthy or aristocratic influences are allowed to bend the rules to suit their own interests - and this goes on all the time behind the closed doors of Whitehall, not just with the Windsors. Documents leaked to Private Eye showed that the permanent secretary to HM Revenue and Customs personally shook hands on a deal that let off the investment bank Goldman Sachs £10m in unpaid interest on a failed tax-avoidance scheme.

The Ministry of Defence is only just staggering away from a scandal in which it emerged, among other things, that a lobbyist who had paid a reported £20,000 in expenses to Liam Fox's aide was granted face time with the arms sales minister. Time and again, private law trumps the public interest, yet we allow ourselves to be distracted by a fairy tale of functioning democracy.

This is no time for sugarplum politics. Behind every modern fairy tale is an ancient fable of thuggery, hierarchy and blood, and the story of modern Britain is no different.

*New Statesman,
6 November 2011*

> It's as if the loveliness of the Duchess, wafting in designer gowns around various official engagements with her subtly balding beau and the international media in tow, were enough to distract the world from a nation creaking with corruption and civic breakdown.

> It is worth noting, in these circumstances, that the word "privilege" actually means "private law". It means that wealthy or aristocratic influences are allowed to bend the rules to suit their own interests.

> Time and again, private law trumps the public interest, yet we allow ourselves to be distracted by a fairy tale of functioning democracy.

There's no merit or honour in glorifying imperial arrogance

Fionola Meredith

There are times when Britain seems like a foreign country to me, an alien place with alien customs. And never more so than at this time of year, when the New Year's Honours list is due to be announced.

Much fuss will be made of the small number of deserving ordinary people included in the line-up: local heroes, charity workers and community volunteers who have slaved away for years without expectation of recognition or reward.

An even greater fuss will be made of the sports people and celebrities who are honoured, not for years of selfless drudgery, but for crowd-pleasing athletic prowess, or simply for being a cuddly old national treasure.

Yet none of this populist sweet-smelling lather should distract us from the fact that the British honours system stinks. It is a grandiose relic of Empire and any cursory examination of the history books shows that this is not something to be proud of.

If you agree to be known as a Commander of the most Excellent Order of the British Empire (CBE), you're getting more than a medal pinned to your chest.

That title may sound like no more than a bland anachronism now, as quaint as the Order of the Thistle or the Garter, but by accepting it you're commemorating — if not implicitly endorsing — the grim and bloody exploitation of millions of people around the world who were colonised and ruled against their will.

And that's a psychic burden I wouldn't want to carry. Almost as offensive as the language and symbolism of Empire, to my mind, is the class-bound, intrinsically hierarchical nature of the system.

Again, don't be distracted by awards given out to unsung heroes. Delighted as these ordinary hard-working people may be to receive them, it's just cynical window-dressing.

Only certain lesser awards are open to supposedly lesser mortals like them, just as the higher-ranking awards are only available to top public service mandarins and the like.

You will never see Sadie the school dinner lady getting appointed Knight Commander of the Civil Division of the Most Honourable Order of the Bath (KCB), as the head of the Northern Ireland Civil Service, Bruce Robinson, was last year.

She simply wouldn't be in the running, because the system does not allow for it. But it does allow for the likes of Roger Carr, the head of Centrica, which owns British Gas, to be given a knighthood, as he was last January. Carr, who earns £450,000 a year, put up gas prices by 7% — even though profits were expected to rise to £700m. Just one more of those "extraordinary people from all walks of life who have made a difference to their community", I guess.

The class prejudice and cronyism of the system has just become more deeply embedded by the re-introduction of the British Empire Medal, or BEM.

SOME ISSUES:

Who do you think deserves to be honoured?

Would you accept an honour from the Queen?

Why?

Are there any other ways to honour or reward people?

See also:
www.completeissues.co.uk

Photo: Lewis Whyld, PA Archive/Press Association Images

Sir Bruce Forsyth is knighted by Queen Elizabeth II

Honour or dishonour?

It was scrapped in 1993 by John Major on the grounds that it was out of date and entrenched class divisions.

Now David Cameron is bringing it back for 2012, ironically enough as part of his Big Society project. He sees it as a way to reward people in the voluntary services. But this is quite clearly a token award for the little people: with the BEM, you don't even receive your medal from the Queen, but from one of her flunkeys.

This is no republican rant — well, not in the Irish sense, anyway. My criticisms of the British honours system are not motivated by nationalist fervour, but rather by a distaste for glorifying — in however a watered-down fashion — imperial arrogance, as well as the blithe sense of entitlement of the Bullingdon Club.

They might never admit it, but I'm sure that some unionists are secretly disgusted by the venality of the system, too.

If they would only just come out and say so, we could have a useful debate about Northern Ireland's complex, ambivalent relationship with Britain — one that doesn't fall into the usual polarised, point-scoring tedium.

But that's just one more of those honest, challenging, breast-baring conversations that people on both sides are simply too scared to have.

Here in Northern Ireland, we are in a unique position, standing at a remove both from the Republic and Britain. It should give us a clearer perspective and afford us the opportunity to speak with interest, but detachment.

When it comes to the British honours system, we should be asking: is this really how we judge a person's merit or worth?

Belfast Telegraph, 29 December 2011

A secret list of 300 top people who have snubbed the honours system by refusing knighthoods and other awards was been revealed. Among those believed to have refused the honours are:

Singer David Bowie

Celebrity cook Nigella Lawson

Comedy duo Dawn French and Jennifer Saunders

Novelist JG Ballard

James Bond leading lady Honor Blackman

Jazz musician George Melly

Author Graham Greene

Artist David Hockney

Poet Robert Graves

Author Aldous Huxley

Writer and journalist Evelyn Waugh

Children's author Roald Dahl

Poet Philip Larkin

Actor Alastair Sim

Painter LS Lowry

Actor Albert Finney

Even film director Alfred Hitchcock refused a CBE in 1962, although he accepted a knighthood shortly before he died.

Disability

The demonisation of the disabled is a chilling sign of the times

There is a climate of hostility towards people for whom life is already difficult and it is being fostered by politicians and journalists

Ian Birrell

Peter Greener endured a barrage of hate from his neighbour. Sometimes, it was eggs thrown at his house, stones thrown at his windows or paint thrown at his fence; more often, it was words hurled in his face: spastic, cripple, scum, scrounger. These assaults went on for months, leaving the former Nissan car-sprayer in floods of tears, feeling suicidal and on antidepressants. He was scared to leave his home in Hebburn in South Tyneside and blamed himself for the upset it caused his wife and two children. "It made our lives hell," he said.

Like many people with conditions such as multiple sclerosis, Greener's regressive condition fluctuates. One day, it affects his memory, the next his speech. Sometimes, he uses a wheelchair; at other times, he can haul himself around on crutches. But this only led to more abuse, with angry shouts he was faking his disabilities and exaggerating his problems to get benefits.

A terrible story to shake our heads over and ponder how a person could be so vile, so inhuman, towards someone already suffering

Yesterday was international day of persons with disabilities, but in this country they remain locked in a state of virtual apartheid.

a tough time. But the real tragedy of the tale is that it is all too commonplace in this country. The only unusual thing is that the inadequate perpetrator was caught and given a comparatively strong sentence last month.

Yesterday was international day of persons with disabilities, but in this country they remain locked in a state of virtual apartheid. They are forced to the fringes of society, ostracised from things the rest of us take for granted such as getting a job or going on public transport. Such is the estrangement that a survey last week found two-thirds of Britons actively avoid disabled people because they have no idea how to act around them.

The idea of treating them like anyone else is obviously too much for most Britons. But the Greener case highlights a new and troubling trend in this supposedly tolerant nation. Note the use of the word "scrounger", the spiteful claim that he was faking his disabilities. This kind of abuse is being increasingly heard. With economic storm clouds darkening, disabled people have become easy scapegoats in the age of austerity.

Polls have found substantial increases in the number of disabled people experiencing aggression and abuse, with evidence that the attitudes of the rest of society towards them are worsening. Many disabled people were already scared to go out after dark or travel on public transport such is their justified fear of encountering hostility.

Little wonder many people with disabilities are downbeat. Alice Maynard, chair of the charity Scope and a lifelong wheelchair user, told me she was terrified by the surly mood. "I'm quite an optimistic person by nature, but are we facing a truly ghastly scenario, in which we will live surrounded by hate and with a very limited social care system?"

It is not just the vicious attacks capturing headlines that dislocate lives. Take David Gillon, a software engineer who helped build Eurofighter jets before losing his job three years ago. He walks with crutches and has been physically attacked and regularly shouted at in the street since he slipped and injured his back two decades ago.

Earlier this year, someone reported him to the government's benefit fraud hotline. Officials dismissed the allegation as soon as they walked in his front door, but his condition, which is stress-related, worsened for several months. Now he feels so threatened he barely leaves his house.

"If I go out, I know I could suffer more abuse," he said. One cruel act – and another person left a virtual prisoner in their own home.

As the parent of a defenceless daughter with profound disabilities, such stories disturb me. They should disturb us all. So what lies behind this harsh new mood towards the disabled?

Unfortunately, much blame rests on the shoulders of the media and certain parts of government. There has been a new dialogue over disability, characterised by the constant drip-drip of stories implying vast numbers of disability claimants are bogus, that benefits are doled out without proper checks and taxpayers fund free cars for thousands of children with minor behavioural disorders.

Many emanate from the Department for Work and Pensions, which has twisted facts, manipulated statistics and distorted data to win support for its drive to cut costs and crack down on benefit fraud. This cascade of spurious claims and scandalously spun stories ends up demonising the disabled. It does no credit to Iain Duncan Smith, the secretary of state, who proclaims himself a compassionate Conservative. Ministers say

No one, least of all those with disabilities, disputes the need to prevent fraud. Every pound stolen by a fake claimant is a pound not spent on vital services or much-needed support.

they cannot be blamed for the actions of the media, but they know how the game is played.

Meanwhile, there has been a significant increase in articles about "cheats", "scroungers" and "skivers" in the media. Not just tabloids, but broadsheets and broadcasters. A recent Glasgow Media Group study revealed a near-tripling of these words in papers, alongside a reduction in reports on discrimination and sympathetic stories about disabled people. Focus groups found people suggesting seven in 10 claimants were fraudulent; in reality, levels of fraud for disability benefits are 0.5%, much lower than for other benefits – and less than the level of errors made by officials.

Among those feeling the coldest chill of this new mood of intolerance are people with mental health conditions, already so often victims of bullying and hate crimes. They may not look obviously disabled, so are targeted as "scroungers". The charities Mencap and Mind have received numerous calls from people distressed by the witch hunt; one person said they felt like an "object of hate and derision with no escape".

No one, least of all those with disabilities, disputes the need to prevent fraud. Every pound stolen by a fake claimant is a pound not spent on vital services or much-needed support. Nor is this an argument about the need or otherwise for cuts. My view is that there remains huge inefficiency in public services, although many poor services are being ring-fenced and cuts imposed in the wrong places. But as people scrap for resources and stresses intensify, resentment is growing against the disabled, undermining any good things the government is doing in this area.

It is grossly irresponsible for journalists and politicians to collude in this manner to create a climate encouraging hatred, hostility and abuse towards people for whom life is already so difficult. This would be true at any time, but especially at a time of such uncertainty, when people are fearful of the future and looking for others to blame for their misfortune. Those with disabilities should not be made scapegoats for other people's sins.

The Observer, 4 December 2011
© Guardian News & Media Ltd 2011

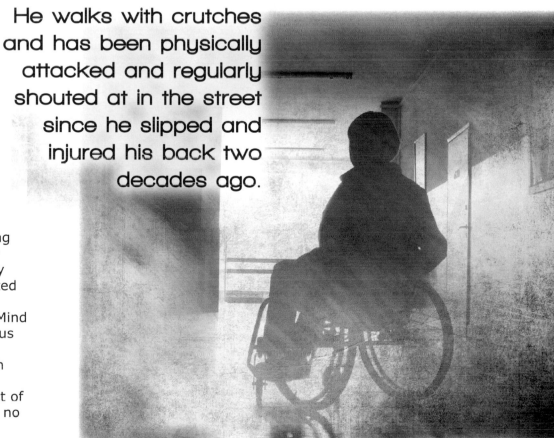

He walks with crutches and has been physically attacked and regularly shouted at in the street since he slipped and injured his back two decades ago.

Why make us cry for help?

To get support, families with a disabled child are forced to describe their lives as thwarted and unhappy.

Leah Wild

Are you happy? Imagine if, in order to be able to do the simplest things – from popping out to the shops to taking a shower, you had to answer, "No" to that question. Imagine if you had to emphasise this unhappiness to complete strangers, who then wrote it down on a sheet to copy and distribute to other strangers. This is what my teenager daughter has had to do, time and again, over the last few months. She is disabled and has just turned 18, which means she has to be assessed for support by adult social care. "Are you happy?" is one of the questions on the assessment form. Unless she repeatedly says "No", she won't get any support.

This week Riven Vincent said she would be forced to put her daughter – who like mine has quadriplegic cerebral palsy – into care if the short term support she so needs is not provided. "We are crumbling," wrote Vincent, hoping that plea will make a difference. I have no doubt that her family's daily life is a struggle, as it is for every family with a disabled child. But I also empathise on another level; I know that the only way to get essential support is to do

as she has done, and evoke a portrait of a family on the edge.

It's obscene that families like mine are forced to give such a bleak account of their lives. I've been asked by social workers if the additional care my eldest child needs means I neglect my two non-disabled, younger children. I refused to say it did. So we never had one hour or one penny of support from social care. We lived with that.

But now my daughter has turned 18, and she is entitled to support in her own right. She has a desire and right to live an independent life, apart from me, replacing my unpaid support with social care. But to get this, she has to claim she is desperate, unhappy, "crumbling". She has to conform to the image of the thwarted disabled girl she – and I – have spent the last 18 years fighting. She has to openly declare her life is a tragedy.

The assessment process is entirely based on what you can't do. In several interviews with social workers, each lasting over two hours, my 18-year-old daughter has had to talk about her inability to wash, dress, walk, sit, get in and

SOME ISSUES:

How do you think these kinds of assessments should be made?

Why might answering these questions be difficult?

Should care be an automatic right?

See also:
The demonisation of the disabled, p22

How will we treat the wilfully ill? p113

www.completeissues.co.uk

out of bed. She has not been given the opportunity to talk about her excellent AS grades, her shopping trips, or helping her younger siblings with their homework.

The first social worker who assessed her was a middle-aged man whom she'd never met before. He arrived with a large form and lots of boxes to tick. Much of my daughter's care is quite intimate. It was difficult for her to talk about this to a male stranger. But it was even more difficult for the stranger himself; he was visibly embarrassed. "We don't need to talk about that," he muttered, flicking to the next page of his form. But we do need to talk about it.

I've spent hours trying to make my daughter feel comfortable and confident in requesting the sort of personal care most of us would balk at. Such honest conversations with carers will need to be part of her life. The social worker made her feel as if she ought to hide it. So she stayed silent, and it didn't go down on the form. As

soon as the social worker left, my daughter burst into tears. Spending over two hours talking about all the things you can't do is hard for anybody. In a world in which being proud, powerful and disabled means challenging every assumption made about you, this is particularly wounding.

I was so worried about the damage this had done that I asked our GP if my daughter could receive counselling to re-boost her self-esteem. Ironically, this counselling would be paid for by the very same primary care trust that is fighting against her support costs. Perhaps if they spent more money on care, they'd have to spend less on counselling those who didn't get it.

There is another way. Instead of strangers with clipboards, the first stage in an assessment could be made by the disabled person themselves. My daughter could have been asked to keep a detailed diary of what she did and what she needed help with. It needn't be written down; it

could be recorded or dictated. This would allow her to paint a rich portrait of her teenage life, which includes going out to see The King's Speech with friends, as well as someone helping her on and off the toilet.

My daughter's life is not an unhappy one. It's as fraught and full as most 18-year-olds'. It's just that she needs support to do some everyday tasks many others take for granted. Sadly, what she can't take for granted is that she is going to get any.

Leah Wild is a pseudonym

The Guardian, 20 January 2011
© Guardian News & Media Ltd 2011

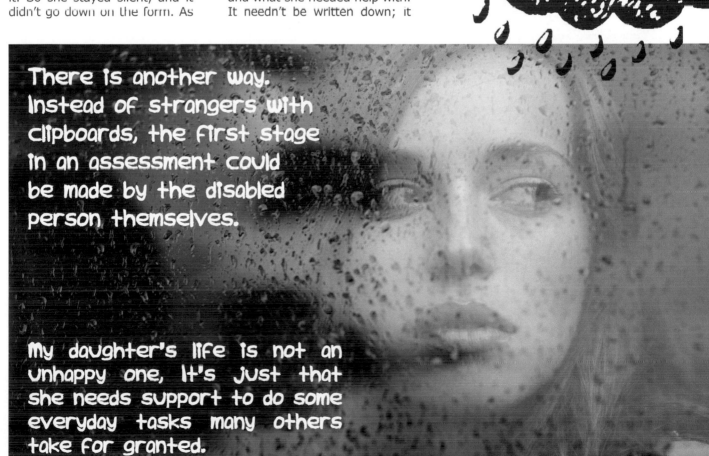

There is another way. Instead of strangers with clipboards, the first stage in an assessment could be made by the disabled person themselves.

My daughter's life is not an unhappy one, It's just that she needs support to do some everyday tasks many others take for granted.

Choosing to sit tight

Photo: Stephen Wallace

Having created a strong identity and personality as a wheelchair-user, Mik Scarlet woke up one day to find he could go back to walking

In 2003 I had to undergo a spinal reconstruction. By this time I had been a full-time wheelchair-user for 22 years, and had built the kind of life most able-bodied types dream of. I toured in bands, was a TV presenter and journalist, an actor and, if I'm truthful, a bit of a media whore. I had a fantastic fiancé who I loved and loved me back. In fact, the only bit of my life that was a bit crap at that time was the amount of pain I was in as my spine collapsed and the amount of strong painkilling medication I had to take for it. It was to stop this pain that I initially agreed to undergo major surgery.

When I came round after 15 hours, I immediately felt something was wrong. It was when I sat up for the first time I realised what it was. When my feet touched the floor I actually

SOME ISSUES:

How sympathetic are you to Mik's decision?

Is he brave? Ungrateful? Clear-sighted?

Why is he proud of being disabled?

How would you react if he were a friend of yours?

See also:
www.completeissues.co.uk

could feel it. I had been able to feel the bed sheets and breezes. I also found that I had loads of movement coming back too.

The medical staff were overjoyed. Not many spinal surgeons can claim to have cured a paraplegic! However, even though my nerves were working better now, I did have other issues. My right hip had dislocated years back, and over time it wore away. So if I was to walk I would need a false hip, that could have been fitted after I had laid in hospital for two months with an open wound, having my muscles and nerves stretched. Hmm. Then it became plain that my bone density wasn't up to walking, so I might also need a replacement knee and then ankle. Double hmm. Then I was told how long the physio might take... between two to four years.

Now, as I said, I really liked my life, but I was also very proud of being disabled (and still am!). I have never held any desire to be more like the able-bodied, and actually feel that becoming a wheelchair-user allowed me to fulfill my dreams and ambitions. My entire identity was as a wheelchair-user.

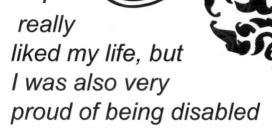

I really liked my life, but I was also very proud of being disabled

I can still remember the face of my surgeon when I told him that I liked being disabled

Waking up one day to find that I had been cured was not the joyous event everyone else seemed to think it was. As the "walk again" pressure grew, my resolve against further painful operations and years of physio grew along with it. I can still remember the face of my surgeon when I told him that I liked being disabled, and would not be going ahead.

So now here I am, probably the first person to have been cured of paraplegia, and to decide to stay in a wheelchair. Because I am disabled, a wheelchair-user and I am proud of it.

Disability Now, August 2010

Photo: Doralba Picerno

Drugs

Lindy McDowell

Would legalising drugs really reap a good harvest?

SOME ISSUES:

Do you think that legalising drugs would make controlling usage easier or harder?

What do you think would be the benefits with regards to crime?

See also:
Where's the Harm?
Essential Articles 14, p54
Breakthrough in Britain's war on drugs
Essential Articles 14, p56
Danger, danger
Fact File 2012, p14

www.completeissues.co.uk

If there's one sector of new business currently outperforming all else, it surely has to be the cannabis growth industry.

Not a day now passes when we don't have news of yet another cannabis factory (or several) discovered somewhere in Northern Ireland. Every back street, every town, every townland even, seems to have had one.

You can't help feeling if only Invest Northern Ireland start-up statistics were on a par...

And these are only the cannabis production plants we hear about because the Police Service Northern Ireland, full credit to them, have busted them.

You have to wonder how much more illicit foliage is still out there being carefully tended in the attics of suburban homes by drug dealers confident of raking it in come harvest time?

Going by the numbers of operations discovered, it looks like the cannabis factory is now about as common a household feature as the old lean-to greenhouse used to be. Or the lettuce cloche.

And the illegal drugs market isn't just growing in terms of farmed pharmaceuticals.

Northern Ireland is awash with all sorts of illicit substances. The problem was once confined mainly to urban areas. Now even the most remote rural area has a habit.

> # The great advantage is that you cut out the dealers and you have control over what precisely people are taking

And while the death of a high profile addict like Whitney Houston might seem a million glittering miles away from what happens in our back yard it all comes down to the same thing in the end. Lives blighted. Lives ruined.

And once again we're back to the debate about whether drugs should be legalised.

Among those arguing for the motion this time round is the 85 year-old Tony Bennett who says: "Let's legalise drugs like they do in Amsterdam.

It's a very sane city now. No-one's hiding or sneaking around corners to get it. They go to a doctor to get it."

I absolutely get the thinking behind the legalise-it argument. The great advantage is that you cut out the dealers and you have control over what precisely people are taking. (Pushers being notoriously unscrupulous when it comes to the additives in their product.)

What bothers me are purely the practicalities.

Who does the state supply to? Only addicts? Or can first time users get some as well?

Can the state legally supply the "softer" likes of cannabis (or allow it to be sold in cafes) knowing it has been scientifically linked to disorders ranging from depression to schizophrenia?

Will users be able to sue if they develop health problems?

And where do you draw the line?

If as Mr Bennett suggests, doctors are to dole out formerly banned drugs will the state, which can't afford some cancer treatments, be able to fund these substances?

Crack cocaine is hardly something you can flog like alcopops.

But then that leads us in turn to the tricky area of alcohol also being an addictive substance which destroys lives.

(And indeed as the deaths of Whitney and Michael Jackson prove, there's also the matter of addictive prescription drugs.)

Most vocal in calling for drugs to be legalised are the older, middle class users who don't have a whole lot of problem with a little recreational stuff.

But what about the real addicts?

What about the poor and the young who use what they can get their hands on to blot out despair or just boredom?

Would the legalisation of drugs make the problem worse for those at the bottom?

I honestly don't know. But since the state with all its bungling bureaucracy has demonstrated impressive cack-handedness in many another field, I'm not sure tasking it with something as sensitive as drug distribution is really our best bet.

Which brings us back to cracking down on the dealers, the factories and the supply chain.

The PSNI deserve full praise for the success they've achieved to date. But their very success is evidence of the scale of the problem we have here.

A growing problem in every sense.

Belfast Telegraph, 16 February 2012

Many agree, none act: to ease untold misery, legalise drugs

The war on drugs is lost, as a global commission is set to admit. But no one in power has the courage for a switch to regulation

Peter Wilby

SOME ISSUES:

Do you think there could be benefits from legalising drugs?

How might legalising drugs affect crime and addiction?

What might the negative effects be?

Do you think the government has a right to decide what drugs people can and can't take?

See also:
Accept the facts – and end this futile 'war on drugs'
Essential Articles 13, p50

www.completeissues.co.uk

In September 1989 Milton Friedman, the man whose views on economics influenced the policies of almost every government on the planet, wrote to Bill Bennett, "drug tsar" to the first President Bush. As Bennett prepared for a new phase in the "war on drugs", launched by President Nixon 18 years earlier – more police, harsher penalties, more jails, more military action overseas – Friedman wrote that "the very measures you favour are a major source of the evils you deplore". He pointed out how illegality made the drugs industry more, not less, lucrative, how crime had flourished during alcohol prohibition in the 1930s and would flourish more under Bennett's plans, and how "crack" might never have been invented had it not been for the drugs war.

Friedman was a firm supporter of decriminalising drugs, and regulating them as alcohol and tobacco are regulated. But however much governments listened to him on economics, they always ignored him on drugs. Many politicians of left and right have accepted the arguments

for legalising drugs – but only before or after being in office. The signatories to a report launched in New York on Thursday, declaring that "the global war on drugs has failed" and that "the criminalisation, marginalisation and stigmatisation" of drug users should end, could hardly be more impressive.

They include former presidents of Brazil, Switzerland and Colombia, a former secretary general of the UN and a former US secretary of state. But the only current office holder is Greece's George Papandreou, who has other things on his mind just now. Other current leaders may be thought sympathetic. David Cameron said that the "war on drugs … has been tried and we all know it does not work". Barack Obama called the drugs war "an utter failure". But they said those things in 2002 and 2004 respectively, long before they got close to political power.

The arguments for legalisation are overwhelming. They do not rest on approval of drugs, or ignorance of their harms, or any wish to see their consumption increase. They are based on the argument that regulation would be less harmful to drug users, less damaging to society and less expensive to taxpayers than outright prohibition. Nobody disputes the dangers of drugs, only the best ways of controlling them.

All drugs become more dangerous when banned. First, because consumers have no protection from adulteration and often have no idea of the strength and quality of what they are buying. And second, because vendors favour more concentrated forms which are less bulky and easier to transport and hide.

Opium, smoked through a pipe, generates, as poets recorded, a drowsy numbness. Converted into pure heroin, a less bulky and more concentrated version, it does far greater harm, and is more addictive. Mixed with drain cleaner or sand – as much illegal heroin is – and injected into the veins with an unsterilised needle, it becomes lethal. During alcohol prohibition in America, consumption of beer fell 70% while consumption of wine and spirits soared. Alcohol was frequently mixed with methylated spirits, which explains the blind blues singers of that era.

Illegal drugs are also dangerous to those who never touch them. Because of the risks, suppliers charge premium prices, though, as in any retail business, new customers get bargain introductory offers. A drug habit is expensive and addicts turn to crime to finance it. Many become suppliers and join gangs which, because they operate in an unregulated market, protect market share and enforce contracts through violence. Estimates suggest over half of UK property crime is to fund drug misuse, and some judges reckon two-thirds of those in prison wouldn't be there if drugs were legal.

The war on drugs, then, is an expensive failure, an extended charge of the Light Brigade. At the time of the Misuse of Drugs Act 1971, the UK had perhaps 10,000 problematic drug users. Now there are at least 300,000. UN figures, quoted in Thursday's report, suggest that in the past decade annual global consumption of opiates is up by 34%, cocaine by 27%, and cannabis by 8.5%. According to the lobby group Transform Drugs Policy, legalisation of cocaine and heroin alone would deliver a net annual saving of £4.6bn (excluding any revenue from taxing these drugs as we tax alcohol and tobacco), even if their use were to double. Portugal, 10 years after it became the first European country to decriminalise the use and possession of all illicit drugs, has experienced only a slight increase in drug consumption, and a decline in heroin.

All drugs become more dangerous when banned.

The arguments over drugs are done and dusted. Any independent body that looks at the evidence comes to similar conclusions. So why do political leaders refuse to countenance more than minor tinkering with the law, such as yo-yoing cannabis between classes B and C? One answer is that as Steve Rolles, senior policy analyst at Transform Drugs Policy, puts it, drugs have been presented as an existential threat and the war against them almost as a religious crusade. In the popular mind, drug users have always been demonised as what sociologists call "the other": Chinese gangsters, Caribbean immigrants, 60s hippies or other threats to the social order. Anyone who proposes ending the war risks being characterised by

Legalisation of cocaine and heroin alone would deliver a net annual saving of £4.6bn (excluding any revenue from taxing these drugs as we tax alcohol and tobacco)

opponents, particularly in the downmarket media, as weak and cowardly, lacking the Churchillian spirit of "no surrender". History does not look kindly on those who lose wars.

But it goes, I think, even deeper than that. Control of drugs is deeply embedded in the DNA of modern government. The criminalisation of drug use, in the west at least, is almost entirely a 20th-century development. Laudanum, a tincture of opium, was in common use in Victorian England and Coca-Cola, invented in 1886, contained cocaine until 1903. No US state banned cannabis until 1915 and it remained legal in England until the 1920s, as did heroin and cocaine. The rise of conscript armies and Fordist mass production prompted the change, briefly affecting alcohol – the US took the first steps towards prohibition during the first world war – along with other drugs. Nobody wanted a drowsy numbness to overcome men marching into battle or clocking onto the production line. Significantly, Asian countries, which still earn their living from traditional manufacturing, now have some of the harshest anti-drug laws.

For most of the world, though, the time has come for political leaders to screw up their courage and rethink their policies. It surely cannot be beyond their spin doctors to present a switch to regulation not as a surrender but as a new phase in the drugs war. It is hard to think of anything that would do more to relieve death, destruction and human misery.

The Guardian, 1 June 2011
© Guardian News & Media Ltd 2011

> **Estimates suggest over half of UK property crime is to fund drug misuse, and some judges reckon two-thirds of those in prison wouldn't be there if drugs were legal.**

Is drug taking just a matter for the individual?

Writers from very different backgrounds think it is a matter of personal choice

Getting high is a basic human right

The "war" [on drugs] is not only wrong in practice, it is wrong in principle.

The right to intoxicate is a fundamental human right, as basic as the rights to worship or to engage in dangerous sports. It's not the state's business to tell us what to do with our leisure as long as we are not hurting others.

Joe Morison, letter to The Guardian, 4 June 2011

In Favour of Drugs

I now don't feel as if I would ever need a drug again, but I do know drugs increase your ability to access hidden realms. Without these things happening to me, I wouldn't have been successful with Creation Records - they changed the way I thought as a person.

What people ingest is up to them, but for me it gave me access to creative worlds whilst running Creation that I would never have got to without the helping hand of the gods.

You only live once, but just maybe you could be living and experiencing 20 other planets at the same time. The only thing that's certain is we don't know...

Alan McGee Founder of Creation Records, in The Huffington Post, 26 January 2012

Taking drugs should be legal but discouraged in the same way as smoking

But the real question is this – given that [drug taking] is bad for you, is the resolution not to take it better made at a personal level, or should it be made at the level of government? In other words, who decides – the high court of parliament, or the high court of conscience? Which is the most effective forum for legislation?

... while smoking has been restricted in public places, it has not been made illegal. If we were to treat the consumption of all drugs in the same way, legal but discouraged, and above all portrayed as unhealthy and unglamorous, the consumption of such drugs would perhaps markedly decline too.

Father Alexander Lucie-Smith, The Catholic Herald, 28 January 2012

HIDDEN DRUG USERS

WHO WON'T BE FOUND BURGLING YOUR HOME TO FUND THEIR HABIT

These detailed new insights reveal that despite media hype around illicit substances, alcohol is the bigger problem – Patrick Butler

SOME ISSUES:

Where do you think stereotypes of general drug users come from?

Why do you think many educated, young people are taking drugs?

Why do you think society is so afraid of the effect of drugs?

Do you think alcohol should be treated like a drug?

See also:
Drug habit
Fact File 2010, p14
www.completeissues.co.uk

You probably know one or two of Britain's "hidden" drug users, and may even be one yourself. They are often young, highly educated, working, sociable and sporty. They feel healthy, happy in their relationships, and confident about the future. They take cannabis, cocaine, MDMA (ecstasy) and, lest we forget, a fair amount of tobacco and alcohol.

They are, by and large, the drug users you rarely hear or read about, at least not in the social affairs pages. You won't find them in a crack den or breaking into your home to fund their habit. Their use of illegal drugs is a lifestyle choice: it

Smart, respectable, holding down jobs in – or preparing to enter – business, banking, public service, the law, even politics.

doesn't define or consume them like some heroin and crack addicts. They don't register as an alert on the public health radar, or as a headline on the law and order agenda.

It is easy to imagine many of them as smart, respectable, economically productive, holding down jobs in – or preparing to enter – the professions, business, banking, public service, the law, even politics. It's easy to think of these "happy" drug takers as unproblematic: as rational, self-regulating,

middle-class "consumers", who are relatively discreet and (on the whole) discriminating in their drug use, and who tend to tidy up after themselves.

This view, the Guardian/ Mixmag survey reveals, is implicitly shared by the police. The status, and perhaps age and skin colour, of our "hidden" drug users means they are not a target – unlike, say black, inner-city youth. They do get stopped and searched, sometimes busted for possession.

But the survey suggests the law is pragmatically uninterested, on the whole, in criminalising their misdemeanours.

It also confirms truths that often get lost in the hysterical media discourse around drugs and public health: that taking drugs is, for many ordinary people, as normal and pleasurable a part of their lives as drinking or smoking.

They balance their desire for drug experiences with the demands of work, study and relationships. They see

WHEN IT COMES TO DRUGS, WE ARE FASCINATED AND HORRIFIED BY THE FASHIONABLE, ILLICIT AND NOTORIOUS. But the deeply mundane finding of our survey is that the most prevalent, damaging and antisocial drug of all — and the one most users want help to kick — is still the one in your fridge and supermarket trolley: BOOZE.

drug use as a choice, with desirable consequences, as well as risks.

This year's survey, conducted by Global Drug Survey, is the biggest of current UK drug use ever carried out, completed by 7,700 UK drug users and 15,500 worldwide, including 3,300 in the US. Its crowd-sourced snapshot of the real-life experiences of a large group of users, male and female, gay and straight, clubbers and non-clubbers, is unique in the scale and detail of its insight into current drug trends, attitudes, practices, risks and harms.

There are detailed, fresh and important insights into drug use and consequences: the unexpectedly high prevalence among drug users of legally prescribed medication – Ritalin, sleeping pills and so on – acquired through the "grey market" of friends and dealers; the reckless use of "mystery white powders" by young hedonists; the consumer backlash against much-hyped drugs such as mephedrone and synthetic cannabis; warning signs of physical harms connected to use of ketamine, for example.

Of course, pleasurable drug use can easily slide into pain: for all that respondents feel happy and in control, most know of at least one friend whose drug use they fear is spinning out of control with all the toxic consequences for their health, relationships and careers. When this happens, it seems conventional help – whether GPs or government-funded drug advice websites – is rarely regarded as trustworthy or helpful.

It's worth noting that while respondents say they block out messages saying "don't take drugs", they would lap up practical, personalised information about dangers and safety tips that enable them to regulate and benchmark their drug intake – the kind of information that Global Drug Survey's Drugs Meter app seeks to provide.

The question for policymakers is how to use this kind of detailed user intelligence data to design and implement appropriate public health responses, based on the evidence of what drugs people take, how and why they consume them, and what consequences they report.

The first policy stop might be that most potent of legal substances, alcohol. Over half of the survey respondents reported drinking at levels that the World Health Organisation would class as harmful (though some of this group believed they were only drinking "average" amounts). Asked which drug they would most like to cut down on, 36% of respondents said alcohol (a figure only exceeded by the 64% who wanted to cut down on tobacco).

When it comes to drugs, we are fascinated and horrified by the fashionable, illicit and notorious. But the deeply mundane finding of our survey is that the most prevalent, damaging and antisocial drug of all – and the one most users want help to kick – is still the one in your fridge and supermarket trolley: booze.

The Guardian, 15 March 2012
© Guardian News & Media Ltd 2011

Education

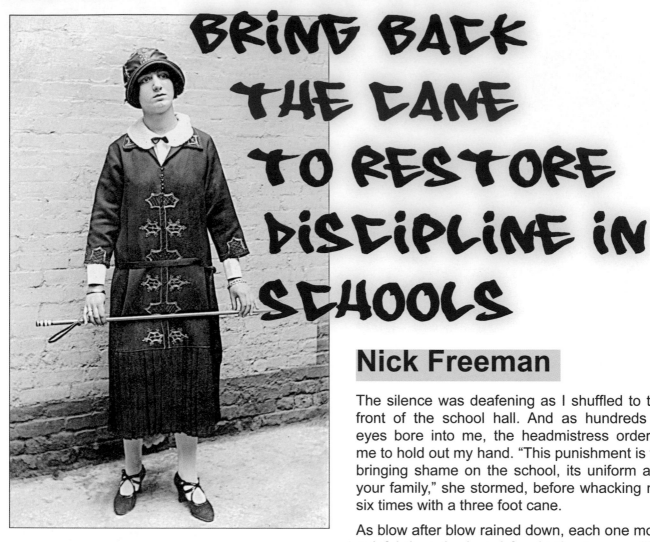

BRING BACK THE CANE TO RESTORE DISCIPLINE IN SCHOOLS

Nick Freeman

The silence was deafening as I shuffled to the front of the school hall. And as hundreds of eyes bore into me, the headmistress ordered me to hold out my hand. "This punishment is for bringing shame on the school, its uniform and your family," she stormed, before whacking me six times with a three foot cane.

As blow after blow rained down, each one more painful than the last, I fought the tears welling inside me. But there was no scope for pity or mercy. A 'crime' had been committed, and I was to be punished.

And the crime? 'Bilking' – trying to dodge paying my bus fare by pretending to the conductor that I couldn't speak English. So, did the humiliation, shame, and red burning mark scorched onto my palm do the trick and ensure my rehabilitation? You bet.

And, believe me, as a deterrent, it worked for everyone else too. This was no blood-thirsty mob surrounding the handiwork of Madame La Guillotine. Every boy in that hall knew he could be next. You could almost taste the fear – let alone the blood.

Now, some may find this kind of corporal punishment barbaric. Yet it did the trick. You'd never find a single teacher at my alma mater quaking in his boots at the prospect of facing a classroom of recalcitrant schoolboys.

SOME ISSUES:

How do you think teachers should maintain order in the classroom?

If a teacher is under threat from a student, what level of force do you think is acceptable for the teacher to use?

Do you think physical discipline has good or bad effects?

See also:
A child will learn nothing from being hit, p62
Classroom crackdown
Fact File 2012, p30

www.completeissues.co.uk

As blow after blow rained down, each one more painful than the last, I fought the tears welling inside me.

Which is why I applaud Education Secretary Michael Gove's move to return power to the teacher by slackening the rules on physical force in school.

The measures will allow teachers to use reasonable force to deal with unruly pupils. But to my mind, this doesn't go far enough.

If we are going to re-establish order in the classroom, end truancy and restore respect

Soft parenting, lack of muscle to discipline and a culture of blame has devastated schooling in this country.

for those in authority, then the only way forward is to bring back corporal punishment.

The current system, driven by politically correct loonies, is totally broken.

A recent series of attacks – ranging from stabbing to rape – are exquisitely eloquent examples of the violent behaviour which is soaring in the classroom.

Fear and pain is the only language that some children understand. Teachers need something in their armoury. Soft parenting, lack of muscle to discipline and a culture of blame has devastated schooling in this country.

Corporal punishment would, I'm certain, lead to a massive reduction in bad behaviour, disruption to other pupils and even the number of expulsions.

That's aside from the net benefit of shaming a hitherto, gung-ho hoodlum who thinks he is untouchable and a hero to his mates.

Break him, break his stranglehold. And that rap on the knuckles may make him knuckle down and show him what he can really achieve.

Manchester Evening News, 5 September 2011

The day my life changed -

Bang! He pinned me against the board. He was vicious and unrelenting

I LOVED TEACHING. On a rare night out with other teachers, I talked shop incessantly. But all that changed on a sunny morning a few weeks ago when I was the victim of a random act of violence. It was lesson two on a Monday. I was happy and confident, cajoling my second Year 9 class of the day.

I had taught the new boy - let's call him Tyson - only once before. I noticed he had his mobile phone out so told him to put it away. He did so. Then, 10 minutes later, I saw that he had it out again.

I was not angry. I did not raise my voice. However, this time I took the phone off him. He removed the battery first, but he did hand it over.

Yet before I had made it to my desk he was out of his seat. He refused to sit back down. He wanted his phone back.

Instinctively, I felt his response was not the norm. His was not the "I'm-going-to-grumble-but-I-know-it's-a-fair-cop" reaction. I decided to lead him to the classroom next door to sit him with my head of department, but she was busy taking mock orals.

I had taught the new boy - let's call him Tyson - only once before. I noticed he had his mobile phone out so told him to put it away. He did so. Then, 10 minutes later, I saw that he had it out again.

SOME ISSUES:

What do you think a teacher should do in this situation?

How do you think students who behave in this way should be treated?

Do you think students should be allowed to bring phones and iPods into school?

Are they a distraction?

What rights should teachers have to protect themselves?

See also:
Teacher Talk
Fact File 2012, p28

www.completeissues.co.uk

I told Tyson that unless he sat back down I would "level 4" him (our school's ultimate sanction where a senior member of staff removes a pupil). He began to walk back into the classroom and I thought the crisis was averted.

What happened next was over in seconds. Tyson thought it would be a good idea to take my bag hostage. He grabbed it, wielding it provocatively in front of him, and swore at me. Some of the class were amused, shouting "He's got miss's bag!"; some were shocked, all were watching. I had no control.

Then, bang! Seconds later Tyson had me pinned up against the board. He attacked me viciously and unrelentingly, swearing at me and promising he would knock me out.

What happened next was over in seconds. Tyson thought it would be a good idea to take my bag hostage. He grabbed it, wielding it provocatively in front of him, and swore at me.

The instinct for fight or flight kicks in at moments like these, but I felt I could do neither for fear of my job. He had me by my wrists. Eventually I did try to kick him off, full of anguish in case I might bruise him. It was only when another teacher entered the room that the attack stopped. I had never imagined how relieved I would be to hear the words: "Tyson, I am going to have to restrain you."

The random act left me bruised down my right side and shocked. Over the next few days my mind raced over events again and again. I gave a statement and was told that I could bring charges. I chose not to - I was frightened I might end up the villain somehow and accused of harming a child.

I coped well for the first few days after the attack, determined to be strong. Every time I saw a phone, I confiscated it. No chances. Instead of avoiding potential conflict I instinctively sought it out. The "random act" had uncovered my inner Clint Eastwood. I was trigger-happy and itching for a fight. Things that had hitherto irritated me mildly now sent me into a rage.

Another teacher's Year 10 class, eating and listening to music on their iPods with their phones out on the desks, made me livid and I would rant when I got home.

One week later I went in to teach the same class where the attack had happened. Some pupils were kind, most the same as usual, but one previously quiet pupil saw me as fair game and did no work.

None of those pupils had come to my help when I was attacked. I survived the lesson but broke down as soon as it was over. The exciting challenge of teaching has changed into a nightmarish battle. I don't know if I have the stomach for it any more.

The writer has chosen to remain anonymous

TES Magazine, 27 May 2011

School was Jamie's only refuge. But not any more

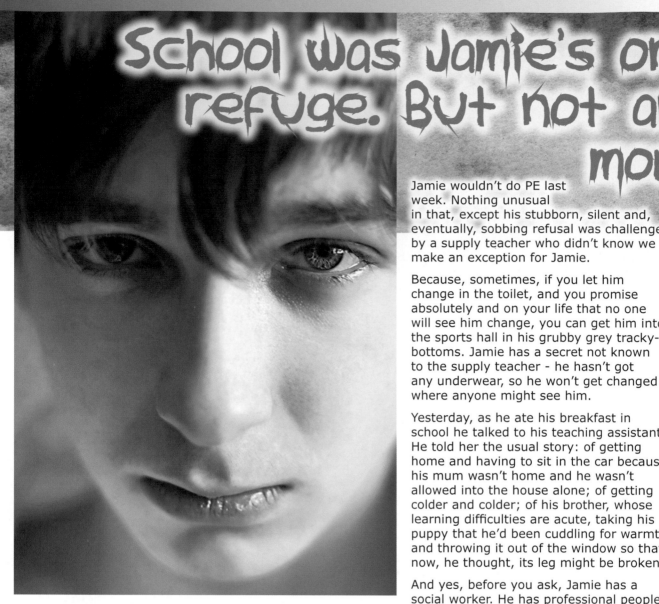

Jamie wouldn't do PE last week. Nothing unusual in that, except his stubborn, silent and, eventually, sobbing refusal was challenged by a supply teacher who didn't know we make an exception for Jamie.

Because, sometimes, if you let him change in the toilet, and you promise absolutely and on your life that no one will see him change, you can get him into the sports hall in his grubby grey tracky-bottoms. Jamie has a secret not known to the supply teacher - he hasn't got any underwear, so he won't get changed where anyone might see him.

Yesterday, as he ate his breakfast in school he talked to his teaching assistant. He told her the usual story: of getting home and having to sit in the car because his mum wasn't home and he wasn't allowed into the house alone; of getting colder and colder; of his brother, whose learning difficulties are acute, taking his puppy that he'd been cuddling for warmth and throwing it out of the window so that now, he thought, its leg might be broken.

And yes, before you ask, Jamie has a social worker. He has professional people who care for him, genuinely care, who try to address his mum's drug habit, who advise that he and his brother and his mum should not share one mattress on the floor of a house, cuddling altogether for warmth.

It is the school which notices and reports the cigarette burn etched delicately into the soft, unwashed skin just below his jaw; it is the school which untangles his hair on to white poster paper that crawls like live newspaper print when we have finished, each word a separate head louse.

It is we who make sure he is fed, attend to his learning needs, report his plight. The school gives him safety and structure and security and, if it can be allowed in such times as these, love. So when last week, his mother, sick of the pressure we exert, sent in the note we knew she would, saying she was exercising her legal right to take her child out of school and educate him at home, it was not just Jamie who cried.

I have not cried before for a child that is not mine, but I cannot see the road as I drive home. I tell the staff we have done all we could and all we should - but how can there be a law that allows these sad, grey children to be kept at home? There are many Jamies, kept away from school, denied the one place where they might find some sort of sanctuary. It makes no sense, and yes, it keeps me awake at night.

The author is a secondary headteacher in the east of England
TES Magazine, 16 September 2011

SOME ISSUES:

Do you think, in situations such as this, that parents should be allowed to take their child out of school?

Who should have rights over this student? The parent, the social worker or the school?

Why?

What would you do to help this boy's situation if you were a teacher?

See also:
www.completeissues.co.uk

Environmental issues

Paradise...

It may be known as a tropical paradise, but the languid ideal hides a far darker and environmentally damaging truth. The Republic of Maldives is, quite literally, in deep water. It is suffering from both rising sea levels and the increasing temperature of the sea. On top of that the Maldives is home the world's largest 'rubbish island'!

The Republic of Maldives is made up of 1,190 islands in 20 atolls spread over 900 km in the Indian Ocean. Only 199 islands are inhabited and the total population is just over 300,000 people. The islands are extremely flat, averaging only 1.5 metres above sea level, the highest natural ground level is only 2.4 metres.

500,000 tourists a year are attracted by its pristine beaches, underwater coral reefs, and spectacular marine wildlife. Its atolls are ringed by reefs which host over 1,900 species of fish, 187 coral species, and 350 crustaceans. But the coral, which is the basis of the economy and is the physical material from which the islands are formed, is under threat.

The post card image of the Maldives does not show just how affected it is by the problems of climate change, a threat we are all dimly aware of but which for the Maldives is becoming

SOME ISSUES:

What do you think the Maldives government should do?

How should tourists take responsibility for the rubbish they leave on the island?

What other solutions can you think of?

See also:
How climate change will affect these lives
Essential Articles 13, p72

A silent crisis and a dire warning
Fact File 2010, p48

www.completeissues.co.uk

Malé, the capital, is one of the world's most densely populated towns: 100,000 people cram into 2 square kilometres

...almost lost

Photographer Elin Hoyland reveals the extent of 'Rubbish Island' in her fantastic images of the islands.
© Elin Hoyland

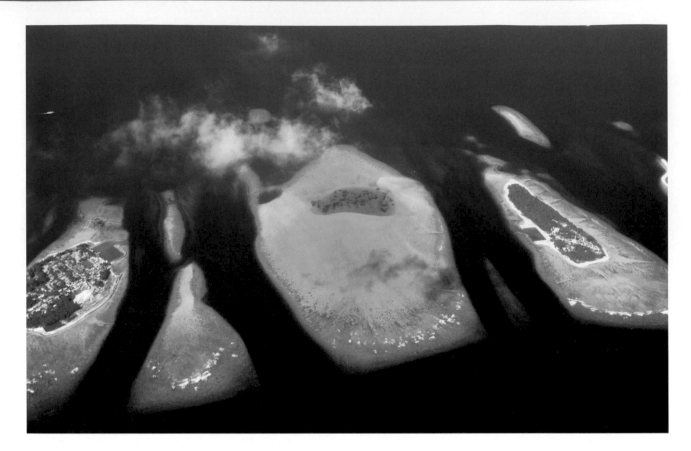

Since 80% of the total land-mass of the islands is only a metre above sea level, within 100 years the Maldives could become uninhabitable.

reality, right now. Over the last century, sea levels have risen about 20 centimetres; further rises of the ocean could threaten the very existence of the Maldives as an island nation. Since 80% of the total land-mass of the islands is only a metre above mean sea level, within 100 years the Maldives could become uninhabitable

It is no surprise, therefore, that it was the first country to sign up to the Kyoto Protocol, which sets targets for cuts in greenhouse gas emissions. It is also no surprise that Malé, the capital, is surrounded by a 3m-high (9.8ft) wall. This took 14 years to construct at a cost of $63m. Unable to foot the bill themselves, the government had to accept aid from Japan, which paid for 99% of the cost.

But the wall offers protection for just one of the inhabited islands - and then only against tidal surges rather than the rising sea level, the longer-term threat.

As well as rising sea levels, rising sea temperatures also threaten the coral reefs, causing bleaching and ultimately the death of these complex, living structures. The most severe damage is in areas that are stressed by pollutants, or damaged by physical disturbance. The coral reefs give some protection to the islands so damage to them worsens the threat from rising sea levels. Some scientists are trying to break this cycle of harm and speed up the recovery of the reefs through cutting-edge techniques to re-grow coral on artificial reefs. While this helps the situation, it is not enough.

Because the Republic of Maldives consists of a chain of islands it actually contains more sea than land. As well as being exposed to the risks of intensifying weather events, such as rising sea-levels and sea temperatures, it also has very limited options when is comes to disposing of its rubbish.

Some scientists are trying to break this cycle of harm through cutting-edge techniques to re-grow coral on artificial reefs. While this helps the situation, it is not enough.

The tourists lured by "bright blue skies, all-year sunshine and fantastic diving and snorkelling in lagoons the temperature of bath water" to quote one brochure, largely support the Maldivean economy but they bring problems too. The Maldives copes with the debris produced by this influx of affluent consumers by dumping and burning rubbish on one of its islands. A few miles and a short boat ride from the capital, Malé, is an island which does not feature in any tourist brochure.

Thilafushi began life as a reclamation project in 1992. The artificial island was built to support industry and to solve Malé's refuse problem but with more than 10,000 tourists a week adding their waste the island is growing. It now covers 50 hectares (124 acres). So much is being deposited that the island is growing at a square metre a day. Environmentalists say that more than 330 tonnes of rubbish is brought to Thilafushi a day. Most of it comes from Malé, which is one of the world's most densely populated towns: 100,000 people cram into 2 square kilometres.

Former president, President Mohamed Nasheed, the country's first democratically elected president, made a film called 'The Island President' in which he attempted to spread the message of what a worrying state the Maldives is in.

Mohamed Nasheed has since been forced to resign and has been replaced by his vice president Mohammed Waheed Hassan. Currently with their own government in an uncertain situation, their environmental plight remains unresolved.

The Maldives are threatened by the climate change produced elsewhere in the world and polluted by the people who come to enjoy its natural beauty. A paradise on the verge of being lost!

Sources: Various

What climate change means for Britain

A government report accepts that climate change is inevitable: bringing major risks – and a few opportunities

It's an old saying that Britain doesn't have a climate it just has weather (and lots of it!). But even in these islands we notice when the weather is unseasonable and in recent years we have been seeing more extreme weather events, which may be just a taste of things to come. The 2009 Cumbria floods, for example, resulted in hundreds of millions of pounds' worth of damage, including the loss of twenty road bridges and long-term disruption for local communities. In 2009 and 2010, long periods of cold weather and heavy snow closed schools and roads. In Spring 2011, a long spell of dry, hot weather meant there was not enough rainfall for some crops, there was an increase in pollution and in some areas forest fires threatened schools and homes.

These may not be isolated events. It is now generally accepted that even if we manage to reduce greenhouse gas emissions, we are locked into a certain amount of climate change simply because the global climate system cannot respond quickly enough to any adaptations we have made to help the environment. The government has conducted an assessment of the problems climate change will pose for the UK with the intention of avoiding them where possible – and dealing with them where it's not.

The UK Climate Risk Assessment Report (2012) accepts that global warming exists: "over the past century there has been a trend towards increasing global average temperatures. Global temperatures are projected to continue rising, which is very likely to cause continued changes in weather patterns, rising sea levels and increased frequency

SOME ISSUES:

How do you think these changes will affect your life?

What do you think we should do about climate change in Britain?

See also:
How climate change will affect these lives
Essential Articles 13, p72
A silent crisis and a dire warning
Fact File 2010, p48

www.completeissues.co.uk

Photo: Bikeworldtravel / Shutterstock.com

and intensity of extreme weather events." It also accepts that it is mainly caused by human activity: " … the recently observed increases are very likely (over 90% likely) due to rising concentrations of greenhouse gases in the atmosphere caused by human activities." But it cannot be quite as confident about the consequences.

It is fairly certain that temperatures will increase in the UK. Winters are likely to be wetter with major snow or rainfall events. It is likely that summers will be drier (though wetter summers are not ruled out). Forecasting is a tricky business but the accompanying Evidence Report attempted to analyse the level of risk (and benefit). The report suggested that by the 2020s we would be seeing greater flood damage and might be seeing the beginnings of problems due to increased temperatures. By the 2080s the consequences of these changes would be more serious and more widespread.

UK business could face disruption to its supply chain because of extreme weather events such as heavy snowfall or flooding

Farms and forests

Drier soil in the summer means that farmers would need to irrigate their land to maintain the amount and quality of their crops. If drought becomes more frequent and water becomes scarce, there will be a demand to take more from rivers and underground stores with irreversible effects on the environment and on wildlife, particularly fish. Forests too could suffer both from lack of water and from new diseases and pests. Warmer and drier conditions could even result in more wildfires.

Increased risk of flooding also endangers agricultural land. It is predicted that the amount of land at risk of frequent flooding (that is, at least once every three years) will increase four fold by the 2080s to make up about 1% of all agricultural land.

There are, however, opportunities in these changes. If water was not in short supply we could have a longer growing season giving better yields and the possibility of introducing new crops and new tree species.

Business

UK business could face disruption to its supply chain because of extreme weather events such as heavy snowfall or flooding. Many businesses rely on the availability of water and would be damaged if the supply was not consistent because of drought. In sectors with large workforces, such as hospitals, schools or shops, high temperatures outside could lead to temperatures inside buildings breaching health and safety regulations resulting in a loss of working hours.

The risks to business relate very closely to what happens in other sectors: availability of water, transport, energy, natural resources all have a strong impact. Disruption to agriculture would obviously affect the food and drinks industry (and vice versa). Most businesses are coping with some of these risks now but climate change means that the disruption could be longer and more frequent.

On the plus side, higher temperatures might mean more opportunities in the tourism and leisure industries. Forward-looking businesses should be thinking about products and services suited to a low-carbon economy.

Health and Wellbeing

An extra bit of sunshine and warmth could increase the health of the nation by encouraging us to spend more time in the open air, increasing vitamin D levels and even easing mental health problems. If the temperature increases in the winter, fewer people may suffer, or even die, from cold.

The drawbacks of increased temperatures, however, are likely to exceed these gains. More time outdoors could lead to more skin cancers – particularly in the south of England. There's more risk of death from extreme heat in the summer. Increased rainfall and therefore flooding would lead to deaths, injuries and mental stress. Increased ozone levels are bad news for sufferers from respiratory diseases. Higher temperatures also increase the risk of water and food borne diseases as well as harmful algae and other organisms in water.

Infrastructure

Like other buildings, hospitals might suffer from overheating, while more frequent flooding, heatwaves and wildfires would increase pressure on all the emergency services.

Both flooding and excess heat could seriously interrupt energy supplies and damage energy infrastructure. Flooding is also a serious risk to roads and railways – particularly to bridges. Buildings are likely to be affected by floods, coastal erosion and by subsidence. Overheating in buildings will lead to a demand for more energy for cooling.

Cities also suffer the Urban Heat Island effetct. Because of the number of buildings, the type of surfaces, such as concrete and asphalt, and the amount of human activity, cities can be as much

Some of the adaptations in place around the world

Toronto, Canada

Disaster control in the face of the urban heat island effect weather alerts to protect vulnerable people from extreme heat or cold, free bottled water, free transport to cooling centres.

New York, USA

Roofs painted white to cool the city down in the summer. Back up power generators moved to higher ground in anticipation of floods.

Andes, Peru

A project (financed by the World Bank) to paint mountain peaks white to cool down the temperature and 'regrow' a lost glacier

Netherlands

Boosting existing defences against rising sea levels and river floods and also finding innovative ways to cope, including houses which are anchored to the ground but can rise with the water.

London

the Thames barrier should be able to protect the city against floods until 2070. There are plans to re-green the city by planting green roofs and increasing green cover.

as 11C warmer than the surrounding countryside. This leads to increased demand for cooling mechanisms and a higher demand for water.

Environment

The natural environment is already under pressure, which is only likely to increase. Any changes in the normal pattern are potentially harmful to the existing environment and the complex ecosystem that maintains it. In summer low water levels may increase the concentration of pollutants, which in turn will damage habitats. Lack of moisture in the soil can both increase erosion and harm biodiversity. Warmer weather would allow the invasion of non-native species, including pests. Native species may be unable to adapt to the fact that their normal habitat has 'moved' or they may be separated from other populations. Changes in seasonal events may disrupt the natural relationships between predators and their prey, causing an imbalance. Warmer rivers, lakes and seas will have an impact on marine habitats, food production and biodiversity.

Forests too could suffer both from lack of water and from new diseases and pests. Warmer and drier conditions could even result in more wild fires.

While higher temperatures will undoubtedly benefit some native plant and animal species, to most they pose at least a challenge, if not a threat.

So what is to be done?

The report concludes that although there are uncertainties about the timing and the scale of climate change the risks are too great to be ignored. While continuing to move towards a low-carbon lifestyle and economy, we also need to adapt to the changes that are now inevitable. Within the next five years we will need to take action on:

- managing flood risk and coastal erosion
- managing crop productivity and biodiversity (pests and diseases, low summer river levels and movement of plants and animals are high priorities)
- managing water resources - particularly where they are likely to be scarce

- Overheating of buildings and infrastructure - especially in towns
- Health risks from heatwaves - especially where they will affect the NHS
- Opportunities for the UK economy

In the face of the complexity of the challenge and the number of agencies involved, the report does not go into detail about specific plans but mentions a National Adaptation Programme, beginning in 2013, to work with the different sectors on identifying and resolving problems. Indeed it makes a virtue of not being specific saying "Adaptation has no prescribed target and is not a one-off but an on-going process" .It emphasises "flexibility and keeping options open."

There's something of a contrast between the urgency in the evidence and the apparent lack of a firm conclusion. But there's no doubting that all of us can expect to feel some effects, sooner rather than later.

Sources: various

CLIMATE CHANGE:

THIRD WORLD REAPS A BITTER HARVEST

A scientific consensus is hardening that extreme climatic events will grow more frequent and more severe as the world heats up – Geoffrey Lean

Photo: radiokafka / Shutterstock.com

SOME ISSUES:

What do you think developed countries should do to reduce the effects of climate change?

Should countries who produce more pollution do more to help the countries who are most affected?

Does this seem fair?

See also:
How climate change will affect these lives, Essential Articles 13, p72

A silent crisis and a dire warning, Fact File 2010, p48

www.completeissues.co.uk

It was, of course, a complete coincidence. Just hours before the latest round of top-level climate negotiations were due to open, Durban was hit by a torrential downpour. High in a precipitous shanty town that clings to one of the hills above this South African coastal city, Sindi Madlala told me how she had been woken at midnight on Sunday by water rushing into her house: she and her family had to take down part of a wall to allow the torrent to flow out the other side. "We have often had rain, but never like this" she said.

She was lucky. Other shacks were swept away – six people died – and even affluent areas were flooded, showing, claimed a local government spokesman, that "even the posh areas are not spared the effects of climate change". Next morning, in the partially waterlogged conference venue, Christiana Figueres, the UN official in charge of the negotiations, called it "unseasonable

IN THE PAST, HE TOLD ME, SEVERE DROUGHTS CAME ONCE A DECADE; NOW THEY HAPPEN EVERY FEW YEARS.

weather of the type we are seeing all over the world as greenhouse gas concentrations in the atmosphere continue to rise".

In truth, no one can accurately attribute any such single storm to global warming, though a scientific consensus is hardening that similarly extreme climatic events will grow more frequent and more severe as the world heats up. But mingling in the city's International Conference Centre among the bureaucrats endlessly haggling over textual minutiae, are people ready to testify, from personal experience, that a change in climate over many years is already taking a terrible toll on some of the poorest people on earth.

Take Mohamed Adow, from a pastoralist family in the dry north east of Kenya, who says he comes "from the front line, where the impacts of climate change are real and devastating". In the past, he told me, severe droughts came once a decade; now they happen every few years. His father lost 60 per cent of his cattle in the last drought, he added, and the whole way of life of a people with one of the lowest carbon footprints on the planet is imperilled.

Agnes Yawe, from Uganda, and Mary Prabhu, from India, say once-reliable rains have become so erratic that farmers can no longer work out when to plant their crops, causing harvests to plunge. Dominica Shumba, from Zimbabwe – who says "the climate has destroyed my life" – agrees: "In the past you could plan and calculate. But now, if you try to plan, the rains will either come late or come too strong and destroy your crops." In Zambia, Wilfred Miga told me, unreliable rains have caused maize, which once yielded eight tons per hectare, to barely produce two.

It's much the same in the Bolivian Andes, adds Rafael Arcangel Quispe Flores, an indigenous people's leader. One of the 10 big glaciers in his area has now entirely

Photo: Bruce Yeung / Shutterstock.com

"IN THE PAST YOU COULD PLAN AND CALCULATE. BUT NOW, IF YOU TRY TO PLAN, THE RAINS WILL EITHER COME LATE OR COME TOO STRONG AND DESTROY YOUR CROPS"

melted away, he says, the rest are about two thirds gone. Water supplies are shrinking while ever hotter weather increases demand. Potato harvests have fallen by 70 per cent and people are having to leave their land and migrate to the cities.

How long can the remainder hold on at this

Photo: Muriel Lasure / Shutterstock.com

POTATO HARVESTS HAVE FALLEN BY 70% AND PEOPLE ARE HAVING TO LEAVE THEIR LAND AND MIGRATE TO THE CITIES.

half the needed emission cuts by 2020. Even the habitually conservative International Energy Agency points out that if there is not a major change of direction by 2017, the two degree limit will be impossible to achieve, as investments in fossil-fuelled power stations and other carbon intensive infrastructure will have locked the world into too polluting a future. Studies show the change can be made with existing technology at reasonable cost, but this would require an unexpected breakthrough in the talks.

Meanwhile, the people here from the Third World – convinced that they are already facing a dangerously altered climate – watch the negotiations with mounting frustration. "They are saying 'let's wait', but we cannot wait", says Agnes Yawe, while Mohamed Adow adds: "Delay costs lives – and threatens the survival of my people."

rate? "Less than 10 years. By 2020 we will all have gone."

As it happens, 2020 is a significant date in the negotiating hall because many of the most highly polluting countries – such as the United States, Japan, Canada, Russia, India and Brazil – are effectively resisting taking further action, beyond what they have already voluntarily promised to do, until after then. But by

that point it will be too late, not just for the people of the Bolivian Andes, but for the world as a whole, if the rise in world temperatures is to be kept beneath two degrees C – the increase which scientists regard as the absolute maximum if runaway climate change is to be avoided.

The voluntary pledges, made by some 80 nations, will – at best – achieve only

The Daily Telegraph,
2 December 2011
© Telegraph Media Group Ltd 2011

MANY OF THE MOST HIGHLY POLLUTING COUNTRIES ARE RESISTING TAKING FURTHER ACTION, UNTIL AFTER 2020. BUT BY THAT POINT IT WILL BE TOO LATE, NOT JUST FOR THE PEOPLE OF THE BOLIVIAN ANDES, BUT FOR THE WORLD AS A WHOLE

Family & relationships

My parents aren't fake

A personal account of adoption

Katherine Eschels is 15 years old. She was adopted when she was 30 days old and wrote this paper explaining her experiences as an adopted child.

SOME ISSUES:

Does it matter if parents adopt a child that has different coloured skin to themselves?

What do you think makes a family?

Are adoptive parents real parents?

See also:
'Brilliant, challenging, gruelling, inspiring, life-affirming...', p60
Finding families
Fact File 2012, p63
All together now
Essential Articles 12, p42

www.completeissues.co.uk

Just because I am not blood related to my parents does not mean they are fake; and my biological parents are definitely not my real parents.

'So who are your real parents?'

Ever since I was young, people have asked me this question. I was adopted when I was only 30 days old. My "real parents", as they have been called, couldn't take care of me so I was adopted by my parents, Mary and Phil Eschels. People have and always will be curious about the why, who, and how of my story, but really, there isn't much to it.

It wasn't until I was in 4th grade (age 9-10) when the first person asked me about being adopted. I was proud to say that my family had wanted a child and they got me. In elementary school, kids were intrigued by why I was dark skinned and both my parents were white. At my school, there was one other boy in my grade who was adopted. However, he was fair skinned like his parents so no one considered that he was adopted like me. I hated how I was questioned about my family and he wasn't.

When I got to middle school, people started to learn more about what it meant to be adopted. They asked deeper questions like, *'Are you ever going to try to find your real parents?'* I have always liked telling people my story but it always stings when people imply that my adoptive parents are not my real parents. I only knew my biological parents for a very short time when I was born. My real parents are the ones I have grown up with all my life. They are the ones who raised me and called me their daughter. When my parents brought me home, all our friends and family came in from out of town to see me. We have many home videos of my first week or two in my new home. Everyone was thrilled for my parents and my new family fawned over having a new baby around. I was baptized a Lutheran when I was barely six weeks old. We changed churches when I was three and the people in that church accepted my family and me instantly. This church made me feel like I had a second family.

I have become very used to people wondering who my parents are when I am with them. When I was trying out some new golf clubs at Golf Galaxy with my dad, a worker was helping us and asked if he was my coach. I think it took the poor worker a while to understand the concept of the white man being the father of a dark skinned girl but

Photo: courtesy of lip magazine

I have become very used to people wondering who my parents are when I am with them.

apparently he finally got the picture because he asked if my Asian friend who was with me was my dad's other daughter. My family and I have gotten used to laughing off comments like this, but I am still shocked at how oblivious people can be about the facts of adoption.

I feel extremely blessed to have such a loving family. There are thousands of children across the globe that do not have homes or families. Some will never be adopted and will be put into a foster home. These children will be forced to leave when they turn 18 if they have not been adopted and even if they have nowhere to go. Most people do not realize how lucky they are to have families that love them. The children that are put up for adoption never know who their biological parents are in most cases and they don't know their story. However, there are also many children who do find homes and families who love and care for them.

I am lucky enough to be one of these people and I now live with a great family, who are my real parents.

lip magazine
February 2012
http://lipmag.com

I think it took the poor worker a while to understand the concept of the white man being the father of a dark skinned girl

'Brilliant, challenging, gruelling, inspiring, life-affirming...'

One adoptive mother's story

SOME ISSUES:

Why do you think more people prefer to have their own biological children, rather than adopt?

How could you encourage more people to adopt?

Would you consider adopting a child rather than having one naturally?

See also:
My parents aren't fake p58,
Finding families
Fact File 2012, p63
www.completeissues.co.uk

I am one of what seems to be a dwindling breed. I am an adoptive parent. Figures released this week suggest that adoption could be becoming less and less of a choice for the childless. Oddly in my view, for I consider myself lucky beyond belief to be raising three amazing adopted children, brighter and more beautiful than anything my sorry genes could produce.

Later today I will be talking to a group of people who are at the beginning of their journey to become adoptive parents. There won't be many of them, but while their childless peers continue to plough the IVF furrow, struggling on with the injections, the drugs and the disappointments in the hope of a "baby of their own", these adventurous few want to hear more about the reality of adopting.

This is one of the ways local authorities try to prepare couples (and individuals) for the adoption process. When I first adopted I remember attending a similar event, and I hung on the adoptive mother's every word – gosh, here was someone who had actually done it and survived to tell the tale! And I suppose what I want to convey, all these years on, is just what an extraordinary, brilliant, challenging, gruelling, inspiring, vital, life-affirming experience it has been.

My kids will have their own versions – of course they will – but from my point of view, this has been the greatest thing I have ever done, or am ever likely to do in my lifetime. Better than scaling Everest, better than winning an Olympic gold or a Euromillions roll-over, it has stretched me, challenged me and rewarded me in every conceivable way.

It may well be the same for any old biological parent, but (I know I'm prejudiced) I can't imagine it. For me everything has been – and

Photo posed by models

Adoption necessarily brings you into contact with different worlds and people who you would otherwise never have come across

care system that gets a persistently bad press, and social workers (so often underpaid, undertrained and overworked) who are habitually pilloried.

Adoption necessarily brings you into contact with different worlds and people who you would otherwise never have come across. There are painful stories and experiences to accept and absorb. It's a difficult, but great thing, to meet your child's birth parents face to face. (I have done it for each of mine, and although it is always incredibly hard – probably the hardest thing I have ever done – it is a profoundly moving and rewarding experience. Everyone in their best clothes, on their best behaviour, trying to do their best for that same child.) And it is quite a thing to get your head around, that this child, who you love and cherish and invest so much in, has a whole other family out there, always and for ever.

Adoption isn't easy, and it's not ordinary. But who wants to be ordinary?

continues to be – a surprise, an adventure, an unexpected bonus and a thrilling voyage into the unknown. My life since adopting children has been lived in brilliantly vivid, HD, 3D, surround-sound Technicolor. Things have gone wrong; I have done things wrong, and things will go wrong again. If the process has taught me anything it has been to expect the unexpected; we think we have some measure of control in our lives, but of course we don't. Things go well, things go badly, and they can turn on a sixpence.

So why don't more people do it? Well, there aren't many babies and people usually want babies (my children weren't babies when I adopted them but they were all under four); there's IVF, of course, with its promise of a peach-perfect newborn baby at the end; there are the bureaucratic obstacles would-be adopters apparently face that we read about in the Daily Mail (too fat, too middle-class, too white); then there's that weird suspicion that surrounds the whole idea of bringing up someone else's child, a child that doesn't share your genes or your background, or anything, in fact. Which in my view is one of the most exciting things about the whole process, though I know others are freaked out by it. Then there's the whole

The author wishes to remain anonymous

The Guardian, 1 October 2011
© Guardian News & Media Ltd 2011

A child will learn nothing from being hit

All smacking shows is that you've lost control when control is the very thing you want to teach

Annalisa Barbieri

SOME ISSUES:

Is there a lack of effective discipline in families?

Does physical punishment of any kind work?

What does work?

See also:
Bring back the cane to restore discipline in schools, p40
It takes more than a slap to teach right from wrong
Essential Articles 13, p82
www.completeissues.co.uk

Well, that David Lammy* has caused a hoo-ha with his talk of smacking children. And a decade ago, I might have agreed with him. But what a lot of learning I've done in 10 years. Here's the thing with children. They aren't born bad. They're not born wanting to harm, or hurt or steal. Circumstances do that to them – adults do.

You want to teach a child about self-discipline, about caring about others, about "doing the right thing"? Smacking won't do it. All it shows them is that you've lost control, at the very point where you're trying to teach them about control. Sure they may do as you say in the short term, because they are afraid or cowed. But they won't stay like that for very long. Ultimately, the fear will turn to anger, then pity if you're lucky, resentment and dislike if you're not. Hope your smacked child will look after you when you're older? Good luck with that.

Furthermore, there is no

Many people hit their children because it's what they grew up with and it "didn't do me any harm". But scratch the surface and there's always damage

evidence whatsoever to show that smacking a child makes them less likely to riot, such as Lammy seems to claim. Plenty to the contrary. Read up, David. A child who has good self-esteem (and cocky arrogance is not having good self-esteem), a child who feels loved and listened to does not riot or loot. Children are not monsters needing the "evil" smacked out of them; reverse that, you might get closer to the truth.

If you hit an adult, you can be charged with assault, even if you don't leave a red mark (a red mark elevates it to actual bodily harm), but if you hit a child and leave no mark, that's deemed OK as far as the law currently stands – unless you hit them above the neck, for which you can still be prosecuted, mark or no mark.

Yesterday, I heard this: "Wishy-washy liberals have ruined child discipline in this country, with their guilt-ridden belief that the rotten, spoilt little brats can do no wrong." Incorrect. It is detached parenting that has done that, and that can have any political or economic background. A detached parent might hit, or shout, or conversely shower the child with presents. But listen, respect, or teach by

example? Nah. Yet how can you teach a child to be empathetic if you show that its feelings count for so little?

Many people hit their children because it's what they grew up with and it "didn't do me any harm". But scratch the surface and there's always damage. Not disciplining your children doesn't mean just allowing them to do what they want, either. There are many

shades of grey: just look at a Farrow & Ball** colour chart.

The way to get a child to grow up to be a responsible adult is to engage with them, be responsive, and love unconditionally. All of this takes time, and courage in today's climate. A smack? Easier, but it teaches the child nothing positive. Nothing.

The Independent, 31 January 2012

* David Lammy is the Labour MP for Tottenham who said, after the riots of August 2011, that parents should be allowed to instill discipline by smacking

** Farrow and Ball make expensive paint in understated colours.

Ultimately, the fear will turn to anger, then pity if you're lucky, resentment and dislike if you're not

"The teacher didn't hit me, but I sure made her want to."

My 14-year-old son is displaying very strong homosexual tendencies

Graham Norton answers all your problems...

SOME ISSUES:

Why do you think the parent is concerned?

Do you think Graham offers good advice?

What advice would you give?

See also:
www.completeissues.co.uk

Dear Graham

My 14-year-old son is displaying very strong homosexual tendencies. He's been regularly looking at gay porn on the internet; I tackled him about this verbally and then by email (I don't live with him), advising him that at his age it doesn't necessarily mean he is gay – it's all part of experimentation and growing up. He seems to have reacted very well to the supportive approach I have taken.

But I can't help thinking that he is definitely gay because he hasn't been visiting heterosexual porn sites and he spoke of urges to kiss his friends at sleepovers. My "public" approach to him disguises my real inner feelings: I am absolutely knotted up inside. I'm not anti-gay; it's just a selfish issue that I am sure most men have with regard to their hopes and visions for their sons. Gay was not on the agenda and it has shaken me up a lot. I feel there is little I can do, however, to alter this (even though deep down I want to and hate myself for thinking that way). He goes to an all-boys' school and lives with his mum and sister. Add to this the fact he is painfully shy and lacking in confidence.

Should I continue to present my public approach of it all being OK if he does turn out to be gay? I really don't want him to think there is anything "wrong" with him. I wonder if maybe I should be buying him some "top shelf" magazines, but then perhaps I shouldn't be encouraging him. Your advice please.

Dave H, Bracknell

Dear Dave

Give yourself a break. Just because you don't live with your son doesn't mean you have to overcompensate by being the best dad in the world ever. Your teenage son is having some issues around his sexuality. No more, no less. I think it's great that the two of you have been able to talk about this and that you haven't freaked out – at least not to his face. Please remember, though, that it is possible to be accepting and supportive of your son while still being a strong parent. Rather than encourage a 14-year-old boy to engage with porn, perhaps you should explain that the images he's seeing are not representative of sex or adult relationships. No one in porn gets rejected. No one gets their heart broken. Make sure he understands this and doesn't blur the lines between fantasy and reality. Kissing random boys on a sleepover will probably not go as well as he hopes. Your fears for your son are perfectly natural. Obviously this wasn't the future you had imagined for him and it will take time for both of you to adjust. Be patient. Just putting the word "gay" in front of "son" or "boy" doesn't alter the fact that he is still a child. What he's going through isn't that different from what you went through when you started stumbling through the sexual undergrowth, so protect him from what you can and prepare him for what you can't. You are doing a great job!

The Daily Telegraph, 18 November 2011
© Telegraph Media Group Ltd 2011

I really don't want him to think there is anything "wrong" with him

Protect him from what you can and prepare him for what you can't.

A letter to... my mother, who I left behind

When I left, I didn't know my desperate actions would scar us both for the rest of our lives. I imagined that my break for freedom would assert my difference to you. I needed to put a distance between the limitations of my childhood and my teenage aspirations for a greater existence. When I look back now, I was so young. At the time, I knew only that I was old enough to fend for myself and make my own life.

The parting wasn't amicable. I had met some people you didn't like. You had already expressed your concerns to my school teachers and despite my exemplary exam results I decided to leave at 16, feeling surrounded and stifled. You asked me to leave home, at the end of your tether with my rudeness and inexplicable behaviour. I think you believed I would be back, sorry for my ways and promising you a daughter more in line with the one you had in mind. But you underestimated my inability to play by your rules, and I never returned.

Proud of my resolve to show you I didn't need you, I found myself so removed emotionally from my life that when I heard you were unwell again I remained solid and unmoved. Years of therapy have taught me that when a child loses a parent at a young age, and is unable to process that grief through conversation, memories and laughter, they will lock that pain very deep inside. When their remaining parent is unwell, it's almost too much to bear.

We rarely spoke about Dad. He was always ill, often in hospital and not very happy. He never did "fatherly" things, but I loved him anyway, as any eight-year-old would. You decided I was too young for the funeral, that it would be too much for me, but it wasn't your decision. You had cancer twice while I was with you and survived. I couldn't take a third time. I bolted before I had to. I'm sorry.

You visited me once. You wrote to me once. You had lived with the guilt of losing your own mother and being blamed for it. Why did you leave me the same legacy?

SOME ISSUES:

Can you understand this writer's point of view?

Who should decide if a child should go to a funeral?

Who is to blame for the sadness and distress in this story?

See also:
www.completeissues.co.uk

> You asked me to leave home, at the end of your tether with my rudeness and inexplicable behaviour. I think you believed I would be back

You had cancer twice while I was with you and survived. I couldn't take a third time. I bolted before I had to. I'm sorry.

Why didn't your wisdom make you fight harder to get through to me and save me from forever living with the same pain? I realised my mistake one morning and rushed to the hospice to see you before it was too late. The nurse told me gently that you had died the previous day. I was 19.

Now that I'm a mother myself, I understand the unconditional love you showered me with when I was young. Every time I hold my children, I know how it feels to be held with such love because of you. When they wake in the night I remember you comforting me when I couldn't sleep.

If we visit Covent Garden I remember our first trip there, the excitement of the two of us on a day out to London. I can still see the earrings you bought me and I can still taste the meal we shared in the restaurant because we couldn't afford to buy two. It all went wrong because I couldn't deal with your pain, you couldn't see mine and there was no one to help us.

You were right about those people. They weren't good for me and I eventually broke free from them as well. I wish you were here to see how much I've learned since you knew me and the person I've become. I think she's much more in line with the daughter you had in mind.

I love you, Mum, maybe too late, but I love you.

AnnaMaria

The Guardian, 7 May 2011
© Guardian News & Media Ltd 2011

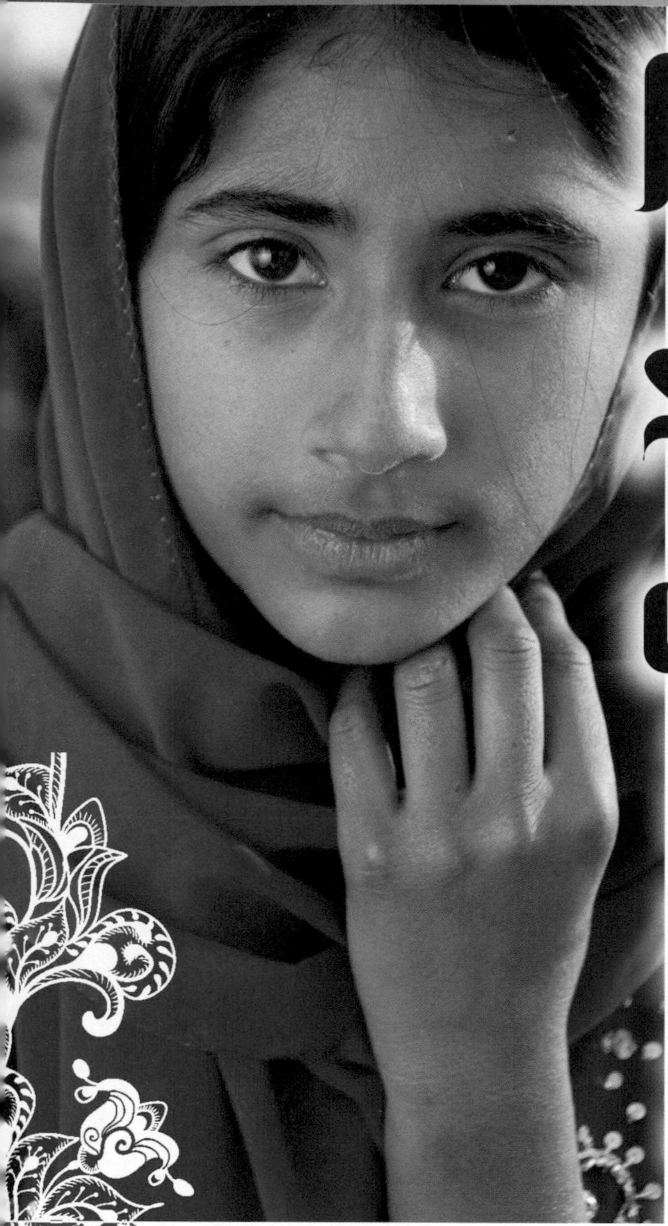

My aunt said I was wicked

Asma Khan grew up in Britain in a traditional Muslim family. She was excited about visiting Pakistan for the first time, aged 11, for a cousin's wedding. But her experience was horrific, and made her wary of family and faith

Photo posed by model

SOME ISSUES:

Did Asma have alternatives to the way she responded to what happened to her?

Did the family have any alternative?

Is keeping quiet a good way to deal with this?

Why would someone who 'will never tell' write a newspaper article?

See also:
I sent my abusive father to jail
Essential Articles 14, p84
www.completeissues.co.uk

If you ask any Pakistani what holds us together, they will say family and faith, but what they won't tell you is that family and faith can also tear you apart. That's what crossed my mind as I sat, holding a photo of a dark-skinned, dark-eyed little girl. I have the photo turned over; I cannot bear to look in her eyes, even though she's done nothing wrong. It's because if I do, I will see the eyes of her father, my Uncle. The last time I saw Uncle, I was 11 and it was my first visit to Pakistan.

I was small and skinny and had yet to show any signs of turning into a woman, either physically or emotionally. I had little knowledge or interest in adult relationships, and things like that are rarely discussed in Asian families.

Although we knew nothing about sex, we all knew about shame, purity and family honour. We have just one word for it in our language, izzat. While there are

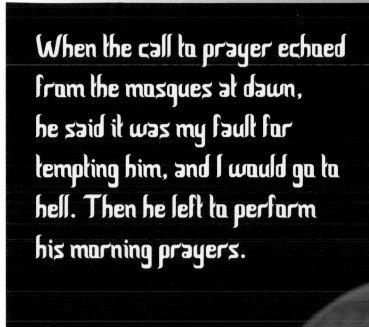

When the call to prayer echoed from the mosques at dawn, he said it was my fault for tempting him, and I would go to hell. Then he left to perform his morning prayers.

Photo posed by model

dozens of words in English to describe its different facets, there isn't an equivalent. Ultimately, it means the worst sin is for a girl not to be pure – in other words, a virgin – before marriage.

Like most of my friends in the UK, our parents were, ironically, much stricter than those of our cousins in Pakistan. They were paranoid about us becoming too westernised, so they kept us cocooned at home. Culture became our religion, and most of our parents were fundamentalists.

Some days I'd be watching TV, and a romantic scene would come, and it would trigger a lecture from my mum. "It's OK for English people, but in our culture we don't have boyfriends, and you are having an arranged marriage, OK?" Sometimes I felt guilty of something before I had done anything.

One day I came home from school and my mum was talking excitedly on the phone in Punjabi. Her youngest sister's marriage had been arranged, and we would be going.

My parents hadn't been able to afford to return home for years, so my mum was excited about seeing her family, and

I was looking forward to seeing the place where she had grown up. I was drawn by her wistful expression as she talked about stealing sugar cane from the fields, and holidays near the mountains. I was a misfit at school, and dreamed that I, too, would find somewhere I could belong. My mum's fantasy had become my fantasy also.

There is no more exciting place for a girl to be than Karachi in the run-up to a wedding. I was excited about wearing traditional wedding clothes for the first time, and my mum glowed with happiness as the sister of the bride.

The first ceremony, the mehndi – or henna party – was what we were most excited about, because that is when everyone dances, and the bride's sisters compete with those of the groom to see who can sing the loudest.

To prepare for the mehndi, we had parties called dholkis – after the dholki drum – which the girls played as the rest of us sang wedding songs from the latest Bollywood films. We used henna paste to decorate our palms, the muddy trails leaving pretty, spider-web patterns on our hands the next day.

My aunts and cousins all knew what he had done, but they all still danced at his wedding and painted their hands with henna.

A week before the wedding, Uncle arrived. On the death of my grandfather, Uncle had taken responsibility for the family and never married. He worked in the Middle East, successfully educated his brothers, and married off his sisters in respectable homes.

He was a large man, dark skinned, with a small beard. Always in white traditional clothes, with prayer beads in hand, he was able to quote lines from the Qu'ran on any subject.

He often cornered me to talk about religion, and how girls growing up in the west were already halfway down the road to sin.

My family was not particularly religious, and Uncle spoke with such authority that I thought Allah was hanging around waiting for me to mess up and prove what everyone suspected all along.

On the night of the mehndi, I fell ill. My cousins were upset that I wouldn't be able to join in and my mother said she'd take me home, but we could tell she was disappointed. "Don't worry," said Uncle.

"Mehndis are for women. I will take her home."

It felt strange being at the house alone with Uncle. It had been so full of people and activity, but now it was silent. Uncle told me to undress for bed and he would check on me later.

I was half asleep and barely noticed him come in. He sat on my bed and placed his hand on my forehead to check my temperature, then began stroking my hair.

As he did so, he talked softly, his voice caring, yet menacing, like honey on a serpent's tongue, and his breath smelled sour, of old cigarettes. I felt scared, but didn't know why. My heart was beating swiftly and I couldn't breathe. He began to caress my back, then his hands slipped under my clothes ...

When the call to prayer echoed from the mosques at dawn, he said it was my fault for tempting him, and I would go to hell. Then he left to perform his morning prayers.

I spent the following day in a daze. I kept thinking I could feel Uncle's touch, like insects crawling over me, and showered over and over again, but no matter how hard I scrubbed, the feeling wouldn't go away.

During the day, he always seemed to be angry with me and I felt like I was walking on eggshells when he was around. Every time I looked up, his eyes were following me. As everyone excitedly dressed up in their sparkly outfits and shared jokes, I was at the edge of the happy picture, not quite a part of it. It was hard to pretend to smile when I knew, as each hour passed, it would be night again and he would return to my room.

Eventually, two days before the final ceremony, I told my cousin Nadia everything. Though I swore her to secrecy, she told her mum. Nadia's mum dragged me downstairs, hissing angrily that I was a wicked girl, and I burst into tears, partly of fear and partly of relief.

My mum couldn't process what had happened and began wailing loudly as her sisters held her. Another aunt asked me if I was a virgin because if not, they would have to marry me off straight away, so I lied and said he had only touched me. Although my aunts were sympathetic, I could tell by their eyes that they were relieved that it wasn't their daughter. I think my mum could tell too.

That night, the elders talked about what to do, but everyone seemed more worried about protecting the family's honour than what was best for me. They worried that any scandal could ruin Nadia's chances for marriage. Everyone decided the best thing would be to pretend it never happened and never to talk about it.

When we returned, my dad hugged us at the airport, thinking we'd had the time of our lives. Looking back, I wonder if he sensed my mum's unhappiness. But I couldn't get the memories out of my head. I couldn't tell anyone because I was ashamed. I stopped writing my diary because the words felt too dirty to be put on the diary's clean pages. My school work suffered and my friends thought I was moody. There was a guy in my class who liked me, but I was horrible to him. Once he touched my shoulder in the canteen and I shouted at him in front of everyone.

At university I became friends with a girl who wore a hijab, who told me she had been abused. I told her what had happened to me and asked how she could stay devoted to her faith after a thing like that. She told me it was her faith that had got her through. I

discovered I'd got it all wrong, that in the Qu'ran It says people like Uncle are the sinners, and in Allah's eyes I was as chaste as a virgin. But nobody ever tells you that. All that time, Uncle had used religion against me and I had let him. My mum became less strict too. What had happened to me had unlocked a repressed memory she had of an uncle abusing her too. She also said she believed me from the start, and regretted not confronting her brother.

I heard rumours about Uncle over the years, that he had reluctantly had an arranged marriage to a woman much younger than him. My aunts and cousins all knew what he had done, but they all still danced at his wedding and painted their hands with henna.

After I graduated, my parents also arranged a marriage for me. Though it was a traditional setup, my husband was brought up here, and he's kind and gentle so we get on well. I am certain he suspects, and has for a long time, but he doesn't ask and I will never tell.

Asma Khan is a pseudonym

The Guardian, 7 May 2011
© Guardian News & Media Ltd 2012

Everyone decided the best thing would be to pretend it never happened and never to talk about it.

Financial issues

QUIDS IN?

are payday loan companies a skint man's best friend – or sharks in digital clothing?

SOME ISSUES:

Why do you think people might resort to loans with such high interest rates?

Do you think there should be a cap set on interest rates to prevent people from getting into a spiral of debt?

Should people sacrifice the things they like if they cannot afford them, rather than resort to loans?

See also:
Deep in debt
Fact File 2012, p74

Debt hotspots
Fact File 2012, p75

www.completeissues.co.uk

"Quickquid", "maketodaypayday", "idosh", "expressloan" and "crisis-loan" – the names tell you most of what you need to know. In this recession, one area of business which is booming is payday loans – instant, easily accessible cash to get you out of a fix, just until you get your wages. The promises attached to the names are seductive: "a loan of up to £1,000 instantly", "Cash in your account in 1 hour", "No hassle. No Fuss." and, significantly, "all applicants accepted", "No credit checks". But the quick and easy instant loan often proves less quick and less easy to pay off and borrowers find themselves trapped into an endless struggle with debt.

There is undoubtedly a demand for the service. According to 3R, a body which represents professionals advising people in financial trouble, 45% of the population struggle to make it to payday and this rises to 62% in the 25-44 year old group. For 38% of those who find it difficult to manage on their regular income the main reason was existing debt –

especially the need to make credit card repayments.

Advocates of this rapidly growing business say that it provides a service for a new generation of borrowers. Wonga, for instance, sees its customers as internet users who are used to getting things instantly, 24/7, and who don't mind paying for the speed and convenience – a group of people for whom traditional loan services are too slow and cumbersome. The head of marketing at Wonga compares their service to taking a taxi rather than a bus – it costs more but it's more convenient. His firm has impressive figures for customer satisfaction and, unlike some, does not accept every customer - in fact it declines about two thirds of applicants. Its interest rates, £1 a day for every £100 borrowed, certainly make sense of the taxi comparison.

A Which? report, however suggests that Wonga's picture of a typical payday loan customer is wrong. It's not convenience but

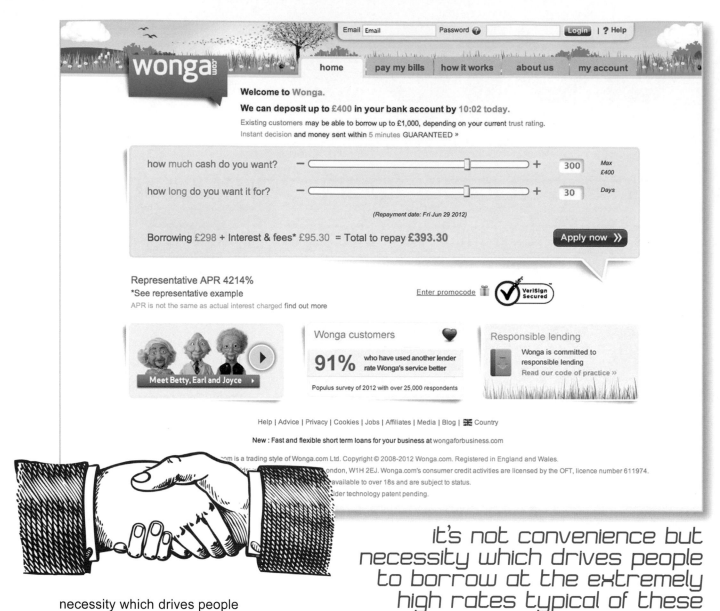

it's not convenience but necessity which drives people to borrow at the extremely high rates typical of these companies

necessity which drives people to borrow at the extremely high rates typical of these companies (and Wonga is not the highest!). Most borrowers need the money for essentials. 60%, according to Which? are borrowing to pay for items such as nappies, food or petrol or in order to pay a household bill. A third of people said they actually had greater financial problems after taking the loan and a fifth were not able to pay it back on time.

The loans are popular – about 4 million people will take out a payday loan in the next six months. The trade body that represents the payday lenders, the Consumer Finance Association, says that 94% of payday customers are satisfied. So who are these customers? Most (two thirds) have a household income of less than £25,000 per year and the average amount they borrow is £300.

Some are grateful for the anonymity, one person posted in response to a Guardian article: "you don't have to humiliate yourself borrowing from friends when you can't make ends meet". Another explained: "No payrise for three years, despite all other costs going up. Partner is a student, ... I recently lost my second job ... which means 140 quid a month less in our pockets. We've not totally cut everything back, but what do you do? Dance with the devil and have the odd payday loan, or my girlfriend stop buying petrol and thus not make it to uni? Or not take the cat to the vet? Or tell the daughter that she can no longer have her dance and piano lessons?"

This is perhaps what lenders mean when they

for someone already in difficulty, one missed payment can be disastrous and the only way out could be further borrowing, accumulating more and more debt.

portray payday loans as a 'lifestyle choice'.

The alternatives – for those who have them – might be to borrow interest free by using an overdraft or a credit card and paying it off. For those, who have no access to other facilities, the payday loan is a lifeline – but an expensive one. Borrowing that average £300 from Wonga would mean an admin charge plus interest of £3 per day, so an extra £97 to pay back after a month. That's if you manage to pay it off at the end of the month.

But some lenders charge much more. Convenience, ease and absence of credit checks come at a price in crippling interest rates – some of which work out at 1000% or 2000% over a year (though of course they are intended to be short-term). There are also extra charges, sometimes as much as £30, for missed payments and around £25 for every reminder letter. The lenders justify these high charges because of the high risk – in other words because they know they are lending to people who will struggle to repay.

For someone already in difficulty, one missed payment can be disastrous and the only way out could be further borrowing, accumulating more and more debt. Quoted in the Guardian, the Citizens Advice Bureau chief executive gave this example: "We recently advised a woman who had a £500 QuickQuid loan, £800 on a Vanquis credit card and £5,000 on an Aqua credit card, but still had £2,000 in rent arrears," he said.

R3 are concerned about the growing number of 'zombie' debtors, people who are only able to pay off the interest on their cards or loans but never manage to pay off the loan itself. In the words of their President: "Remaining on this treadmill carries no provision for outside factors making things worse" and "Struggling onwards each month with high interest charges on personal debt, and with no capacity to pay back, means you are simply tipping water into the sand."

In the R3 survey of payday loan users, 68% said they took out a payday loan because they could not get credit elsewhere. Only 13% said it had had a positive influence on their finances while 48% said it had made their financial situation worse.

So is there a way out? As a nation we have been using large amounts of credit for some time now and it seems unlikely that we will return to the habits of previous generations and learn to 'save up' (sounds quaint!) before buying. This is especially unlikely since student loans make high levels of debt the norm for a mass of young people. One alternative is more credit unions and community based financial cooperatives – though these are more likely to encourage old-fashioned saving rather than reckless spending, which isn't always what people want. Another, supported by some MPs, is a legal limit on interest charges. Naturally this is not favoured by the payday lenders who argue that it would drive legal lenders out of business and force desperate people to go to illegal lenders – loan sharks.

So, for the moment, for those with little or no alternative, you pays your money and you takes your choice, then you pays your money again, and again and again ...

Sources: Various

only 13% said it had had a positive influence on their finances while 48% said it had made their financial situation worse

It's the inequality, stupid

Katherine Trebeck

We know so much about the growing inequality in the UK.

We know that it is getting worse – in Scotland, for example, two fifths of the increase in income during the last decade has gone to the richest 10% of the population).

We know that it is worse than most other European countries – the UK is up there with Greece, Bulgaria and Lithuania.

Many of us know that now the greatest inequality seems to be not between those in work and those out of work, but between those in work – between those who earn mountains and brag about it, and those who earn an hourly wage so low they remain below the poverty line.

And we know that, combined with decreasing social mobility, the **UK's inequality means people have no hope of ever climbing an increasingly steep and sparsely-runged ladder.**

What is so amazing is the lack of appreciation of how interconnected the talons of inequality are with our various social and environmental problems.

In an unequal society, in which resources are owned, enjoyed and controlled by the few rather than being shared amongst more people, the (often not very subtle) message to those at the bottom of the hierarchy is that they have lost the competition. Worse, there is an implicit assumption that they deserve their lower status because they are somehow less able, less talented, less gifted.

This ignores the opportunities, privilege and support showered on those who already 'have' – the education, the social connections, the resources, the confidence, the

SOME ISSUES:

Do you think that you live in an unequal society?

What signs of inequality do you see around you?

How do you think this can be tackled?

See also:

Time to stop glossing over these artful tax dodgers
Essential Articles 14, p92

Fair play on fair pay
Essential Articles 14, p191

www.completeissues.co.uk

Photo: Nick Reynolds Photography / Shutterstock.com

exclusive access to jobs and so on. I often wonder why we don't expect more from such people than 'socially useless' work in finance or wallowing in inherited wealth. What happened to 'from those to whom much is given, much is expected'?

But there is a much more profound, longer term impact of inequality.

Firstly, **it corrodes our social institutions that make us civilised and humane.** The more distant we are from each other – the more we inhabit different worlds, live in different localities, send our children to different schools, shop in different establishments, experience different health care –, the less we recognise each other.

The less we recognise each other, the less we appreciate our connections with each other.

The less we appreciate our connection with each other, the less we empathise for each other.

The less we empathise with each other, the less we care for each other.

And the less we care for each other, the less willing we are to contribute to shared support systems.

Hence we should start recognising the growing tax evasion and the paring down and tightening up of our mechanisms of social protection as a function of our increasingly unequal society. These shifts will also make inequality far, far worse.

Secondly, **inequality fuels materialism that leads to conspicuous consumption** – people try to demonstrate their status outwardly through possessions that denote conformity to some social grouping. Materialistic pursuits crowd out our time and emotional energy for more valuable pursuits such as community involvement. It can also lead to debt. And such consumption is completely rubbish for the environment – in every sense of the word 'rubbish'!

And finally, **inequality generates angst and anxiety about one's status.** Evidence from around the world shows that living with stress, anxiety and a sense of alienation leads to socially destructive behaviours and premature death. **Inequality really is a matter of life and death.**

When looking aghast at the state of the world, we could do worse than remind ourselves that it is the inequality that underpins so many of our dire problems.

oxfamblogs.org, 27 January 2012

The hypocrisy of the filthy rich

James Bloodworth

The benefits of being rich are numerous, and probably don't need a great deal of explanation from me. The ability to travel the world at the drop of a hat is, I imagine, one of the many advantages great wealth brings, as is the possibility of doing away with a number of the banal inconveniences that plague everyday life. Not having to get out of bed at the crack of dawn for work has its appeal, as does eating the best food and never having to cook any of the damn stuff.

Just as important as jet-setting and attending "exclusive" parties these days, however, is the obligatory portfolio of charity work that comes with being incredibly wealthy. One is far more likely to turn on the television today and hear a member of the global elite talking about a project for clean water in Africa than about their recent purchase of a mock-Tudor mansion in Hertfordshire. And rarely does a week go by without the appearance of a member of the super-rich in a distressed part of the world with their shirt sleeves rolled up – if not actually trying to save the world, then usually throwing a great deal of money at a small proportion of it.

There is no doubt of course that some of those fortunate enough to be wealthy are genuinely concerned with the plight of the poor. Just as there are conservatives with nothing to be conservative about, so there are aristocrats, "entrepreneurs" and

> Another type among the super-rich... is the wealthy individual who very publically gives generously with one hand while ruthlessly seeking to minimise what they pay in tax with the other.

those that are simply swimming in cash who do have a well-developed and genuine social conscience.

Another type among the super-rich, however – some would say the dominant type – is the wealthy individual who very publically gives generously with one hand while ruthlessly seeking to minimise what they pay in tax with the other. The moralising hypocrite, you might call this lot.

Perhaps the most well-known figure in this mould is Bono, the lead singer of U2. As well as being the frontman of one of the world's biggest rock bands, Bono fancies himself as something of an anti-poverty activist, and can often be heard urging people to give generously to a number of causes. Bono has even been nominated for the Nobel Peace Prize several times for his charity work.

In 2006, however, on the back of the massive Live 8 concert the year before – which U2 played a large part in organising and which was supposed to "make poverty history" – Bono's band moved part of their tax liability from Ireland to the Netherlands. The move came after Ireland scrapped tax breaks that allowed musicians and artists to avoid paying taxes on royalties. When asked about the decision, U2's lead guitarist David Evans, aka "The Edge", said that of course the band were trying to be tax-efficient, because "who doesn't want to be tax-efficient?"

The answer, at a guess, would be those who spend a great deal of time moralising about the world's poor. Away from the self-congratulatory press conferences where Bono smugly demanded we send our money to the dispossessed, U2 were simultaneously cutting the feet from under their own government's ability to help the world's most desperate people – the same people Bono was proclaiming such grave concern for.

The hypocrisy of the super-rich is nothing new of course. What is astonishing is that they are so consistently let off the hook for it. Nobody bats an eyelid today at a campaign against homelessness featuring a politician who would sooner sell his own mother than interfere in the exploitative buy-to-let market; or a coffee chain publicising its fair trade credentials while preventing its own workers from joining a union. Both will stand on a soap box and espouse their unflinching dedication to the downtrodden – and both will be given an extraordinarily easy-ride by the media when doing so.

It is quite possible that we have the late Princess of Wales to thank for at least a portion of this fetishisation of charity above all other virtues. Her death at a young age saw perhaps the closest thing Britain has ever seen to mass hysteria; and with it the passing into folklore of the belief that her goodness was tied up to a large extent with the notion that she "did a lot for charity" – despite the fact that she left her entire estate to her own super-rich family.

It feels like all of this has been preparing the ground in some way for David Cameron; for if there is one thing which seamlessly gels Cameron's conservatism together, it is the belief that poverty is best left to wealthy individuals to remedy, rather than government. His "Big Society" approach to social provision can perhaps best be summed up with the phrase: do it yourself, because we don't care.

It would be an extremely brave or stupid person who said there was not a long way to go in terms of democratising the way public funds are spent by governments and treasuries. Government spending does, however, at least give us, the public, at least a degree of a control over where money is spent. Certainly a great deal more than when we rely for the solving of our social problems on the mood swings of a global financial elite – the same elite who threaten to pull down the roof whenever the prospect of paying a few extra pence in the pound in income tax is proposed.

As Clement Atlee pointed out some half a century ago, "charity is a cold, grey, loveless thing. If a rich man wants to help the poor, he should pay his taxes gladly, not dole out money at a whim."

The Independent,
19 January 2012

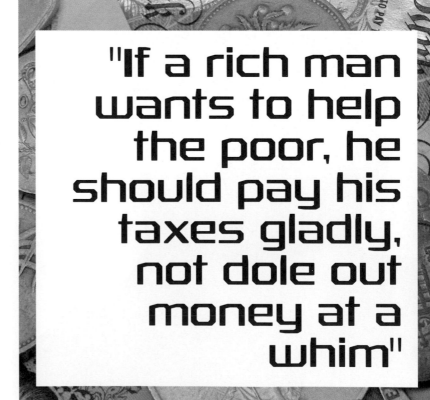

"If a rich man wants to help the poor, he should pay his taxes gladly, not dole out money at a whim"

Food & drink

Why are children so fat? Check their morning cereal

Jackie Annesley

The foodies on Mumsnet call it crack for kids. Krave is the latest offering from Kellogg's to persuade children to eat a breakfast that is 30 per cent pure sugar. The TV ads feature bouncing cereal shells gobbling up chocolate, while the packets entice you to play Krave Krusaders on Facebook. Children love it.

Which is obviously why no one at Kellogg's is taking a blind bit of notice of Health Secretary Andrew Lansley's Call to Action for the food industry to cut calories "in many products" as the country faces an obesity epidemic.   If he really wants to understand why 28 per cent of children aged two to 10 are overweight, Lansley might do well to wander around his local supermarket, not forgetting to check out the cereal aisle.

I did last night. If you are partial to death-by-chocolate at 7am, you really are spoiled for choice. Look, here are some Weetabix Minis Chocolate Chip ("built for family life"), and just 21 per cent sugar. And there are chocolate-flavoured Oats So Simple, only 14 times more sugar than boring old plain

SOME ISSUES:

Who is responsible for a child's food choice?

Who is responsible for increasing levels of obesity?

The website says 'Enjoy Krave as part of a healthy, balanced diet', has the company done enough by saying this?

See also:

Bad breakfast
Fact File 2011, p92

www.completeissues.co.uk

If you are partial to death-by-chocolate at 7am you really are spoiled for choice.

porridge. (There's sweet cinammon flavour too!) And over there is Ready Brek - no longer central heating for kids but chocolate-flavoured and 21 per cent sugar, while Kellogg's Coco Pops Choc'N'Roll has a big tick next to its claim of "9 per cent GDA of sugar" above a smiley face of a monkey. They forgot to mention that was for an active adult, not a three-year-old.

But the big daddy of them all is Choco Puffs, cousin of Sugar Puffs, which spawned the memorable Honey Monster's "Tell them about the honey, Mummy" ad campaign. I suppose "Tell them about the 43.3 per cent sugar content, Mummy" doesn't have the same ring to it. Why should we care? And if parents are idiotic enough to buy this stuff, why should the Government intervene? You only have to look at its bill for Type 2 diabetes, an obesity-driven epidemic, to find the answer. Treating it costs taxpayers £14 million a day, 10 per cent of the NHS's entire budget.

Historically, governments are useless at protecting the public from damaging food industry claims. If you have a spare 58 minutes and really want to know why child cancers have been growing at up to 1.5 per cent a year for decades, check out a lecture on YouTube (http://tinyurl.com/6zhr43f) by Professor David Servan-Schreiber from Pittsburg University. Cancer cells feed only on glucose (sugar), and to explain the sudden spike in sugar consumption after the war the professor shows a classic American ad from the 1950s. "For a better start in life, start cola earlier" is written next to a picture of a

mother and a chubby-faced baby, sponsored by The Soda Pop Board of America. At about the same time, cigarette manufacturers in Britain were still allowed to advertise the supposed health benefits of their product, free from warnings that nicotine could turn your lungs black and kill you. When lung cancer rates shot up and NHS bills mounted, government finally got a grip. Soon it might just dawn on Lansley that allowing food manufacturers to sell children's breakfast cereal with a 43 per cent sugar content is just as ruinous to the nation's health, and equally unaffordable to the NHS.

I crave the day.

London Evening Standard, 14 October 2011

A **NEW BREED** OF **CHOCOLATE CEREAL** IS **HERE!**

"WE NEED TO MAKE SURE THAT ... ARE GIVEN THE OPPO... TO LEARN ABOU ... EATING HABIT ... E STILL YOUNG, ...'RE SORTED ... OLIVER

WE'VE BETRAYED CHILDREN WHO CAN'T USE CUTLERY

Rosamund Urwin

Poor Jamie Oliver. Not only has his noble fight to stop the nation's youngsters chowing down on chips slipped out of the public consciousness, but now a study suggests he might have been better concentrating his message beyond the school canteen. According to research from Pennsylvania State University, how children eat at home has a much more marked effect on obesity than the food they can buy at secondary school.

The study was done in the US but the same conclusion would surely be drawn here. If children eat 21 meals a week, five of them will be at school, and eating patterns develop before they even start school. If they are loading up with sugar-laden cereals in the morning and munching their way through Domino's for dinner, how much difference can a healthy meal in the middle really make?

SOME ISSUES:

How can you persuade people to eat healthily?

Is fast food to blame for obesity?

What does it say about somebody if they can't use a knife and fork?

See also:

www.completeissues.co.uk

Just over a year ago, the catering giant Compass invited me to eat in one of its schools. No more Turkey Twizzlers, I was told: post-Jamie the company's approach was radically different - would I come to Stockley Academy in Uxbridge and see?

Given the small sum it was able to spend per pupil, I was impressed. Every option was fairly

WE CAN'T STOP THE RATE OF CHILDHOOD OBESITY RISING UNLESS PARENTS CHANGE WHAT THEY GIVE THEIR CHILDREN

healthy and the majority of meals were made from scratch. What interested me most, though, was speaking to the head chef, a charming man keen to spread the message about good food. He told me that the school taught nutrition, as pupils had little understanding of what they should be eating, and that some turned up at secondary school not knowing how to use cutlery because they had only ever eaten fast food.

We can't stop the rate of childhood obesity rising unless parents change what they give their children. We seem to believe that good quality food is invariably expensive and that eating well is a snobby activity, yet some of the best cuisines in the world were born out of poverty. It is never going to be politically popular to say it, but parents - however busy they may be - need to get back in the kitchen.

They're not entirely to blame, though: the Government needs to be tougher with fast-food sellers too. Last year I spotted an advert for KFC that read: "Called your teacher 'Mum', but GOOD NEWS!" Underneath this, was a picture of chips and chicken spheres. The news so good it had to be in capital letters was that this "snack box" only cost £1.99.

THEY'RE NOT ENTIRELY TO BLAME, THOUGH: THE GOVERNMENT NEEDS TO BE TOUGHER WITH FAST-FOOD SELLERS TOO.

KFC says this portion of "popcorn chicken" has 630 calories. It also claims it doesn't market to children - but I'm guessing most of us only had teachers when we were under 18.

If you give children five healthy meals a week, it's a good start. But eating healthily needs to begin on the street - and at home.

London Evening Standard, 19 January 2012

YOUNG CARNIVORES SHOULD BE TAUGHT THE TRUTH

Meat-eating children need to learn about how the animals we eat end up on our plates
Jemima Lewis

At a time when many schools no longer dare organise field trips, for fear that someone might chip a nail and sue, you'd think Shirley Stapleton would be hailed as a national heroine. On Wednesday, the headteacher of Ashbeach Primary School, in Ramsey St Mary's, Cambridgeshire, despatched a class of 10-year-olds on an evening "wildfowling" trip.

What that means, for the uninitiated, is that they got to tiptoe across the local marshes in the gloaming, looking for ducks, and then watch one being shot out of the sky and retrieved by a gun dog. Darkness. Bogs. Firearms. It could hardly get more exciting if the Hound of the Baskervilles hoved up.

Yet instead of marvelling at Mrs Stapleton's chutzpah, some parents have accused her of traumatising their children. Ray Poolman, 46, claims his daughter came home in tears after the "harrowing" experience of seeing a duck shot. "They allowed children to witness the death of an animal," huffed the outraged paterfamilias. "Ramsey might be rural but we have a Tesco – people don't need to walk around killing animals to survive any more."

Now, strictly speaking this may be true. Here in London, too, we don't usually "walk around killing animals" for the table. There wouldn't be much to choose from anyway, apart from rats and weapon dogs. But – and it surely shouldn't be necessary

to explain this to a country-dweller – just because you buy your meat shrink-wrapped, doesn't mean you're not a killer.

The reality is that, if you eat any meat at all, you have blood on your hands. No animal wants to be killed and eaten. Whether the creature in question gets hooked out of a river, blasted out of the sky or strung up by its ankles and electrified before having its throat slit, you really can't claim to be doing it a kindness.

So if you're going to be part of the carnivorous majority, you ought to at least be realistic about what that entails. When Jamie Oliver was criticised for killing a lamb on a 2005 TV show, he defended himself on the grounds of honesty. "A chef who has cooked 2,000 sheep should kill at least one," he retorted, "otherwise you're a fake."

But it's not just chefs: it's anyone who's partial to a bit of Peking duck, a crispy sliver of

THE REALITY IS THAT, IF YOU EAT ANY MEAT AT ALL, YOU HAVE BLOOD ON YOUR HANDS.

bacon or a chicken sandwich. You cannot eat an animal without participating in its death; to pretend otherwise is pure hypocrisy.

Granted, there are advantages to letting the experts do the slaughtering. A friend of mine once announced that, for a year, he would eat nothing he hadn't killed himself. Even for a practical and unsentimental countryman, this proved extraordinarily difficult. For the first six months, he ate a lot of winkles. Then rabbits.

Finally, just when he thought he might go mad with longing for a proper roast, a farmer gave him a live sheep. After a prolonged tussle, my friend managed to slit its throat – but

the intimate experience of slaughtering a large mammal as it fought for its life put him right off his chops. For the rest of the year, he murdered nothing but broccoli.

Nevertheless, most of us would be better carnivores for getting a bit closer to the action. The more you know about an animal's life and death, the more humane your meat-eating is likely to be. Some years ago, my restaurateur husband took me to visit a chicken farm; I haven't been able to touch a battery-farmed nugget since.

The idea that children are too delicate to cope with the realities of the food chain is, in my experience, sentimental nonsense. My four-year-old son, George, loves nothing better than cross-examining his father about whatever's for supper.

"What are sausages made from, Daddy?" "Bits of pig, minced up and stuffed into little skins made from stomach lining." "How do they kill the pig?" "They clonk it on the head so that it can't feel anything, and then they cut its neck with a knife so all its blood pours out." "Where is its head now?" "I'm not sure. It's probably been chopped up and turned into catfood." "I'd like a sausage with a head on it."

In the same spirit of openness, George has seen a whole pig being butchered, held its eyeball in his hand,

helped to pluck a pheasant, eaten sushi made from a freshly caught, twitching mackerel, and (his favourite) learnt to prise a limpet off a rock and eat the raw mollusc inside.

So far – and I realise it's early days – this hands-on experience of carnivorism doesn't seem to have turned him into a sadist, or a vegetarian. I hope it means he will grow up with some understanding of, and respect for, the animals he eats.

Shooting a duck is a hundred times more morally sound than tucking into, say, an intensively reared pig. If you let your children grow up thinking of meat as a disembodied protein that comes coated in breadcrumbs and shaped like a T. rex, you are not protecting them from anything – except their own responsibilities.

The Daily Telegraph, 1 December 2011
© Telegraph Media Group Ltd 2011

THE IDEA THAT CHILDREN ARE TOO DELICATE TO COPE WITH THE REALITIES OF THE FOOD CHAIN IS, IN MY EXPERIENCE, SENTIMENTAL NONSENSE.

MY BEEF ISN'T WITH BEEF: WHY I STOPPED BEING A VEGETARIAN

To be vegetarian is to be a pacifist, avoiding the fight against animal cruelty. Eat meat from sustainable farms, and we will win.

Jenna Woginrich

I was a vegetarian for a long time – the bulk of my adult life, actually. When I realised how most of the steaks got to my plate (and how pumped-full of antibiotics and growth hormones they were), I put down my fork and took a vow to never be a part of that system again. My research into the brutal American factory farm system and its effects on the environment was a life-changing stumble down into the rabbit hole; I discovered a twisted world of assembly-line death camps, crippled animals, radiated carcasses and festering diseases. I don't have to get into the specifics, but clearly it wasn't a compassionate way to get my suggested 46 grams of protein a day. So I stopped eating meat, cold Tofurkey.

Nearly a decade later I'm no longer a vegetarian. In fact, I couldn't be further from the produce aisle. Nowadays I own and operate a small farm where I raise my own chicken, pork, lamb, rabbit, turkey and eggs. I had a serious change of heart, and it happened when I realised my aversion to meat wasn't solving the animal welfare problem I was protesting about. My beef, after all, wasn't with beef. It was with how the cow got to my plate in the first place. One way to make sure the animals I ate lived a happy, respectable life was to raise them myself. I would learn to butcher a free-range chicken, raise a pig without antibiotics and rear lambs on green hillside pastures. I would come back to meat eating, and I would do it because of my love for animals.

Every meal you eat that supports a sustainable farm changes the agricultural world. I cannot possibly stress this enough. Your fork is your ballot, and when you vote to eat a steak or leg of lamb purchased from a small farmer you are showing the industrial system you are actively opting out. You are showing them you are willing to sacrifice more of your paycheck to dine with dignity. As people are made more aware of this beautiful option, farmers are

SOME ISSUES:

Does it matter how the animal lived if it is going to be killed anyway?

Is it better for the animal to live a comfortable life?

Do you think the meat industry can ever be fair?

Is vegetarianism the only right option?

Can small farmers feed the world?

See also:

Young carnivores should be taught the truth, p86

Cooking up a storm
Fact File 2010, p92

www.completeissues.co.uk

CLEARLY IT WASN'T A COMPASSIONATE WAY TO GET MY SUGGESTED 46 GRAMS OF PROTEIN A DAY

coming out in droves to meet the demand. Farmers markets have been on a rapid rise in the US thanks to consumer demand for cleaner meat, up 16% in the last year alone.

It's a hard reality for a vegetarian to swallow, but my veggie burgers did not rattle the industry cages at all. I was simply avoiding the battlefield, stepping aside as a pacifist. There is nobility in the vegetarian choice, but it isn't changing the system fast enough. In a world where meat consumption is soaring, the plausible 25% of the world's inhabitants who have a mostly vegetarian diet aren't making a dent in the rate us humans are eating animals. In theory, a plant-based diet avoids consuming animals but it certainly isn't getting cows out of feedlots. However, steak-eating consumers choosing to eat sustainably raised meat are. They chose to purchase a product raised on pasture when they could have spent less money on an animal treated like a screwdriver.

"There is a fundamental difference between cows and screwdrivers. Cows feel pain and screwdrivers do not." Those are the words of Temple Grandin, the famed advocate responsible for making the meat industry aware of animal suffering. But how many of us consumers think of that steak in the plastic wrap next to the breakfast cereal and laundry detergent as just another object? A product as characterless

as a screwdriver? We seem to be caught in a parted sea of extremes when it comes to how we see food – either we're adamant about where our food comes from, or completely oblivious. I don't think the world needs to convert into a society of vegans or sustainable farmers, but we do need to live in a world where beef doesn't just mean an ingredient; it means a life loss. I never thought of my beans or hummus like that. Now every meal is seasoned with the gratitude of sacrifice. For me, it took a return to carnivory to live out the ideals of vegetarianism. Food is a complicated religion.

It may mean spending more money, but the way small farmers raise their sheep, goats, cattle and hogs on pasture is the polar opposite of those cruel places where animals are treated like a cheap protein and "quality" is a measure of economic algorithms, not life. If cruelty is bad for business, business will simply have to change. When consumers demand a higher quality of life from the animals they eat, feedlots will become a black stain of our agricultural past.

I'm sorry my vegetarian friends, but it's time to come back to the table. You can remain in the rabbit hole and keep eating your salad, but the only way out for good is to eat the rabbit.

The Guardian, 19 January 2011
© Guardian News & Media Ltd 2011

WE DO NEED TO LIVE IN A WORLD WHERE BEEF DOESN'T JUST MEAN AN INGREDIENT; IT MEANS A LIFE LOSS

Would you eat a burger grown in a laboratory?

A Dutch scientist has created 'meat' from stem cells – and wants Heston Blumenthal to cook the first batch.

Steve Connor reports on the ultimate in culinary experimentation

The world's first hamburger made with a synthetic meat protein derived from bovine stem cells will be publicly consumed in October 2012 after being prepared by a celebrity chef, according to the inventor of the artificial mince.

Heston Blumenthal is the favourite to be asked to cook the €250,000 (£207,000) hamburger, which will be made from 3,000 strips of synthetic meat protein grown in fermentation vats. Dr Mark Post, of Maastricht University in the Netherlands, said the anonymous backer of his research project had not yet decided who would get to eat the world's most expensive hamburger, which will be unveiled at a ceremony in Maastricht.

Dr Post told the American Association for the Advancement of Science that a hamburger made from artificial beef protein was a milestone in the development of novel ways to meet the global demand for meat, which is expected to double by 2050.

"In October we're going to provide a 'proof of concept' showing that with in vitro culture methods that are pretty classical we can make a product out of stem cells that looks like, and hopefully taste like, meat," Dr Post said.

"The target goal is to make a hamburger and for that we need to grow 3,000 pieces of this muscle and a couple of hundred pieces of fat tissue. As long as it's a patty the size of a regular hamburger, I'm happy with it," he said.

A handful of researchers has been working for the past six years on the technical problem of extracting stem cells from bovine muscle, culturing them in the laboratory and turning them into strips of muscle fibres that can be minced together with synthetic fat cells into an edible product.

The technical challenges have included giving the meat a pinkish colour

Animals are very inefficient at converting vegetable protein into animal protein. Yet meat demand is also going to double in the next 40 years

and the right texture for cooking and eating, as well as ensuring that it feels and tastes like real meat.

Dr Post admitted to being nervous about the final result. "I am a little worried, but seeing and tasting is believing," he said.

Although some animals still have to be slaughtered to provide the bovine stem cells, scientists estimate that a million times more meat could be made from the carcass of a single cow, compared with conventional cattle rearing. As well as reducing the number of beef cattle, it would save the land, water and oil currently need to raise cattle for the meat trade, Dr Post said.

"Eventually, my vision is that you have a limited herd of donor animals that you keep in stock in the world. You basically kill animals and take all the stem cells from them, so you would still need animals for this technology."

One of the economic incentives behind the research is the increasing cost of the grain used to feed much of the world's cattle. This is helping to drive up the cost of meat.

"It comes down to the fact that animals are very inefficient at converting vegetable protein [either grass or grain] into animal protein. Yet meat demand is also going to double in the next 40 years," he said.

"Right now we are using about 70 per cent of all our agricultural capacity to grow meat through livestock. You are going to need alternatives. If we don't do anything, meat will become a luxury food and will become very expensive.

"Livestock also contribute a lot to greenhouse gas emissions, more so than our entire transport system. Livestock produces 39 per cent of the methane, 5 per cent of CO2 and 40 per cent of all

the nitrous oxide. Eventually we'll have an 'eco-tax' on meat."

Growing meat in fermentation vats might be better for the environment. And it might be more acceptable to vegetarians and people concerned about the welfare of domestic livestock, Dr Post said. "There are many reasons why people are vegetarian. I've talked to the Dutch vegetarian society, which has said that probably half of its members will eat this meat if it has cost fewer animal lives and requires less intensive farming," Dr Post said. Growing artificial meat would also allow greater control over its makeup. It will be possible, for example, to alter the fat content, or the amount of polyunsaturated fats vs saturated fats, according to Dr Post.

"You can probably make meat healthier," he said. "You can probably trigger these cells to make more polyunsaturated fatty acids, just like grass-fed beef has more polyunsaturates than grain-fed beef. You could make any type of meat, you could make mixed meats. I'm pretty sure you could even make panda meat."

Dr Post declined to reveal who his backer was, except to say that he was well known but not a celebrity – and not British. "It's a very reputable source of money," he said. "He's an individual. There may be two reasons why he wants to remain anonymous: as soon as his name is associated with this technology he will draw the attention to himself and he doesn't really want to do that."

Dr Post added: "And the second reason is that he has the image of whatever he does turns into gold and he is not sure that may be the case here so he doesn't want to be associated with a potential failure."

The Independent, 20 February 2012

LAB-GROWN MEAT, THE CASE FOR & AGAINST

Pros:

- Billions of animals would be spared from suffering in factory farms and slaughterhouses

- Would reduce the environmental impacts of livestock production, which the UN's Food and Agriculture Organisation estimates account for 18 per cent of greenhouse-gas emissions

- Could reduce by 90 per cent the land- and water-use footprint of meat production, according to Oxford University research, freeing those resources for more efficient forms of food production

- Would provide a more sustainable way to meet demand from China and India, whose growing appetite for meat is expected to double global meat consumption by 2040

- Lab-grown meat could be healthier – free of hormones, antibiotics, bacteria such as salmonella and E.coli, and engineered to contain a lower fat content

- Would reduce the threat of swine and avian flu outbreaks associated with factory farming

Cons:

- Consumers may find the notion of lab-grown meat creepy or unnatural – a "Frankenstein food" reminiscent of the Soylent Green at the heart of the 1973 sci-fi film of the same name

- For some vegetarians, in vitro meat will be unsatisfactory as it perpetuates "meat addiction" – rather than focusing on promoting non-meat alternatives, and changing our meat-heavy diet

- Although the fat content can be tinkered with, other risks of eating red meat, such as an increased threat of bowel cancer, remain

- It's not cruelty-free – animals will still have to be slaughtered to provide the bovine stem cells

- There could be unforeseen health consequences to eating lab-grown meat

- As a highly processed, "unnatural" foodstuff, lab-grown meat is a step in the wrong direction for "slow-food" advocates, and others who believe the problems in our food system have their origins in the distance between food production and the consumer.

The Independent, 20 February 2012

Gender

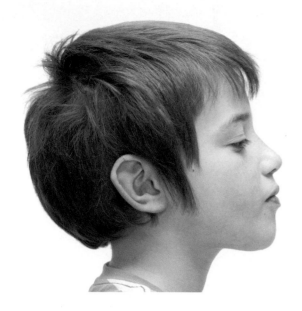 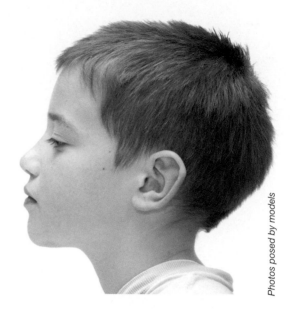

Photos posed by models

Blue for a boy and pink for a girl. Is it beige for a gender-neutral baby?

SOME ISSUES:

In these cases we are looking at boys dressed as girls, would girls dressed as boys provoke the same reaction?

Are parents right to use their children to demonstrate their viewpoint?

Do you think people treat children differently because of their gender?

How might this affect the child?

See also:

Gender unknown
Essential Articles 14, p107,

**Keeping up appearances
Essential Articles 14, p108**

Boy or girl? You choose
Essential Articles 13, p104

www.completeissues.co.uk

"I don't mind, just as long as it's healthy!" How often have you heard that answer from an expectant parent when asked if they hope for a boy or a girl? Yet gender is an absorbing topic for expectant parents, friends and relatives. "What sex?" usually comes before any other question following a birth.

Gender matters

Once the gender is known, a whole range of unspoken assumptions and expectations come into play. Consciously or unconsciously people select clothes, buy toys and even alter their language to match what they feel is appropriate for a girl or a boy. As they do this, they begin to shape the behaviour, appearance and even the nature of the child to fit those assumptions. They mould the child into the pattern they see as appropriate for their gender. Since most children respond by conforming to that pattern, this reinforces the notion that it is right, proper, natural – an inborn part of the child's make-up.

This circle, vicious or not depending on your point of view, is being challenged. There are a few parents, in different countries, who are so opposed to these conventional assumptions that they are trying to raise their children 'gender neutral'. One way of preventing other people behaving towards the child in a gender specific way is for parents to refuse to reveal the sex of their offspring in babyhood and beyond.

Sweden

In Sweden a couple referred to their baby as 'Pop' and kept the gender secret for more than two years saying "We want Pop to grow up more freely and avoid being forced into a specific gender mould from the outset. It's cruel to bring a child into the world with a blue or pink stamp on their forehead."

Canada

In Canada, Kathy Witterick and David Stocker decided to keep the gender of their third baby a secret. They named the baby Storm and emailed friends and family explaining their decision as: "A tribute to freedom and choice in place of limitation, a stand up to what the world could become in Storm's lifetime (a more progressive place?)".

The result was a media siege of their home, abusive letters and even people shouting at them from cars.

These parents, like others, believe children should have the freedom to choose who they would like to be, unconstrained by what's expected of males and females. Their eldest child Jazz, for example, loves to wear dresses and says pink is his favourite colour and has (inevitably perhaps) been teased over these choices. But he also has a range of friends who attended his fairy-themed birthday party.

His parents hope that the discussion about their choices will lead to conversations on broader issues, such as how strict gender expectations result in gender-based bullying.

Media feedback

Reporters in their local paper, The Toronto Star, expressed opposing views: Columnist Heather Mallicjk was supportive: "They are raising their three children to be intellectual adventurers. They have the next 80 years to be obedient wage slaves and vote Conservative. Which they'll probably do when they rebel against their parents' tiresome freedom…. they're starting out with a sturdy independence. Their parents aren't forcing them, they're giving them a choice. I suspect they'll choose the social norm, children being Nature's joiners. But perhaps not."

Children should have the freedom to choose

Another reporter, Catherine Porter, disagreed, quoting her own son, Noah, as an example of how gender differences are inescapable, "I am a boy," he says. "My friends are boys." Despite this, Catherine Porter agrees that too many parents just accept gender restrictions, asking: "Why can't boys wear pink and paint their toe nails, too?" But she feels Storm's parents are leaving their child without essential guidelines about how to behave and react. "I think they are trapping Storm in an endless discussion. For Noah, inside and outside the house, being a boy is just one thing that defines him. Will the same be true for Storm?"

UK

Similar massive media coverage occurred in the UK case of Beck Laxton and Kieran Cooper who kept the gender of their son Sasha a secret from everyone, but close family, for the first five years of his life. Their motivation was similar and their views were equally strong. "I wanted to avoid all the stereotyping," Beck Laxton told the Cambridge News.

For her, putting a child into a 'male' or 'female' box is idiotic, and potentially damaging. "It affects what they wear and what they can play with, and that shapes the kind of person that they become… it's not just a harmless bit of silliness, like horoscopes, it's actually harmful."

When she found she was pregnant Beck didn't want to know the sex of the child, "It's like opening your presents before Christmas, and I worry that people start making all these presumptions about what the child's going to be like." And even after the birth she asked the midwife not to reveal the sex to her so that for the first half hour she could be sure

> She can't climb a tree because she's wearing a skirt, so then she can't climb very well. But you did that, because you shaped her environment. You shaped what she could do!"

that she herself was not reacting to the new born in a way that was based on gender.

Beck referred to Sasha simply as 'the infant' in her blogs and only revealed his sex to strangers when he went to school. But she had an early experience of hostility to this decision. At her mother and toddler group: "I was the last person to introduce myself and I said: I'm Beck, and this is Sasha." To questions about the baby's sex, she replied 'I'm not going to tell you.' which earned the label of 'that loony woman who doesn't know whether her baby is a boy or a girl'.

Sasha has always worn both girls' and boys' clothing and has chosen to wear a blouse from the girls' uniform list to school.

Limitations

Beck is scathing about the way mothers dress girls in elaborate clothes with complicated fastenings which inhibit their play options: "Fussy things, impractical things, uncomfortable things that restricted their movement and that they have to look after. ...She can't climb a tree because she's wearing a skirt, so then she can't climb very well. But you did that, because you shaped her environment. You shaped what she could do!"

Beck defends her own standpoint by saying: "I don't think I'd do it if I thought it was going to make him unhappy, but at the moment he's not really bothered either way. We haven't had any difficult scenarios yet. I just want him to fulfil his potential, and I wouldn't push him in any direction. As long as he has good relationships and good friends, then nothing else matters does it? All I want to do is make people think a bit."

Forced to conform

In contrast, some parents feel it is their duty to persuade their children to conform to accepted standards. Lorraine Candy, editor-in-chief of Elle magazine's U.K. edition, has also had a son who preferred to wear girl's clothes. She wrote in the Daily Mail about her son Henry who, for the first five years of his life, loved dresses and wouldn't play football because it involved wearing 'boys' clothes. "His favorite game was wearing his elder sisters' sequin party dresses while running his imaginary boutique 'Slinx' or greeting customers in his hairdressing salon 'Slapchicks'," his mother said.

But Candy was not in favour of 'gender neutral parenting'. Although she acknowledged that 'some children do not conform to the conventional behaviour expected of their gender anyway.' She was not prepared to let Henry's unusual choices continue: "There came a time when I had to put a stop to my boy's 'girlish' instincts. I knew it was my duty as a parent to make it stop."

Her decision was supported by the parenting books she read which told her that all children need to belong to a peer group. They need that approval and security to aid their development and confidence. At first, Henry's peer group was his two older sisters – he copied their behaviour and dress. However, once he had started school, his parents intervened "From now on, you need to wear boys' clothes and sleep in boys' pajamas."

His mother says this is not because she herself has any objection to his cross dressing: "Remember, I work in fashion," but she feared the consequences if he continued: "Allowing my son to continue down his feminine path would only incur ridicule and hurt."

Despite their different viewpoints, all these parents feel they are doing the best for their children – like Lorraine Candy by avoiding the possibility of ridicule or like Kathy Witterick, David Stocker and Beck Laxton by expanding the choices children could make in the future. Does the fact that people in general have opinions on how a child, not their own, is dressed prove Candy's view that conforming to gender matters? Or does it show, as the supporters of gender-neutral upbringing would suggest, that we are so conditioned we are unable to think differently?

It seems unlikely that the trail-blazing parents in Sweden, Canada and the UK will see many following them in the near future. The importance of gender is shown in a new trend, recently imported from the US, for those who know the sex of their baby before birth to hold a 'reveal party'. Guests are invited to guess the baby's gender before the prospective parents cut a cake whose colour coded interior reveals the sex of their imminent arrival. The interior is, of course, blue for a boy and pink for a girl.

Sources: Various

Don't primp children out of their innocence

The advent of Trendy Monkeys, a beauty and hairdressing salon for children in Essex, is not a welcome innovation, says Jenny McCartney.

SOME ISSUES:

Is this harmless fun or encouraging a life of insecurity and reliance on beauty regimes?

Should little girls be allowed to use make-up and beauty treatments?

Do you think that make-up and beauty treatments have positive or negative effects on people?

Why?

See also:

Keeping up appearances
Essential Articles 14, p108

Beautiful and feminist
Essential Articles 13, p100

www.completeissues.co.uk

There is a word that comes to mind when one sees pictures of the junior clients of Trendy Monkeys, the newly opened beauty salon for little girls in Essex – their tiny faces set in moues of adult concentration as they scan the menu options of spray tans, hair straightening, make-up, ear piercing or mani-pedis. That word is "Yeuch!"

The mild revulsion is not at the children themselves, but at what they are being beckoned into in the name of fun: the world of relentless female grooming, which has already assumed rather too tyrannical a presence

Photo: © East News

concern about the "sexualisation" of young girls – witness this month's government report, which recommended, among other things, that shops must not sell overly risqué clothing to the under-age.

There is a very good reason for that concern, but it is important not to become hysterical. Mothers who grew up in the 1970s and early 1980s, as I did, might do well to cast their minds back to the Britain of their youth, which was by no means some kind of Famous Five era of childhood innocence. The dance troupe Hot Gossip regularly writhed its way across Top of the Pops in outfits that would make an archbishop choke on his claret: admittedly, it wasn't quite at the level of Rihanna energetically straddling a bemused female fan on stage, as she did recently, but it wasn't too far off. And remember a grotesque 1983 programme called Minipops, in which heavily made-up pre-pubescent children performed cover versions of adult hits, complete with pseudo-provocative gyrations? It was a monstrous success, particularly with children themselves, until adult condemnation had it stopped.

in the lives of many young women. What was once breezily called "making the best of yourself" has transformed in some cases into a full-time job, spurred by a virtually permanent state of anxious self-loathing.

The owner, Michelle Devine, has opened her salon in the midst of rising public

It is necessary to remember that young girls perceive the world of sexuality very differently from how we might like them to, and they always have done. They scent

> **We adults might envy them their charming innocence, and yearn for them to hang on to it: they can't wait to appear older than they are.**

At 13, my friend and I actively lamented that we were not cute little blondes, for whom life was significantly easier. On reflection, I am grateful that I wasn't: while the class beauties emitted an aura of prematurely preening self-regard, the rest of us were forced to concentrate on working on the rather knottier task of building up our "personalities."

The difference, back then, was that our mothers didn't fret much over how we were perceived, aside from murmuring occasional reassurances. There wasn't the obsession with dressing children up and parading them that exists today, even in the most well-meaning households. The adult world, by and large, was either unconcerned about, or actively disapproving of, little girls acting like grown-up women.

the power of sexual attraction, without really understanding it, and they are clumsily eager to imitate it. We adults might envy them their charming innocence, and yearn for them to hang on to it: they can't wait to appear older than they are.

I was very cross, at the age of nine or 10, that I looked exactly like a skinny boy, with curly hair that my mother kept cropped for easy management. There is a snapshot in which I can see that I have painted my toenails bright red, as some kind of desperate, flailing signal of my true identity. At 11, I prevailed upon my parents to let me get my ears pierced, for similar reasons. That evening, on a walk with my father, we met a bluff friend of his, who took one look at me and said kindly: "And what age is your son?"

In the past decade, however, a number of powerful forces have entered the picture: the rise of beauty salons, the popularisation of cosmetic surgery, the ubiquity of pornographic imagery. All of these are exerting their pressures on women, and now their influence is trickling down to little girls. Instead of shielding their daughters, and acting as a form of restraint, mothers are eagerly leading them into this new world under the pretext of "pampering" or "being girly together", or "learning to look pretty". Please let us stop the primping by proxy, and let our daughters once again claw their own awkward, curious way into womanhood.

The Daily Telegraph,
11 June 2011
© Telegraph Media Group
Ltd 2011

Helen, 28, has some thoughts on Page 3

Women's groups appear at the Leveson inquiry to talk about media sexism.

Helen Lewis Hasteley

Woe betide any woman who dares complain about sexism in the media. When Clare Short first protested about Page 3 girls in 1986, she was monstered – and The Sun was still harassing her a decade and a half later when the subject came up again. In 2003, she recounted in her autobiography, the paper mocked up pictures of her as "a very fat page 3 girl" and sent what it would probably refer to as "scantily clad lovelies" to the house she shared with her 84-year-old mother. "It is hard not to conclude that The Sun sets out to frighten anyone who might dare to agree that such pictures should be removed from newspapers," she wrote.

Nearly another decade on, and representatives from four women's groups appeared at the Leveson Inquiry into press standards and ethics to talk about how much things had changed. (Joke!)

Their testimony made for depressing viewing: Page 3 girls are cutesy cheesecake compared with the "upskirt shots" and "nipple slips" that hordes of photographers follow young women round in the hope of capturing for today's papers and celebrity websites.

Google (if you dare) the final edition of the Daily Sport from April, where the entire front page is taken up with a borderline gynaecological view of Cheryl Cole taken by the paper's "dwarf paparazzo" Pete. The Sport might have gone the way of the dodo but its approach to female celebrity genitalia (ie to be as close as possible to them, preferably with a wide-angle lens) lives on in a dozen celebrity websites.

The Daily Mail's website, meanwhile, is a vast, teetering edifice of wardrobe malfunctions and women "flaunting their bikini bodies", even as the paper itself gets its chastity belt in a twist over "X Factor raunch" and Irene Adler in the nip on Sherlock.

The Daily Mail's website, meanwhile, is a vast, teetering edifice of wardrobe malfunctions and women "flaunting their bikini bodies"

SOME ISSUES:

Are celebrities 'fair game' for photographers?

Is this just harmless fun or something else?

What sort of impression do you think this media representation of women will have on young girls?

See also:
A paparazzo speaks
p128

It's our obsession with celebrity that's on trial
p130

Bikinis or bingo wings?
Essential Articles 12, p33

www.completeissues.co.uk

It's a pervasive press culture where women are routinely naked, their bodies pored over, found wanting, and put up for grabs as a subject for public discussion.

Of course, it's not just a few jaunty nipples: it's a pervasive press culture where women are routinely naked, their bodies pored over, found wanting, and put up for grabs as a subject for public discussion. You can't escape by dressing sensibly: only this week, a photograph of Theresa May in a sober skirt and jacket was reproduced alongside an article which wondered how she could be taken seriously while going for a "cover girl look".

One of the most astonishing lines to come out of Leveson was that the evidence offered - from British papers, available at your friendly local newsagent alongside the fruit pastilles - was censored by the inquiry lawyers, so explicit were its depictions of women. You certainly wouldn't want to open that front page of the Sport on your monitor at work – it's so NSFW (Not Suitable For Work) I haven't linked to it – so god knows how parents felt hustling their children past it on the news stand.

One of the suggestions made, by Anna Van Heeswijk of Object, was that the papers should observe some form of watershed, in the same way that broadcasters do (almost all British newspapers and magazines get very f***ing queasy about bad language, after all).

While there might need to be allowances made for images with significant news value - I'm thinking of the pictures of a dead Colonel Gaddafi, which proved the tyrant was toppled - there's a germ of a good idea there: and although the Sun might squeal, how could the Mail object? Or, as the supremely patronising News in Briefs column might put it: "Helen, 28, from London, thinks that if you're going to complain about tits on telly, you shouldn't be allowed to use them to flog your paper."

*New Statesman,
24 January 2012*

Photo: Ben Sullivan

Cheryl Cole: not quite the view of her the Sport gave its readers
*Photo: Featureflash /
Shutterstock.com*

Laurie Penny:
A woman's opinion is the mini-skirt of the internet

You come to expect it, as a woman writer, particularly if you're political. You come to expect the vitriol, the insults, the death threats…

After a while, the emails and tweets and comments containing graphic fantasies of how and where and with what kitchen implements certain pseudonymous people would like to rape you cease to be shocking, and become merely a daily or weekly annoyance, something to phone your girlfriends about, seeking safety in hollow laughter.

An opinion, it seems, is the short skirt of the internet. Having one and flaunting it is somehow asking an amorphous mass of almost-entirely male keyboard-bashers to tell you how they'd like to rape, kill and urinate on you. This week, after a particularly ugly slew of threats, I decided to make just a few of those messages public on Twitter, and the response I received was overwhelming. Many could not believe the hate I received, and many more began to share their own stories of harassment, intimidation and abuse.

Perhaps it should be comforting when calling a woman fat and ugly is the best response to her arguments, but it's a chill comfort, especially when one realises, as I have come to realise over the past year, just how much time and effort some vicious people are prepared to expend trying to punish and silence a woman who dares to be ambitious, outspoken, or merely present in a public space.

No journalist worth reading expects zero criticism, and the internet has made it easier for readers to critique and engage. This is to be welcomed, and I have long felt that many more established columnists' complaints about the comments they receive spring, in part, from resentment at having their readers suddenly talk back. In my experience, however, the charges of stupidity, hypocrisy, Stalinism and poor personal hygiene which are a sure sign that any left-wing columnist is at least upsetting the right people, come spiced with a large and debilitating helping of violent misogyny, and not only from the far-right.

Many commentators, wondering aloud where all the strong female voices are, close their eyes to how normal this sort of threat has become. Most mornings, when I go to check my email, Twitter and Facebook accounts, I have to sift through threats of violence, public speculations about my sexual preference and the odour and capacity of my genitals, and attempts to write off challenging ideas with the

SOME ISSUES:

Were you aware that writers received this much abuse?

Why do you think people respond in such ways?

How should the law address these issues?

Why do you think women attract more negative responses to their writing then men?

See also:
Internet trolls
p133

The faceless virtual mob spreading spite online
Essential Articles 13, p124

www.completeissues.co.uk

> *The implication that a woman must be sexually appealing to be taken seriously as a thinker did not start with the internet: it's a charge that has been used to shame and dismiss women's ideas since long before Mary Wollestonecraft was called a "hyena in petticoats"*

declaration that, since I and my friends are so very unattractive, anything we have to say must be irrelevant.

The implication that a woman must be sexually appealing to be taken seriously as a thinker did not start with the internet: it's a charge that has been used to shame and dismiss women's ideas since long before Mary Wollestonecraft was called "a hyena in petticoats". The internet, however, makes it easier for boys in lonely bedrooms to become bullies. It's not only journalists, bloggers and activists who are targeted. Businesswomen, women who play games online and schoolgirls who post video-diaries on YouTube have all been subject to campaigns of intimidation designed to drive them off the internet, by people who seem to believe that the only use a woman should make of modern technology is to show her breasts to the world for a fee.

Like many others, I have also received more direct threats, like the men who hunted down and threatened to publish old photographs of me which are

relevant to my work only if one believes that any budding feminist journalist should remain entirely sober, fully clothed and completely vertical for the entirety of her first year of university. Efforts, too, were made to track down and harass my family, including my two school-age sisters. After one particular round of rape threats, including the suggestion that, for criticising neoliberal economic policymaking, I should be made to fellate a row of bankers at knifepoint, I was informed that people were searching for my home address. I could go on.

I'd like to say that none of this bothered me – to be one of those women who are strong enough to brush off the abuse, which is always the advice given by people who don't believe bullies and bigots can be fought. Sometimes I feel that speaking about the strength it takes just to turn on the computer, or how I've been afraid to leave my house, is an admission of weakness. Fear that it's somehow your fault for not being strong enough is, of course, what allows abusers to continue to abuse.

I believe the time for silence is over. If we want to build a truly fair and vibrant community of political debate and social exchange, online and offline, it's not enough to ignore harassment of women, LGBT people or people of colour who dare to have opinions. Free speech means being free to use technology and participate in public life without fear of abuse – and if the only people who can do so are white, straight men, the internet is not as free as we'd like to believe.

The Independent,
4 November 2011

> *Most mornings, when I go to check my email, Twitter and Facebook accounts, I have to sift through threats of violence*

Laurie Penny is a feminist, socialist writer who runs her own blog http://pennyred.blogspot.co.uk and also contributes regularly to publications such as New Statesmen and The Independent

THESE 'SLUT WALK' WOMEN ARE SIMPLY FIGHTING FOR THEIR RIGHT TO BE DIRTY

True liberation is women wearing what they like and abandoning the Hoover
By Germaine Greer

www.completeissues.co.uk

The Toronto policeman who in January told a "personal security class" at York University that "women should avoid dressing like sluts in order not to be victimised" said nothing unusual. What made news was what happened 10 weeks later, when a thousand people hit the streets of downtown Toronto in a "slut walk".

That was surprising, but not as surprising as what happened next. Within days, all over North America, in Britain and even in Australia, women came together to organise slut walks of their own. Throughout the English-speaking world, it seems there are hordes of women prepared to sashay round the streets provocatively dressed, making a defiant display of their inner slut.

The mind police were not amused. The most sanctimonious of our newspapers solemnly intoned that "women need to take to the streets to condemn violence, but not for the right to be called 'slut' ". But it was not heeded. The women (and men) who are set to prance the streets of dozens of cities in underwear and fetish gear for weeks to come will be taking liberties. That's where liberation begins.

Slut-walkers are apt to say that the purpose of their action is to "reclaim the word". It's difficult, probably impossible, to reclaim a word that has always been an insult. And yet here are women spontaneously deciding to adopt it. Before we decide that thousands of our sisters are simply stupid or misguided, an attempt must be made to understand what's going on. The slut walk manifesto states: "Historically, the term 'slut' has carried a predominantly negative association. Aimed at those who were sexually promiscuous, be it for work or pleasure, it has primarily been women who have suffered under the burden of this label. We are tired of being oppressed by slut-shaming; of being judged by our sexuality..."

A little knowledge here misleads. Historically, the primary attribute of a slut is not promiscuity but dirt.

Photo: Padmayogni / Shutterstock.com

Photo: michael rubin / Shutterstock.com

The word denotes a "woman of dirty, slovenly, or untidy habits or appearance; a foul slattern". A now obsolete meaning connects it with a kitchen maid, whose life was lived in soot and grease. She was too dirty to be allowed above stairs, but drudged out her painful life scraping pans and riddling ash, for 16 hours a day, and then retreated to her squalid lodging where hot water could not be had. The corner she left unswept was the slut corner; the fluff that collected under the furniture was a slut ball. People who thought of sex as dirt suspected the lazy kitchen maid of being unclean in that way as well.

If the kitchen maid's life was made wretched by the struggle against dirt, the life of the housewife was hardly less so. A woman who didn't hang out her washing when everyone else did, who didn't scrub her front doorstep and windowsills, who didn't scour everything that could be scoured at least once a week, but preferred to gossip with her friends or play with her children in the sun, would

also be suspected of being no better than she should be. A man married to a sloven needed to take her in hand if he was not to be generally despised.

Twenty-first century women are even more relentlessly hounded and harassed by the threat of dirt. No house is ever clean enough, no matter how many hours its resident woman spends spraying and wiping, Hoovering, dusting, disinfecting and deodorising. Women's bodies can never be washed often enough to be entirely free of dirt; they must be depilated and deodorised as well. When it comes to sex, women are as dirty as the next man, but they don't have the same right to act out their fantasies. If they're

"We are tired of being oppressed by slut-shaming; of being judged by our sexuality..."

Girls don't have the option of not minding. Dirty house equals dirty woman equals tramp.

to be liberated, women have to demand the right to be dirty. By declaring themselves sluts, they lay down the Cillit Bang and take up the instruments of pleasure.

Men already enjoy the right to be dirty. In the usual rugby house, unwashed dishes can be found festering under beds as well as piled to chin height in the sink. The rubbish bin will contain an impacted mess of stomped-down rubbish. The lavatory would be only too accurately described as a bog. The filth becomes a challenge; the first man to crack and grab the Hoover is a sissy. In mixed digs in our tolerant universities, it's the women who are forever cleaning the shared facilities, because the men won't. The con is a simple one. If you don't mind that the toilet's disgusting, then don't clean it; if you do, then do. Girls don't have the option of not minding. Dirty house equals dirty woman equals tramp.

If women are to overthrow the tyranny of perpetual cleansing, we have to be able to say: "Yes, I am a slut. My house could be cleaner. My sheets could be whiter. I could be without sexual fantasies too – pure as the untrodden snow – but I'm not. I'm a slut and proud." The rejection by women of compulsory cleansing of mind, body and soul is a necessary pre-condition of liberation. Besides, taking part in what looks like an endless "vicars and tarts' street party is not just bad-ass. It's fun.

The Daily Telegraph, 12 May 2011
© Telegraph Media Group Ltd 2011

The rejection by women of compulsory cleansing of mind, body and soul is a necessary pre-condition of liberation.

Photo: Padmayogini / Shutterstock.com

LET'S HEAR IT FOR THE BOYS ...

ARE BOYS AND MEN FACED WITH HIDDEN DISADVANTAGE AND DISCRIMINATION?

SOME ISSUES:

Do you think it seems fair to say that women are taking the place of ambitious men?

Why do you think men suffer more with their health and relationships?

How do you think boys can catch up with girls in education?

See also:

Prejudice isn't what keeps men out of nurseries
Essential Articles 12, p206

Man of the house
Fact File 2012, p66

Missing women
Fact File 2012, p188

Worlds apart
Fact File 2012, p174

www.completeissues.co.uk

Women finally won the full right to vote in 1928 and the Equal Pay Act was passed in 1970. These were among the milestones which have made women's lives incalculably better and more equal than they were. But has women's progress been achieved at the expense of men?

One person who argues that this is the case is the Minister for Universities and Science, David Willetts. He says that equal education and work for women has impeded the progress of some men. In his analysis, women who would otherwise have been middle class 'housewives' have taken places in university and high-powered jobs, blocking the prospects of ambitious working class men. Since well-educated women tend to marry well-educated men this means some households now contain two people who are financially successful meaning others now contain two people who are struggling. He says, "This transformation of opportunities for women ended up magnifying social divides. It is delicate territory because it is not a bad thing that women had these opportunities, but it widened the gap in household incomes because you suddenly had two-earner couples, both of whom were well-educated, compared with often workless households where nobody was educated".

It is a controversial view but there are some statistics which support it.

At every level of education girls are doing better. Girls regularly achieve better GCSE grades overall than boys and significantly more girls than boys are taking A level exams – 466,000 girls in 2011 compared to 394,000 boys: boys are selecting themselves out of higher education. Consequently, for some years more women than men have been accepted into UK universities: in 2011 45.1% of entrants were male and 54.9% female. Similarly women have long outnumbered men in medical schools, meaning that by 2017 it is likely that the majority of doctors will be female.

This distinction starts from the outset. At the end of their reception year in school only 10% of girls can't write simple words, but writing "cat", "dog" or "mum" is beyond 19% of five-year-old boys. Girls out-perform boys in every area of early development including reading, communicating, basic numeracy, social skills and physical awareness.

So are women really on the way to having the upper hand?

Support for the theory of men's oppression comes from South African philosophy professor David Benatar who, in his book The Second Sexism, argues that men's concerns are now routinely overlooked. He claims that discrimination against men is often not recognised and never discussed. While he agrees that there are more men at the top of society he says there are more at the bottom too: more boys drop out of school, fewer men earn degrees, more men die younger, are in prison, are homeless.

While women have made advances in many 'male' professions, men are still routinely excluded from or made to feel unwanted in the care of young children. A male midwife is still a rarity. Pre-

WOMEN WHO WOULD OTHERWISE HAVE BEEN MIDDLE CLASS 'HOUSEWIVES' HAVE TAKEN PLACES IN UNIVERSITY AND HIGH-POWERED JOBS, BLOCKING THE PROSPECTS OF AMBITIOUS WORKING CLASS MEN

school groups are still often referred to as 'mother and toddler groups'. Men are a tiny minority among primary teachers (and a slightly larger minority in secondary schools). This is also reflected in family life. Men are far less likely to be given care of their children after divorce – with the courts still presuming that the natural, primary carer is the mother, no matter how much a father has been involved, or how much he loves his children.

Men, generally, do the most gruelling jobs, the ones with the most physical danger and little security. They work longer hours. While it is becoming more common for women with children to have flexible working hours it is unusual for men to be offered this.

In general men develop heart disease earlier than women, suffer more from stress-related illnesses and have a lower life expectancy. In both physical and mental health contexts men are less likely to seek treatment in good time. The mental health system requires people to seek help – which is not a male characteristic. Young men are more likely to commit suicide than young women, an imbalance which could perhaps be altered if the system worked differently.

These are all areas where inequality exists but does not draw comment.

In addition, men are now the subject of widespread condescending humour. In many advertisements women patronisingly comment on the ineptness and incapability of their men folk – their inability to clean up or cook, their susceptibility to 'man flu'. While the portrayal of women in the media has drawn criticism, this patronising view of men seems to have been accepted and absorbed into the general culture.

It is still easy to point out the many areas in

which men dominate – finance and government being among the most prominent. And even in those professions where women are the majority (education, medicine) the top positions are generally occupied by men. But Benatar claims that is a false comparison. If we compare the most successful men and the most successful women then women appear to be disadvantaged. If however we look at the other end of the social scale men, in general, appear to be worse off.

If, as seems to be the case, we have a social structure that disadvantages both men and women, perhaps we need to look more closely at the behaviour we think is appropriate for each gender and at what we mean by success. Psychologist and journalist Susan Pinker examined the issues in The Sexual Paradox, Men, Women and the Real Gender Gap. She says:

"Health, happiness, the richness of one's human relationships, job satisfaction and how long one lives are also important values. Men are lagging behind women in all those areas."

Sources: Various

"HEALTH, HAPPINESS, THE RICHNESS OF ONE'S HUMAN RELATIONSHIPS, JOB SATISFACTION AND HOW LONG ONE LIVES ARE ALSO IMPORTANT VALUES. MEN ARE LAGGING BEHIND WOMEN IN ALL THOSE AREAS."

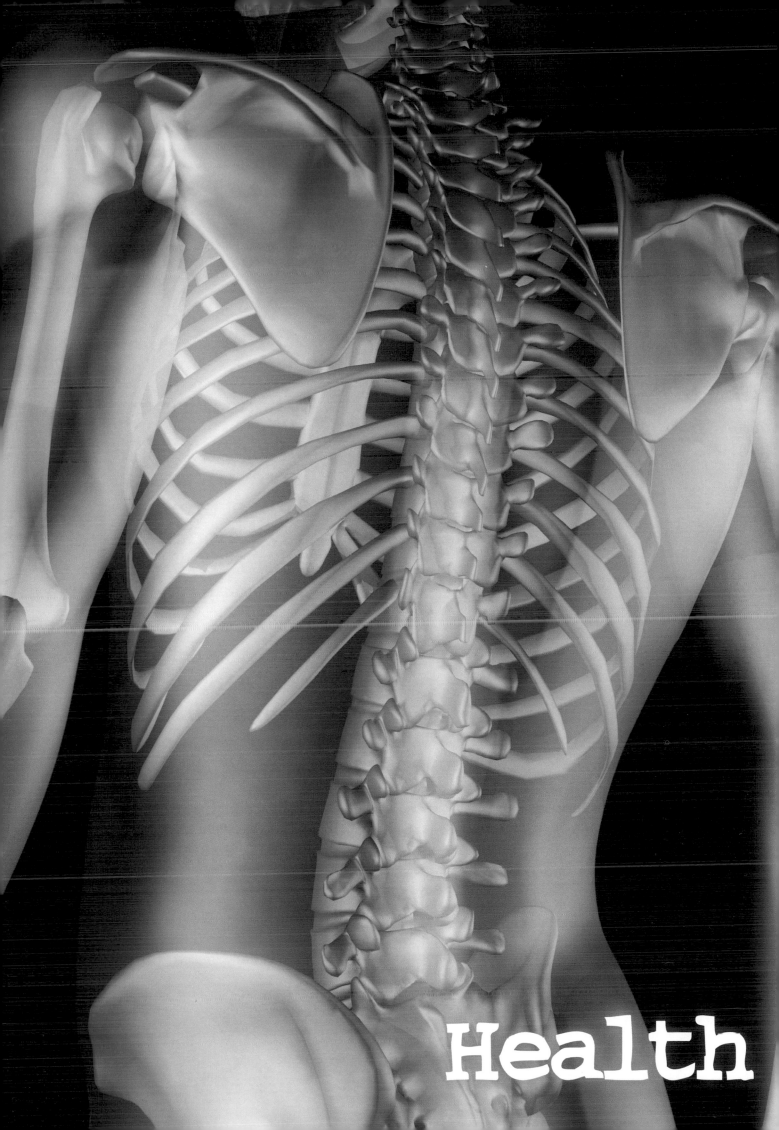

Health

"I think I have an eating disorder"

By Ilona Burton

You don't have to weigh five stone, have bones protruding like angry Himalayas or have lived by water and green tea alone for weeks on end to have an eating disorder.

You don't even have to fit neatly into one of the doctor's tick-lists; their tidy criteria used to label you as anorexic, bulimic or a binge eater. Every single person who has the courage to take that leap of faith and mutter the sentence "I think I have an eating disorder" deserves to be taken seriously and treated with respect.

There are many reasons why eating disorders are something that are often kept secret for months or

SOME ISSUES:

What sort of behaviour shows a normal attitude to food and what sort of behaviour would you classify as an eating disorder?

How could you help a friend who seemed to have such a problem?

Every single person who has the courage to take that leap of faith and mutter the sentence "I think I have an eating disorder" deserves to be taken seriously and treated with respect.

even years before a person confides in someone or asks for help. In the early stages of the illness, many people who are affected will be in denial and not even be aware themselves that they have a problem; they will shake off the fatigue, the headaches, the dizziness, the turmoil and be adamant that they are 'fine', especially if challenged. But even as the penny drops in slow motion and flips on the floor sending ripples of fear, as the awareness flicks a switch and eyes widen, acceptance is hard to swallow.

Is power over food really a power or is it a weakness? You thought you were in control, but look at you now; is sickness control or is it the opposite? Where is the happiness that you thought this quest to 'be thin' would bring you? Where is the joy in dragging your exhausted body to the gym at 6am? Is that pride you see in the mirror as your eyes water and mascara stains after throwing up that child's portion of dinner? Is this level of self-denial really an achievement? How do you feel now? Admit it – you feel like shit.

Looking back at my 'worst' stage of Anorexia (one of many 'worst' parts I hasten to add), even now I feel nostalgic sometimes. I miss that sense of achievement that I got from knowing that I was strong enough to resist anything and everything. But that wasn't strong, that was me being dictated to by a mental illness that could have killed me and has killed many others like me.

Real strength comes through holding your hands up. Real strength is saying those words out loud for the first time. Real strength is admitting that you can't do this alone; that you need help.

Breaking point for me came years after people first started to notice, make comments and voice their worries. For years I batted them away, told those closest what they wanted to hear, that it was just a phase – I'll be fine, I'll be fine, I'll be fine. I was a

But there's no point in doing that, addressing it for a while and then letting it peter out into weeks, months, years of more whispers and sneaking – the secret wins. 'BREAKING THE SILENCE' ONCE IS NOT ENOUGH.

'fine' robot. Perhaps they gave up trying. My parents later told me that living with me back then was like treading on eggshells. They were desperately worried and wanted to help, but didn't know how. They wanted to talk, but didn't know how. They were scared I would snap and bite their heads off at the slightest mention of food or weight. They were called into school after friends expressed concern to the deputy head. I was annoyed because all they ever talked about was make-up and the bloody Special K diet – how could they tell me to eat?

Eventually, I went to the GP with my mum. I reluctantly admitted whatever charges were put to me, lulled in the chair staring at the dial as the wet-lettuce woman GP did my blood pressure. She weighed me. Underweight. A few more questions. The result? "As long as you're having your periods you're fine." Years later, my consultant stared in disbelief as I recounted this. She had treated girls with a BMI of

11, still menstruating. To me, this doctor's appointment was a green light. I was right – I was fine.

Of course, I wasn't. The seeds had been sown and the next few years of my life would see me eat less, exercise more, lose more weight and become increasingly miserable. Ultimately, it ended in me getting so ill that I was told I could have a cardiac arrest at any minute.

I sometimes wonder 'what if?' What if that first GP had said something different? What if I had shown a bit more willingness to cooperate if she had? Hindsight is a wonderful thing – but for the record, I so much wish that I had been able to ask for help earlier. If you're in that position now, I urge you to do it – tell someone, anyone.

But this isn't just for those who have never told anyone about their illness. This is for those working towards recovery, those struggling to keep a hold, those who have come so far and are 'stuck', those who are recovered and are having an 'off day'. Telling someone for the first time may be the most daunting thing – but there's no point in doing that, addressing it for a while and then letting it peter out into weeks, months, years of more whispers and sneaking – the secret wins. 'Breaking the Silence' once is not enough. Eating disorders can only be beaten if we start the wheels turning and keep them going. Honesty and openness in spite of whatever the voices in your head tell you. The illness will scream at you to keep quiet. Scream louder.

The Independent Blogs, 21 February 2012

The illness will scream at you to keep quiet. SCREAM LOUDER!

How will we treat the wilfully ill?

I'd rather not pay for pillow-plumpers for Britain's fattest woman

Cristina Odone

I spent last Saturday comforting a friend, Sue, whose mother had been taken to Accident and Emergency following a fall. Sue's mother, a 78-year-old widow, lives on her own outside Oxford. Sue and her family live in London, where she and her husband hold down full-time jobs. She immediately took a week off work, but after that, her mother would have to rely on social services: carers will visit her twice a day to help her wash and dress in the morning; practise walking with her new stick; and make sure she doesn't slump into depression.

I was happy to know that my taxes were being used for this pensioner's welfare. The infirmities of age come to us all, and, to use an old-fashioned term, this was a deserving case.

The crack-head, the woman with faulty breast implants, the teenager with a tattoo that's grown gangrenous: when it's a matter of life and death, the health service does not distinguish between the deserving and undeserving ill

I feel differently about Brenda Flanagan-Davies. Britain's fattest woman weighs 40 stone. That's more than my refrigerator, double bed and desk combined. Brenda has reached these gargantuan proportions by chomping her way through nine chocolate bars and three fizzy drinks per day. Now immobile, she needs help to turn in bed, wash, dress and relieve herself.

A team of carers is on hand to do just that. Every day they come and cater for a 43-year-old who for decades has deliberately indulged her cravings for Twix and crisps. Paid for by my taxes, the carers make this obese woman's existence as pleasant as her 40 stone will allow. They plump her pillows, massage cream into her fleshy folds and cook her meals. I begrudge her the team's assistance, I'm afraid: in my eyes, she belongs to a growing number of the "undeserving ill".

The term is adapted from the Poor Law of 1601, which drew a distinction between the "deserving poor" who wished to work but couldn't find a job, or were too old, ill or young to work; and the "undeserving poor" who were able-bodied but lazy. A "poor rate" was levied to raise money to support the former, but there were no hand-outs for the latter.

Today, millions who are elderly and infirm rely on the equivalent of a "poor rate" for support. Their condition is not the predictable consequence of a foolish choice. As in the case of my friend's elderly mother, it is part of the natural process, or the debilitating result of an accident or a disease. However, there are millions of others who, having embarked on lifestyles that carry huge risks, look to the state for support in their distress. They are the "undeserving ill".

If a drug addict were rushed into A&E with a suspected heart attack, I know that the hospital must offer him or her its best treatment, state of the art equipment and illustrious specialists. Our publicly funded hospitals do not turn away patients at death's door simply because their affliction may have been self-inflicted. The crack-head, the woman with faulty breast implants, the teenager with a tattoo that's grown gangrenous: when it's a matter of life and death, the health service does not distinguish between the deserving and undeserving ill.

"After extensive X-rays and blood tests, we've confirmed what we already suspected-- you're not big-boned, you're fat."

But what about when the drug addict – or the binge drinker, or the Jordan wannabe – is not actually at death's door, but simply carrying on with their risky lifestyle? I don't want to support men and women who make potentially harmful choices – either about what they ingest or what they do to their breasts. I'm happy for my taxes to fund the long list of programmes to help addicts kick their habits; but I don't want to contribute to a team of carers who make things easy and cosy for the risk-taker. Everyone is free to live unhealthily; but they must live with the consequences too. And not at my expense.

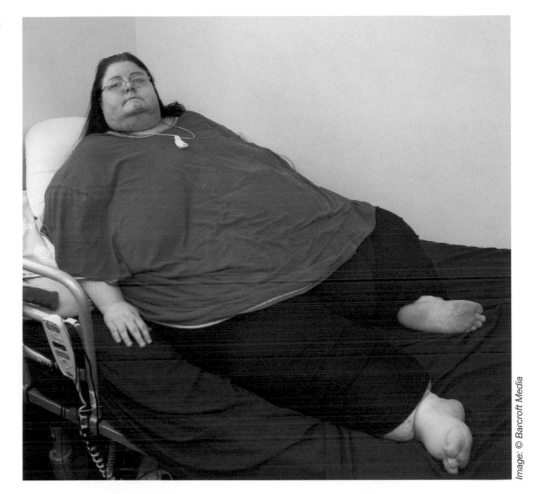

Image: © Barcroft Media

The "undeserving ill" is only in part a question of the rights and wrongs of self-inflicted damage. Rationing is another consideration. Forecasts of this country's demographics are alarming: thanks to remarkable technological advances, more and more of us are growing older and older. But while the pool of needy elderly is set to grow enormously, there is no similar trend among carers. Health and safety regulations, health authority cuts and gruelling work: the carer's lot is unenviable, and already in certain areas, demand outstrips supply.

When the ageing population makes the shortage of carers even more acute, the state will have to choose between providing Brenda with her carers, and assisting a septuagenarian widow after an accidental fall. Let Brenda plump her own pillows.

The Daily Telegraph, 18 February 2012
© Telegraph Media Group Ltd 2012

But what about when the drug addict – or the binge drinker, or the Jordan wannabe – is not actually at death's door, but simply carrying on with their risky lifestyle? I don't want to support men and women who make potentially harmful choices

A moment of kindness

Katie Elliott

Almost exactly a year ago, an extraordinary thing happened to me. It was a gloomy, cold December and I was really, really unhappy. I'd like to be able to say that feeling unhappy was the extraordinary thing, but that wouldn't be true. Looking back, I can spot a recurring pattern of mood swings which began when I was about twelve, but it took until my mid-thirties before I was diagnosed with bipolar disorder and started to understand what was going on.

Sinking feeling

By last winter, I had lived through many depressive episodes and I was finding them increasingly difficult to deal with. All those years of thinking myself a bad person rather than an ill one had taken their toll – I had learned to be intolerant and critical of myself, which only ever made things worse. On top of that, I was experiencing a dose of festive anxiety – the sinking feeling that comes from convincing yourself that everyone else is perfect and in control and you're not. Surely I'm the only one who just missed the last posting date yet again? Surely I'm the only one who just yelled at their partner and stormed out of the house, locking themselves out in the process? Surely I'm the only one huddled amongst the crumbs on the kitchen floor, crying and hoping her kids won't find her? Have you ever seen Nigella Lawson do that on her BBC Christmas special? Exactly.

SOME ISSUES:

Are there enough people prepared to listen to others?

Why are people reluctant to talk about depression – or about feelings?

See also:

Freddie Flintoff: the hidden pain of sporting stars p169

Dark Blues
Essential Articles 13, *p109*

Someone to talk to
Fact File 2012, p60

www.completeissues.co.uk

> *One day, despairing and lost, I found myself doing something I'd never done before. I started talking about how I felt with someone I barely knew.*

All in all, things were shaping up to be pretty miserable. I'd fallen out with some of the people I loved most. I was tired of roller-coastering from crazy schemes and sleepless nights to depression and anxiety over and over again. I didn't seem to get on with any of the medication I tried. And I couldn't see how I was going to be able to hang in there if this was how life was going to be. One day, despairing and lost, I found myself doing something I'd never done before. I started talking about how I felt with someone I barely knew. I didn't mean to. If I'd thought about it in advance I would have stopped myself. I'd had experiences before of opening up to people and it going wrong - I wouldn't have had the nerve to consciously risk that again, especially when I felt so bad. But I didn't think - I just spoke and everything came flooding out. How I believed myself to be impossible to live with. How I was scared that I was unfit to bring up my children. How I was so very tired of it all. It was then that the extraordinary thing happened. The person I barely knew, who probably had lots of other more important things to do, listened. She didn't judge or pity me. She let me speak until I'd said all I needed to say and then she told me about her experiences. She didn't have a diagnosed mental health problem herself but she still understood about mood swings, about anxiety, about perfectionism, about all sorts of things. And yet she seemed really normal and lovely and not at all like me.

Kinder

Something in the experience of letting myself be completely vulnerable, of being listened to and then confided in, changed everything. I felt accepted. And as I did so, something switched in my brain. For the first time I can remember, it occurred to me to accept myself. Since then, life has felt very different. The mood swings still come and go, but what has changed is that now I'm a little kinder to myself. Being kinder has helped me to get stronger. And as I've grown stronger I've talked with more and more people and listened to their stories and realised that I'm

Image © Alastair Johnstone

not alone in experiencing the things I do. Which has meant that I've been able to accept myself a little more, and be little kinder and get stronger and on and on...

Meet me in Winter

I'm lucky. I found someone to listen when I most needed it. But many don't. Many are right now feeling isolated and scared to reach out for help because mental health issues are still so difficult to admit to. For that reason, I have promised myself that I will do everything I can to work towards a society in which we can all speak openly without fear of discrimination. A society in which it is as easy to ask for help for mental health problems as it is to get a broken arm fixed. I started a project called Meet Me in Winter which brought together thousands of people from around the world. We made a single and a music video to raise money for charities including Mind (one of the two mental health charities who run Time to Change), and we got people talking about mental health issues. If you go to the website, you can watch our video and see how that one small but extraordinary moment of kindness has made a big difference, not just in my life, but now in many others' lives too.

time-to-change.org.uk
23 December 2011

'There was someone who needed it...' 60 lives, 30 kidneys, all linked in longest donor chain

Organ donation to stranger starts an amazing series of events across 11 US states

JEREMY LAURANCE

SOME ISSUES:

Is this a good way to increase organ donation?

Were some donors in the chain more generous than others?

Were some recipients more deserving?

Who would you donate an organ to?

See also:
The Biggest Gift
Essential Articles 14, p123

Organ Donation
Fact File 2011, p98

www.completeissues.co.uk

It began with an electrical contractor in Riverside, California called Rick Ruzzamenti who, after chatting to someone in his yoga class, decided to donate a kidney to a stranger.

Four months and 60 operations later, the longest kidney transplant chain in the world – with 30 patients receiving a kidney from 30 living donors – was completed when Don Terry, a diabetic who lives in Chicago, received a new organ at the Loyola University Medical Centre.

The extraordinary feat, which involved military-style planning, saw operations carried out over four months in 17 hospitals across 11 states, with newly-donated kidneys being flown coast to coast to ensure organs were matched to the right recipient.

It was made necessary because none of the patients in the chain was a good match for the loved one who had agreed to donate to them. So each donor agreed to give their kidney to a stranger on the understanding that their loved one would receive a kidney from another donor.

A similar feat would not be possible in the UK. British surgeons have decreed that transplant chains involving unrelated donors and recipients may only be established where all operations can be carried out on the same day. They fear that donors may drop out once their relative or friend has received a kidney, if there is a delay before they give their own organ, bringing the domino arrangement to a halt.

The US chain began with an altruistic donor – Mr Ruzzamenti

The chain went on from there with children donating for parents, husbands for wives and sisters for brothers.

– who expected nothing in return. It was then sustained, as the New York Times reported, by a mix of selflessness and self-interest as each donor gave up their organ in return for another to be given to their loved one by someone else.

It depended on some remarkable acts of generosity. David Madosh, 47, a tree surgeon from Michigan agreed to donate a kidney to help his ex-wife, Brooke Kitzman, 30, despite their split. He did so, because he did not want their two-year-old daughter to lose her mother.

Chain 124, as it was named by the National Kidney Registry, almost fell apart several times. The first operation on Mr Ruzzamenti took place on 15 August 2011. His kidney was flown from Los Angeles to New York where it was taken to Saint Barnabas Medical Centre in Livingston, New Jersey, and transplanted into a 66-year-old man.

His niece, a 34-year-old nurse, had wanted to donate her kidney to him but they had different blood groups and turned out to be a poor match. Instead she gave her kidney in exchange for Mr Ruzzamenti's, and it was flown to the University of Wisconsin Hospital, Madison,

where it was transplanted into 30-year-old Brooke Kitzman. The chain went on from there with children donating for parents, husbands for wives and sisters for brothers.

Nine days after Mr Ruzzamenti's operation, when the first five transplants had been completed, disaster struck. A donor dropped out saying he could not take the necessary two to four weeks off work to recover from the operation.

In late October there was another setback when a donor backed out citing unexplained "personal reasons," putting the 23 patients that lay behind him at risk. On each occasion the NKR struggled to find replacements. It succeeded, but not without nail-biting delays.

After John Clark of Sarasota, Florida, got his transplant on 28 September at Tampa General Hospital, his wife Rebecca had to wait more than two months before it was her turn to give up her kidney in return. Mrs Clark admitted she had thought about dropping out, but had resisted.

"I believe in karma and that would have been really bad karma. There was someone out there who needed my kidney," she said.

The Independent, 23 February 2012

Our youngsters are doing much better than parents in shunning booze and fags

Kate Higgins, Blogger

SOME ISSUES:

Why do you think newspapers make a bigger deal of bad news?

Do you think teenagers drink too much?

Do you think adults drink too much?

Is this a problem or not?

See also:

I am an actual human being
Essential Articles 14, p203

Let's be realistic about teen drinking
Essential Articles 13, p14

Road to recovery?
Fact File 2011, p8

www.completeissues.co.uk

The parents never tire of telling it. Aged 16, and on my first local pub foray with friends, one thought it would be funny to buy me doubles all night.

I arrived home to go to the midnight church service but only managed to greet the church-goers in between vomiting episodes on the front steps of our house.

The parents spent all night with me checking I wasn't going to choke and die mid-huey. At 7.30am I bounced into their room, fully recovered; they meanwhile felt like they'd been the ones on the batter.

Safe to say, I have never drunk vodka, lime and lemonade since: the thought of it still makes me shudder. And sadly, most of us have a tale to relate from our yoof involving alcohol that, many years hence, still has the ability to turn us a shade of crimson.

Sometimes we adults need to remember this when rushing to condemn the latest statistics on the consumption of substances by teenagers. Last week, the headlines screamed that one in seven youngsters "drank regularly".

A phone-in focussed on this national disaster with appropriate doom-laden sonorousness. We adults queued up to express our shock and surprise and what we are all doing to "address the problem" both as parents and professionals.

I'm afraid I rather rolled my eyes at it all. There's nothing like the realisation that today's teenagers are behaving just as we all did in our teenage years to unleash a sense of hypocritical moral panic.

Indeed, I'd be more worried at the prospect of today's youth turning out just like us and maybe that's where the debate should be concentrated. Frankly, we 30 and 40-somethings are the most irresponsible generation I know.

Addled with debt, addicted to good times, still ingesting too many substances than can possibly be good for us, avoiding maturity for as long as we can: if we want to work out what's going on with the junior generation, perhaps we should take a long hard look in the mirror. After all, children see, children do.

In the last week, how many adults can say, hand on heart, that they did not have an alcoholic drink?

But it's only when you pare back the research that you realise how misleading the media portrayal has been. The survey findings actually contain an awful lot of good news.

Teenagers smoke much less than they did in the 1990s; indeed, the figures are at their lowest since 1982. There is also a downward trend in alcohol consumption, with fewer 13 and 15 year olds ever having imbibed. The trend for drug use is also downward.

Overall, what the findings show is that only a tiny minority of teenagers use (and therefore misuse) substances on a regular basis. What no one bothered to report – because good news is no news – is that for the one-third of 15 year olds who had a drink in the last week (apparently that means regularly to headline writers) there were two-thirds who did not.

Fess up here people – in the week December 14-21, how many adults can say, hand on heart, that they did not have an alcoholic drink?

Most of us would be toiling to stay within the recommended consumption limits, given the Christmas party season was at its peak. Maybe we should be conducting parallel research with adults on substance use, to give us a useful yardstick. I'd bet right now that teenagers' consumption habits pale into insignificance compared to grown-ups.

None of this is to belittle the findings, but simply to try and apply a sense of perspective.

The small minority of children and young people with serious misuse issues relating to alcohol, tobacco and drugs need better support.

It is in scant supply and a media focus on this scandal would be helpful. As would a better understanding – and appropriate support services – of the reasons why some children try to obliviate themselves in drugs and alcohol. Scratch the surface and abuse, neglect and violence will be hidden beneath the veil of substance misuse.

Moreover, the data shows where to target resources to address consumption spikes. Tobacco use leaps between 13 and 15 year olds: surely we should focus preventative efforts at this age group?

But ultimately, we should take heart from these findings. Our young people increasingly turn their nose up at ingesting substances. Fewer smoke, take drugs or drink, despite the pressures on them and the prospects of becoming part of a lost generation dangling enticingly before them.

Such moral fortitude in troubled times suggests greater resilience than their elders and supposed betters. And that is the kind of good news that should be shouted from the rooftops.

This article was originally published in the Herald Scotland Online, 28 December 2011

Kate Higgins also writes for burdzeyeview.wordpress.com/

'Nurses helped my Gran to die'

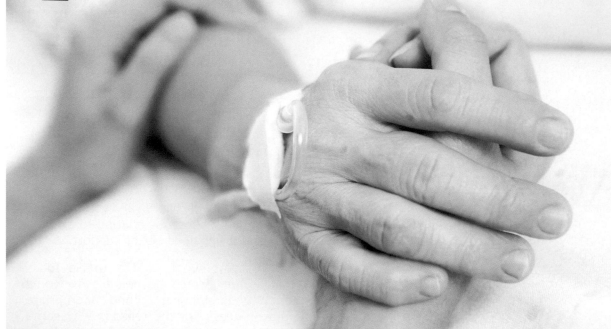

Nurses withdrew my Gran's medication - but don't call the police.

Max Pemberton

SOME ISSUES:

Do you think people should ever be assisted to die?

Who should make the decision?

See also:
Why preserve a life with no meaning?
Essential Articles 13, p18

The big question
Fact File 2010, p112

www.completeissues.co.uk

A few months ago, my Gran died. She had terminal cancer, so it was expected. She slipped away quietly in a side room on a medical ward of a provincial teaching hospital, with my sister and me holding her hand and talking to her gently. It was a delicate, humane and peaceful end. On her death certificate, it says she died of septic shock, pneumonia and metastatic lung cancer. But that's not what killed her. She was killed by a nurse.

Now, before anyone panics and calls the police, what the nurse did was perfectly legal and all according to a plan my Gran had set out before she was admitted to hospital. In fact, my sister and I asked the nurse to do it. As my Gran slipped into unconsciousness, the medical team stopped giving her any medication and discontinued the drip that was giving her fluids.

Over the next 24 hours, her body quickly began to fail. A consultant came to visit us and we had "the talk". As a doctor, I have had this talk with many relatives of patients before,

Doctors routinely help people facing death, such as my Gran, to end their own lives

but it was strange to be on the receiving end. It's never easy talking about death, but he did it with compassion. Euphemistic phrases such as "keeping her comfortable" were used, but it was clear what was really being said: there would come a point when, in order to ensure that she was not suffering, larger doses of morphine would be needed, which would have the knock-on effect of depressing her breathing to the extent she would die. In essence, the consultant was checking with us that we realised that, when the time came, they would kill her. He never said that explicitly, but we understood what was implied.

Later that day, as she was beginning to experience some distress, a nurse administered a dose of morphine. It didn't appear to have the desired effect, and my Gran remained distressed. "We could give her another dose ..." said the nurse. Again, we understood what he was saying and nodded: "We promised her she wouldn't die in pain." Another dose was administered. Five minutes later, she stopped breathing.

There is nothing unusual about this: similar scenes are played out up and down the country – and I'm pleased they are. Medicine's aim is to alleviate suffering.

I thought about my family's experience when I read the report published last week by the Commission on Assisted Dying. Under the plans, doctors would be able to prescribe drugs to end the lives of terminally ill people who request it, who are deemed to have the mental capacity to make that decision, providing they have less than 12 months to live. To safeguard the vulnerable, those with disabilities, dementia or depression would not qualify for help in killing themselves.

Those still opposed to these changes denounced the Commission – whose research is funded by campaigner Sir Terry Pratchett (he has Alzheimer's) – claiming they were a "self-appointed group" who excluded anyone who opposed legalising assisted suicide. This may be true, but then those who oppose assisted suicide are similarly self-appointed, taking it upon themselves to impose their beliefs on the rest of us.

We should be cautious when it comes to considering such changes in legislation, but we also need to be honest about what's already happening. The main arguments from opponents to any change are that they are the "thin end of the wedge". Yet they fail to appreciate that the wedge is already in place.

Doctors routinely help people facing death, such as my Gran, to end their own lives. That this is rarely publicly acknowledged gives the false impression that the Commission's proposals represent a significant shift in current practice. Certainly, it is different, conceptually at least, for doctors to help terminally ill people die before death is imminent. But it's not that different.

Assisted suicide is illegal in this country. At present, those physically able and wealthy enough can go to Switzerland where physician-assisted suicide is possible. The alternative is to remain here and do it yourself. I'd far rather a doctor was on hand to ensure things go smoothly than witness a painful or slow death as a result of a botched suicide attempt.

For me, this is about individuals choosing when and how they will die, and enabling doctors to ensure this does not result in extra suffering. As a doctor, I like the idea of people feeling empowered at a time of their lives when so much can seem out of their control. I want people with a terminal illness to have the kind of death my Gran had, when they choose it.

The Daily Telegraph
9 January 2012
© Telegraph Media Group
Ltd 2012

OUR HATRED OF 'OLD DEARS' MUST BE TACKLED LIKE RACISM OR SEXISM

THE DISMISSIVE LANGUAGE USED ABOUT OLDER PEOPLE IS A SYMPTOM OF A DEEPER FEAR AND VISCERAL DISGUST

GERALDINE BEDELL

SOME ISSUES:

As a society, do we value older people?

How much does the way you speak to or about people matter?

Is it more important for nurses to be skilful, efficient or kind?

See also:
Population pyramid
Fact File 2012, p138
Age concern,
Fact File 2010, p168

www.completeissues.co.uk

My father-in-law recently died in a hospital ward where he had developed appalling bedsores. Patients were often to be found wandering confused and unattended, the nurses seemed more interested in their computers than their patients and – on the two occasions we finally managed to speak to a doctor – we got conflicting stories of whether he was dying or being cured.

This is not an unusual experience. The elderly are being let down in large numbers, the Commission on Improving Dignity in Care for Older People has concluded. Compassion needs to become central to nursing. Well, there's a revelation.

Still, it needed saying, because there is an epidemic of abuse. Since Gransnet launched last May, this has probably been the most frequently discussed issue on our forums. Many of

Give people half a chance and they'll see the older patient, as someone without identity or personality

our users have elderly parents alive, or have seen for themselves (for example) the patient in the next hospital bed called an "attention-seeker" by nurses for asking to be propped up.

Individually, the examples are relatively trivial; together, they amount to a systematic reducing of older people to less-than-human. The father whose hearing aid was removed because its whistling bothered hospital staff: immediately rendered less than competent. There was the mother left for an hour and 40 minutes after she asked to go to the toilet; eventually, she wet the bed. When a nurse finally turned up, she said: "We all have these little accidents." But this woman wasn't incontinent, just humiliated.

Some, no doubt, will mutter that the Commission's insistence that no one should be allowed to say "old dear" is political correctness gone mad, the thought police at it again. But, as so often, dismissive language is a symptom of deeper fear and hatred. Ageism seems to be in a similar state to what sexism was when I was a child, or homophobia in my teens: so ingrained that, most of the time, we don't even notice it.

"Do you walk with a stick at home, dear?" one of our members was recently asked as she made her way down the ward after an operation. No, she said tartly, "at home, I ride a bicycle". Another advises: "Always take a photo of yourself surrounded by your grandchildren to put by your bed." Give people half a chance and they'll objectify the older patient, see them as someone without identity or personality.

So, are nurses to blame? Have they, as is suggested, become "too posh to wash"? This argument holds that things have gone downhill since nursing became a degree subject and Matrons disappeared, along with their strictures to young nurses who dared to look under-occupied.

The draft report, which was put together by the NHS Confederation, the Local Government Association and Age UK, goes some way to endorsing this view, pointing out that the NHS would do well to learn from John Lewis and recruit people who have the right values, then give them the skills. A degree is no guarantee of empathy, sympathy or, that most unfashionable virtue, kindness.

It's not simply that a cohort of go-getting nurses has lost

Increasingly we are warehousing people in large care homes, tended to by poorly paid (though sometimes devoted) staff

interest in paying attention to people, or got too grand to sit and talk to the patient who has no visitors. The Royal College of Nursing has found that older people's wards typically have one registered nurse to between nine and 10 patients, whereas adult general and surgical wards have one to six patients.

This is completely the wrong way round. It ignores the fact that older people's needs are much more likely to be complex. It's the little things that get overlooked as a result – like forgetting to give people their spectacles, or getting patients out of bed to change the sheets then not getting round to it all day, so they have to take their nap in a chair. Small things, perhaps, but they add up to a pervasive air of neglect and disdain.

These too-few nurses are overwhelmed by administration. To transfer a patient from hospital to a care home, it is necessary to fill out a 70-page form. It's no wonder that so many of us have stood at nurses' stations waiting for someone to look up – and, when they do, to behave as if we might have something useful or interesting to say.

There is, of course, nothing wrong with inspections and setting standards of performance (just as there is nothing wrong with nurses taking on responsibilities that used to be managed by doctors), but it's human nature then to deal with the more measurable things first. Hospitals assess how many people fall over on their wards but not the quality of patients' experience.

Most old people aren't in hospital for months on end. The long-stay geriatric wards of the past are gone; these days, older people are shipped out to care homes. This is not inevitably a bad thing – hospitals with their 50-bed wards and lack of calm, quiet rooms to talk to relatives are not well-designed for the old. But care homes, even where publicly funded, are privately run, and there is no requirement to employ qualified nursing staff even if what is really needed is nursing care.

Increasingly, we are warehousing people in large care homes, tended to by poorly paid (though sometimes devoted) staff where we can do our best to forget abut them until our turn comes. It is inhumane, and it's small wonder that

most people dread the prospect.

This latest report is not the first broadside against the dreadful care of older people. It follows other well-researched protests by the Patients' Association and the Care Quality Commission. Last week, the National Pensioners Convention published a not dissimilar set of Dignity In Care guidelines.

What they're all saying shouldn't need to be said. Why wouldn't nurses and carers look after people properly, when it's their job? If similar cruelties were visited on children, the stories would never be off the front pages. But we inhabit a world in which speed and youth and the ability to earn money are prized above all qualities, where an ageing population is seen as a burden as well as, more viscerally, faintly disgusting. Until we can censor ourselves and stop thinking about "old dears" rather than vivid personalities, about a drain on resources rather than people who have something to teach us, there is no hope.

Geraldine Bedell is the Editor of Gransnet: www.gransnet.com

The Independent,
1 March 2012

Internet & media

Leveson inquiry –
A paparazzo speaks

Paparazzi may not rank highly in public opinion, but it is public appetite for celeb pics that creates the market snappers serve

KEVIN RUSH

> **It's OK everyone taking the stand at the Leveson inquiry and demanding paparazzi be regulated but none of them offered workable solutions...**

SOME ISSUES:

Do you think people deserve the right to privacy away from photographers?

Do you think that famous people should expect to have photographers follow them?

Does this seem like an appealing profession?

See also:
Helen, 28, has some thoughts on Page 3
p100

It's our obsession with celebrity that's on trial
p130

www.completeissues.co.uk

As a paparazzo I'm well aware I'm down there with traffic wardens in the court of public opinion. I've had eggs and flour thrown at me and more abuse than I care to mention. It doesn't faze me; and if it did I'd have to get another career. In the same way, if I got too bogged down with ethical conundrums every time it came to picturing people such as the Dowlers I'd have to quit.

It's our job to take pictures of the top stories of the day, whoever they may be. It's the moral decision of the newspaper editors whether they print them or not. While there is a market and a public appetite there'll be paparazzi, whatever Leveson eventually decides.

If he completely banned such photos in Britain the photographers wouldn't go away, they'd just sell abroad or to websites. I wish we could go back to the days before digital cameras when it was just film. Back then you needed to be a proper photographer,

> You hear all these celebrities complaining about being chased, but the fact is if they don't try and get away then photographers don't need to chase them. Simple.

now anyone can go out and buy an £800 camera and stand outside Nobu and take pictures of the rich and famous.

Some youngsters starting out don't know how to operate properly, driving like lunatics and turning what should be a simple photo into a free-for-all. It's the worst at night; things can get quite aggressive as everyone is fighting to get the best shots, the ones that will sell. You hear all these celebrities complaining about being chased, but the fact is if they don't try and get away then photographers don't need to chase them. Simple.

I've worked all over the world as a paparazzo and Britain is different because celebrities tend to hire these big entourages and that means photographers have to fight harder for the shots. In Hollywood Reese Witherspoon, for example, will go out shopping with a friend accepting she might get her picture taken and there's no issue. Security teams just escalate the situation.

Kate Moss is someone who has a good relationship with photographers: she knows she's a supermodel and that she'll get papped going about her daily life. If a picture appears of her stumbling drunk out of a club so be it, she shrugs it off.

To some extent photographers in London have made a rod for their own back because even the most minor D-lister gets mobbed. Celebrities complain about long-lens photographs but they're the least intrusive of all. A good photographer would ideally take a shot without leaving their car and the target wouldn't even know they'd been there.

The recession hasn't helped matters. In the last two years the value of photos has dropped at least 30%. Some pics will make as little as £10 online and it's rare to see even big exclusives fetch more than £10,000. A full-time paparazzo in London is struggling to take home £2,000 a month. It makes them desperate and so push the boundaries. The News of the World shutting down hasn't helped – they were the best payers.

> Some pics will make as little as £10 online and it's rare to see even big exclusives fetch more than £10,000.

I have an NUJ press card but most paparazzi don't. Gerry McCann's idea that photographers would need signed permission before publishing pictures taken in public is effectively gagging the media. What about if I'm taking a photograph of a policeman taking a bribe? It's not like I can walk on over after and ask him to sign on the dotted line. Plus, technology means everyone is a photographer of sorts. Would regulation apply to a thousand screaming fans with cameraphones outside the Odeon Leicester Square? What about if some chased after Johnny Depp's car afterwards?

If you're in the public eye you have to accept that the public will want to know about your life. The more you try to hide it, the greater the hunger will be.

The Guardian, 25 November 2011
© Guardian News & Media Ltd 2011

It's our obsession with celebrity that's on trial

Blame the hacks if you like, but what about the sources in hospitals, police stations and hotels?

CHRISTINA PATTERSON

Sienna Miller arrives at the Leveson enquiry, at the High Court in central London
Photo: Matt Crossick EMPICS Entertainment

SOME ISSUES:

Do you think people deserve the right to privacy away from photographers?

Should the press look into people's private affairs for the sake of news?

How far should an investigation go?

See also:

Helen, 28, has some thoughts on Page 3, p100
A paparazzo speaks
p130
www.completeissues.co.uk

It was, in its moving and sometimes funny way, as English as roast beef. First, the suburban couple *[parents of murdered schoolgirl Millie Dowler]* whose dead daughter's hacked phone messages triggered this inquiry, as modest and dignified as grieving human beings can be. And later, the performance of his life from an actor world famous for his English understatement, but who had decided that understatement was no longer enough.

There was nothing funny, of course, about the Dowlers' testimony to the Leveson Inquiry on Monday, the first time they had spoken publicly about the events that made them think their dead daughter was alive. Sally Dowler didn't, she told

the court, sleep for three nights after hearing that her daughter's phone had been hacked. "You replay everything in your mind," she said. She was thinking back, she said, to those moments when she'd thought "something untoward is going on".

"Something untoward" was certainly going on, something that meant she could suddenly hear her daughter's voice on her voicemail, and that someone could print a photograph of a walk that no one except she, her husband, and the police knew about, a walk retracing their daughter's last steps. The photograph, she said, made her "really cross", and so did the fact that whenever she went out of her front door, she "had to be on guard".

But when she met the chairman of the media company whose employees had made her life even more of a hell than it had been before, she wanted to be fair. Rupert Murdoch was, she told the court, "very sincere". She and her husband were, she said, "ordinary people", with "no experience in such a public life situation".

"We tried," she said, and it's hard to hear the words without wanting to cry, "to be as balanced as we could."

You couldn't really describe Hugh John Mungo Grant, as we learnt he's called, as an "ordinary" person. You couldn't really say that he has "no experience" in "a public life situation". If he ever thought that playing a bumbling bachelor in films that turned out to be unexpectedly popular would mean a few staged interviews and photoshoots, and a private life that was free as a bird, he soon learnt he was wrong. You don't, in fact, get all that much more public than having the police mugshot taken of you when you were found performing "a lewd act" in a car with a prostitute splashed on the front pages of papers around the world.

Grant, to be fair, which lots of people don't seem to want to be, including Piers Morgan, who tweeted on Monday that he hoped Nelson Mandela was watching the inquiry, "so he could understand what real persecution is all about", seemed to take the whole thing in his stride. He kept his appointment on an American chat show, which was booked

What is the Leveson Enquiry?

The Leveson Inquiry is a public inquiry into the culture, practices and ethics of the British press. Prime Minister David Cameron appointed Lord Justice Leveson as Chairman to look into the specific claims about phone hacking at the News of the World, the failure of the initial police inquiry and allegations of illicit payments to police by the press. A second inquiry would review the general culture and ethics of the British media.

51 victims were named by the Inquiry up to November 2011, including members of the public, politicians, sportsmen, other public figures, who may have been victims of media intrusion.

Hearings into the relations between press and public took place between November 2011 and February 2012 with testimony about press intrusion and press behaviour and freedom. These were followed in February 2012 by hearings into relationships between the press and police.

a few days later, and told Jay Leno, with the honesty that seems to have become his trademark, "I think you know in life what's a good thing to do and what's a bad thing, and I did a bad thing. And there," he said, "you have it." And when he was invited, on the Larry King show, to come up with some kind of explanation for his behaviour, he wouldn't. "I don't," he said, "have excuses."

On Monday, 16 years after the arrest that made him even more famous, he said it again. "I was arrested," he said, "it was on public record. I totally expected there to be tons of press, a press storm. That happened," he said, "and I have no quarrel with it." What he did have a quarrel with, he went on to say, was the fact that his flat was burgled, and nothing in it stolen, just before a full description of its décor appeared

in a tabloid newspaper, and the fact that medical symptoms, reported during a trip to Accident & Emergency, appeared in a tabloid newspaper, and the fact that when a girlfriend was mugged, and they called the police, it was the photographers who came round first.

And the fact that when an ex-girlfriend went into hospital to have his baby, which no one knew about except her parents, who didn't speak English, and his cousin, who he says wouldn't have told anyone, he didn't dare visit his own first child "because of the danger of a leak" bringing a "press storm down". Which, when he couldn't resist "a quick visit", which you can kind of understand, is exactly what happened. Since then, the mother of his child, who never sought the life of a "celebrity", and isn't his partner, and probably didn't plan to have his

When people rush out to buy newspapers that plaster the secrets of people's sex lives, and medical records, and interior décor, and unannounced pregnancies, and private walks in their dead daughter's last steps, where do they think they come from?

child, has been unable to leave her home without being chased. Her life, she says, has become "unbearable".

Newspapers, he said, claimed that "celebrities" deserved to have their sex lives exposed because they were trading on false images. "I wasn't aware," he said, "that I was trading on my good name. I've never had a good name. I'm the man who was arrested with a prostitute." He didn't want, he said, to see "the end of popular print journalism", but there was "a section of our press" that had been allowed to become "toxic".

Yes, there is a section of our press that has become "toxic", but this isn't just about the press. When people rush out to buy newspapers that plaster the secrets of people's sex lives, and medical records, and interior décor, and unannounced pregnancies, and private walks in their dead daughter's last steps, where do they think they come from? Do they think the "celebrities" involved are just so thrilled to be "celebrities" that they can't resist phoning tabloid hacks to spill more beans? Do they think it's done on a nice cup of tea and a handshake? Blame the hacks if you like, but what about the "sources", in hospitals, and police stations, and clinics, and hotels, and restaurants, who see any whiff of a "celebrity" life as a fast track to a fast buck?

There is a system for ensuring that people's phones aren't hacked. It's called the law. If the police who were meant to be upholding it had acted on the evidence they had, then quite a lot of this horrible, ugly, shameful exploitation of what ought to have been private grief, and, in Grant's case, private joy, wouldn't have happened. But it wouldn't change a culture that

What was discovered?

Evidence was taken from 184 witnesses which lead to tabloid newspapers being accused of "blackmail, intrusion, harassment, hounding... and bullying" by a barrister representing victims of their behaviour.

In a detailed and, at times, devastating attack on the popular press which lasted over three hours, David Sherborne told the inquiry those practices were "systemic, flagrant and deeply entrenched".

The enquiries revealed that phone-hacking at the News of the World was commonplace, including hacking into the phone of murdered schoolgirl Millie Dowler – leading her parents to believe she was alive and picking up messages from her phone.

Gerry and Kate McCann, gave evidence explaining how they felt "mentally raped" when the NoW ran the contents of a private diary Kate had written to her daughter following her disappearance, without their permission.

Actress Sienna Miller told of how she was spat at and verbally abused and had to endure high-speed car chases. She told of how journalists would turn up to meetings she'd arranged on her mobile phone and that she later discovered her phone and computer had been hacked. She also told of the intimidation saying "Take away the cameras and you've a pack of men chasing a woman".

Author JK Rowling told the enquiry how she was outraged when one evening she found a note from a journalist in her five-year-old daughter's school bag.

Actor Hugh Grant explained how his flat was broken into – the details of this flat were subsequently published in a newspaper.

makes "celebrity" a god, and one to be envied, and destroyed.

If Hugh Grant is a King Canute, trying to fend off the lapping tides of an ocean that threatens to drown us, an ocean where every single aspect of the life of anyone you've heard of is public property, then good for him. He's big enough to look after himself, but he isn't, I believe, just thinking of himself. He's thinking of the people who are suddenly thrust into the

limelight, and tossed to the lions, or wolves. He's thinking, in fact, in what you might say was quite a plucky English way, of the underdog.

The Leveson Inquiry is about much, much more than the press. It's about what Grant appealed to, and the Dowlers embodied: "Our British sense of decency." It's also about what we used to call fair play.

The Independent, 23 November 2011

Internet trolls

In the January issue of The Believer, Meghan Daum wondered whether the writers of today "have ever really been able to express anything—in print, on a blog, on Facebook, wherever—without on some level bracing themselves for mockery or scorn or troll-driven pestilence." I don't have to wonder, because she's talking about me. Well, not just me – you too.

Last year I had an article in a high-profile US newspaper. I was thrilled, obviously, and sent the link to my mum. Everything was going swimmingly until she scrolled down to the comments – which called me stupid, snobby, close-minded and a hack. Worst of all, they called me "Kristy".

My mum wanted to track down each of the commenters and respond to them personally, with the general theme of HOW DARE YOU, MY CHILD IS A GENIUS. You've never seen Mama Logan on the warpath, but trust me when I say that if you upset her children, she will fry up your heart with some onions and Worcestershire sauce. And then afterwards she'll knit a nice scarf.

I laughed it off, telling her that nasty comments were just how it goes. We're creative people. We eat rejection for breakfast. We have the hides of rhinos and the egos of Kanye West. We make things, they go out into the world, and then anonymous strangers tell us that we're stupid. Just how it goes. But does it have to be that way?

It would be great if everyone who commented had thought carefully about what they'd read and wanted to share their opinion – whether agreement or disagreement. But often it's "tl;dr" (too long; didn't read) followed by screeds of scorn with little or nothing to do with the article.

> **In the Olden Days (also known as the years BB, Before Blogs), people who hated your work might call you an idiot – but you'd never know it.**

In the Olden Days (also known as the years BB, Before Blogs), people who hated your work might call you an idiot – but you'd never know it. If they really cared they'd write a letter to the editor – but you'd only see it if they were articulate enough for the editor to publish. Now there are no gatekeepers. By the time an article has been up for a day, it's so choked with arguments that rational, thoughtful people don't want to wade into the shitstorm. Life is just too short.

But aside from bracing ourselves, what can we do about it? The internet is a free and open forum. We shouldn't change it, no matter how many trolls or non-thinkers clutter it up. The ability to comment anonymously is a beautiful thing, and everyone's opinion is valid, whether they've really thought it through or not. Right?

SOME ISSUES:

Should all writers just expect criticism?

Should everyone have the right to comment?

Does the thought of being criticised stop people from expressing their opinions?

See also:

www.completeissues.co.uk

Kirsty Logan, 8 February 2012
www.ideastap.com

The best solution to game addiction? Maturity and strategy

WENDY KAYS

SOME ISSUES:

Do you think you can be 'addicted' to playing these types of games?

How long do you think is an acceptable time to play each day?

What are the pros and cons to playing these games?

Does it affect your 'real' life?

See also:

What good is information if our children can't understand it
Essential Articles 13, p128

I fear the wii folk are playing a dangerous game
Essential Articles 12, p128

www.completeissues.co.uk

While it's tempting to use the "addiction" label to explain the rude behaviour of Alec Baldwin* after being refused a plane seat because he wouldn't turn off his phone game "Words with Friends," there is a less simple and more sobering explanation.

Game addiction is real. It's a behavioural addiction like gambling, thrill seeking, or sex addiction. It happens when instead of taking a drug like cocaine into your body, you abuse the naturally existing chemicals in your glands and brain by repeatedly cutting straight to the most exciting part of an experience. When you stop artificially inflating your adrenaline and internal reward drug, dopamine, you feel depressed. This is because your body has put up a fight to save you from the stress you've put on yourself by adding dopamine receptors in your brain to deal with the overload and calm you down. So when you go back to a normal level, you feel terrible. You want to feel good again. You want to play again, just like wanting another hit of a drug.

However, there is another reason Mr. Baldwin may have reacted the way he did. Rich Vogel, a veteran and respected game designer, has called the design features in a game that keep us interested as "sticky"

The inflated sense of achievement, ownership, and the immersion we feel while gaming gives us pleasure and distracts us from our surroundings.

factors. Games, both complex and simple, are designed to keep us involved. The inflated sense of achievement, ownership, and the immersion we feel while gaming gives us pleasure and distracts us from our surroundings.

It gives the player a sense of urgency and importance that doesn't match the mood of what's actually going on in the larger world. When pulled suddenly from the small world into the larger one, the typical response of a gamer is to react with annoyance and rage.

The best solution? Maturity and strategy. Schedule your gaming, and try to show a little compassion to those who don't have the controls.

Wendy Kays is the author of 'Game Widow'

The Independent, 8 December 2011

* *The actor was rebuked by a flight attendant for using his mobile while waiting for take off. According to the airline he refused to turn it off and became annoyed and abusive. He was told to leave the plane.*

"Video gamers are like gambling addicts"

Startling headlines followed the publication of a report looking at the brains of young people who often played video games.

The researchers studied 154 healthy 14 year olds: 72 boys and 82 girls. The young people were then divided into two groups: frequent gamers, who played for more than the average nine hours a week, and infrequent gamers who played less. When the brain structure of these two groups was compared it emerged that the area involved with rewards and decision-making was larger in frequent video game players. There were no differences in other parts of the brain.

This area – the ventral striatum – is usually activated when people anticipate or experience something positive such as good food or winning money, releasing a 'feelgood' chemical. It has also been associated with drug addiction.

The researchers also found more brain activity in the frequent gamers when they were losing – similar to the process that keeps problem gamblers betting.

But were the shocking headlines justified?

The study did not prove that gaming changed the brains of the young people. It could be that the frequent gamers already had the enlarged brain area which made gaming more rewarding.

Dr Simone Kuhn of Ghent University in Belgium, who led the research, said: "Although our subjects were not addicted to video games in the strict diagnostic sense, the current result seems to suggest that video gaming is related to addiction."

The researchers now plan to ask adults who have never played video games to start gaming to see if this has any effect on their brains.

Sources: various

We won't let fear rule the street
**DEFEND
TO PROTEST**
www.....ttoprotest.org

FREE
FRANK
FERNIE!

Law & order

the Stephen Lawrence legacy:

On 22nd April 1993, Stephen Lawrence, aged 18, was stabbed and died. In January 2012, two people were found guilty of his murder. This case has highlighted huge issues involving race, society and the law.

the background

On 22nd April 1993, Stephen Lawrence, aged 18, was stabbed to death by a gang of white youths while waiting for a bus. The only motivation for the unprovoked attack was that Stephen was black.

The initial investigation by the police was slow to start and plagued by errors such as failure to contact witnesses or to arrest and question suspects. In May the Lawrence family complained that the police were not doing enough. After this, arrests were made and murder charges were brought against five men but in July the Crown Prosecution Service said there was not enough evidence to go to trial and the prosecution was dropped.

In September 1994 the Lawrence family began a private prosecution against the five men. Charges against two of them were dropped and in 1996, when it came to court, the remaining three were acquitted by the jury.

In 1997 there was an inquest into Stephen's death which ruled that he had been unlawfully killed in an unprovoked racist attack by five white youths. The five original suspects were called to the inquest but refused to answer any questions. On 14th February The Daily Mail printed pictures of all five on the front page, branding them murderers and inviting them to sue the newspaper and prove it wrong.

Also in 1997, the Home Secretary set up the Macpherson Enquiry into the handling of the case. It found that the original investigation had been incompetent and came, famously, to the conclusion that the Metropolitan Police was 'institutionally racist'. The Enquiry also recommended a change in the law so that someone who had been acquitted of murder could be tried again if new evidence came to light. This came into force in 2005.

In 2006 the police began a cold case review which found forensic evidence of minute particles of blood and hair from Stephen Lawrence on the clothing of Gary Dobson and Stephen Norris, two of the original five suspects. Dobson could only be tried again because of the change in the law recommended by Macpherson.

In January 2012 these two were found guilty of the murder of Stephen Lawrence.

The murder of Stephen and the campaign for justice by his parents highlighted racism in British society but also brought about major changes. The Metropolitan police set out to reform its practices and an ancient tradition of British common law was changed.

But did the changes affect the ordinary life of young black people? Two young Londoners give their opinion.

Sources: Various

SOME ISSUES:

How do you think the Stephen Lawrence case might have affected race relations in the community?

How might it have affected the law?

See also:

'My tram experience' is shocking – but should it be cause for arrest?
p14

www.completeissues.co.uk

nineteen years after Stephen's murder, stop and search is poisoning race relations:

Story of a 'suspect'

Photo: jon le-bon / Shutterstock.com

For Feyi Badejo, stop and search is a part of life. In Peckham, south London, the 17-year-old says his peers are used to being targeted.

"I'm doing nothing wrong, on my own, sometimes I'm in front of my house when I am stopped. There's not many people around here who have not been." He has no doubt that he is targeted because he is black. "It causes a lot of frustration. You're doing nothing and then you're stopped and searched, labelled as a criminal. That makes some people hostile towards the police. For some it gets psychological: they become more aggressive towards the police, their attitude changes, they actually become criminals because they keep getting targeted."

He says that, too often, police use the tool to intimidate. "If you are stopped and don't give your name, the intimidation will worsen, they start making threats. Sometimes the police are relaxed, other times they are aggressive. Sometimes it's just because something has happened down the road. It's quite obvious that it has nothing to do with me." The tactic, he says, is most evident with younger targets. "Between the ages of 13 and 16 they pick on you. They tend to search you less when you get older, but they definitely put pressure on younger kids."

The single most effective way to avoid being stopped, he said, is to change dress sense. "When I was younger I was wearing tracksuits, trainers, baseball cap, but I changed the way I dress and as I got older became less targeted."

not everybody's experience of London today is the same:

my London is so different from Stephen Lawrence's

For Inez Sarkodee-Adoo the case of Stephen Lawrence feels like a grim glance into the city's history

Stephen Lawrence was murdered before I was born. And yet his name was in the air when I was growing up. I can recall events in the news as the case developed and remember asking my mum what had happened. And I would overhear the conversations of relatives, provoked, perhaps, by reflections on Stephen's death, as they shared the sorts of struggles they'd experienced in a London far less tolerant than the one I've known.

Photo: Aija Lehtonen / Shutterstock.com

the London I know has never been a place where I fear for my life because of the colour of my skin

However, being too young to draw much meaning from it all, I suppose I grew up unaware of the true tragedy of Stephen's murder. Also, I felt like a stranger to the challenges faced in the London of that time, the London of 1993. In fact, the case of Stephen Lawrence feels, in many ways, like a grim glance into the history books of the city, where true hatred existed in an almost casual fashion and tensions could become inflamed in the most heinous fashion.

My worries when travelling to and from school on my own – I live in Edmonton, north London, and go to school in neighbouring Hackney – or when going out with friends have never had anything to do with possible racial attack. The London I know has never been a place where I've feared for my life because of the colour of my skin, so it's massively disconcerting to imagine a time when it seemed routine for people to feel that way. Far more prominent in my memory are the warnings of my parents to keep my mobile phone out of sight.

So, from my perspective, it's tempting to consider the days of racial hatred as a ghastly chapter of London's history. But perhaps racism has taken on more subtle forms.

So, from my perspective, it's tempting to consider the days of racial hatred as a ghastly chapter of London's history. but perhaps racism has taken on more subtle forms.

What's more, it's perhaps easier for me to take an optimistic view than it would be for my male peers. The disproportionate number of black and ethnic minority males who are stopped and searched is certainly a reality that my male friends and family members can testify to. I've heard of countless occasions when friends have felt wrongly stereotyped. They describe stop and search as an unprovoked and humiliating ritual.

Still, I'd like to think the London of today is a far less sinister place than it used to be. Instead, my experience is of an emphasised appreciation for the advantages of diverse, tolerant and cohesive communities. I have friends from a range of ethnicities, religions and backgrounds. Any differences between us don't tend to run along any of those lines. I take pride in the fact that where I live, go to school and work are not places dominated by a single group of people, but host a pretty harmonious mix.

And, in truth, as an 18-year-old living in inner-city London, I'm principally absorbed by a whole number of challenges that, on the surface at least, have little to do with race relations. Where will we find jobs? And the prospect of increased university tuition fees is not a particularly exciting one.

An ideal London, then, is a long way off. But it doesn't feel like the place it used to be – it's a place with problems, sure, but problems of a different order and I don't mind admitting to optimism about the direction in which we're heading.

The Observer, 8 January 2012
© Guardian News & Media Ltd 2012

Photo: Lewis Whyld/PA Wire/Press Association Images

Riots in England: political protest or lawless trolley-dash?

SOME ISSUES:

What do you think caused the riots?

Do you think the reasons given justify what happened?

Is there ever a good enough reason to riot?

See also:
I predict a riot
Fact File 2012, p120

Restrain, contain – and duck
Essential Articles 14, p144

www.completeissues.co.uk

In August 2011 England suddenly appeared to be a different country. People – young and old – looked on in disbelief as city after city was taken over by hordes of looters. Buildings burned, police were attacked or stood by powerless to stop the mayhem. Teenage girls told interviewers how much fun they were having as they swigged from stolen bottles of wine. People too young to work claimed to be 'getting our taxes back'. The nation watched, live, as cities fell into lawlessness.

What actually happened ?

On Thursday 4 August 2011, in Tottenham, Mark Duggan, a 29 year old black man, was shot by police officers who said they were trying to arrest him. On Saturday 6 August, his family and supporters, about 120 in all, marched to Tottenham police station to protest about the shooting. It was a peaceful protest but, later in the evening, violence broke out and by the early hours riots were spreading. By Sunday 7 August, 12 areas within London had seen rioting and by Monday 8 August the riots had spread to other cities such as Manchester, Liverpool and Birmingham as well as smaller towns. Eventually, 66 areas of England saw some rioting.

Over five days, more than 5,000 crimes were committed, including arson, criminal damage, burglary, disorder and violence against the person. The vast majority of the crimes (68%) took place in London. Hundreds of people lost homes and businesses and five people lost their lives in 254 separate incidents.

What caused the riots ....

The rioting may have been sparked by the shooting of Mark Duggan but as the events grew more remote in both geography and time there was less and less connection with that original incident. Youths speaking to reporters in Salford mentioned the shooting but had no idea of the name of the victim or the circumstances. So why did the riots spread like wildfire? After the spark, what fanned the flames?

Photo: Peter Byrne/PA Archive/Press Association Images

Over five days, more than 5,000 crimes were committed, including arson, criminal damage, burglary, disorder and violence against the person.

There was a definite sense in on-the-spot media interviews that rioters felt deprived of something they were entitled to - whether it was a job and a future or a flat screen TV. Tottenham, where the riots began, has a high level of social deprivation, poor housing, high youth unemployment and little hope to offer disaffected young people. Government cuts to youth services were frequently mentioned by people trying to explain the numbers of young people willing to join the mayhem.

Resentment against the police in particular came through in those rioters who were interviewed. They spoke of 'payback time' and 'pissing off the police'. The Citizens Inquiry into the Tottenham Riots, mentions 'toxic relations with local police' and the Riots Panel heard a great deal of resentment from young black men about 'Stop and Search'.

Government cuts to police numbers were given as one reason why the authorities were unable to contain the trouble. As the rioting broke out late on Saturday and into Sunday, there were 3,480 police officers on duty in London trying to contain events in two areas. By Sunday/Monday 12 areas were affected but only 800 more officers were on duty. The scale of events continued to overwhelm police numbers until Tuesday/Wednesday by which time 16,000 police officers (many brought in from other regions) were available.

An impression of the difficulties the police faced can be gained from the Metropolitan Police Strategic Review. Chief Inspector Ade Adelekan says: "I watched my local officers get chased down a side street by a baying mob who I believe would have done them some serious harm had they caught them...waves of bottles, petrol bombs, wheelie bins set alight and a host of street furniture were being thrown at us. These officers went on to complete, at the minimum, a fourteen hour tour of duty outside the police station. They were completely fatigued by the time I dismissed them."

The ineffective first police response meant that many joined the riots simply because they saw that they could. The sheer numbers involved meant that each person had a smaller chance of being caught. Seeing others get away with looting gave people the confidence to join in. Once a critical mass of rioters had assembled the police were unable to stop the looting and destruction. The widespread, instant, TV, radio and internet coverage also added to the momentum. Actually witnessing the mayhem, and the inability of the authorities to control it, brought more people onto the streets. Social media could also bring together loosely connected groups to a particular spot for it all to 'kick off'.

Who were the rioters?

Between thirteen and fifteen thousand people were involved in the riots. One of the most bewildering aspects for those watching was where such numbers of criminally minded people had suddenly emerged from and how they had gathered together.

If disturbances are to be avoided in the future, it is essential that people have a reason not to riot, that they are included in society and that they too have something to lose when their community is damaged.

As part of an attempt to understand and explain the events, the Riots Communities and Victims Panel was set up by the government. Its report "After the riots" was published in March 2012. It stated that those involved were not a fixed, identifiable group but could be placed into categories based on how they acted during the riots and what they wanted to get out of them.

The five broad categories of behaviour they identified were:

Organised criminals, often from outside the area.

Violent aggressors who committed the most serious crimes, such as arson and violent attacks on the police.

Late night shoppers – people who deliberately travelled to riot sites in order to loot.

Opportunists – people who were drawn into riot areas through curiosity or a sense of excitement and then became 'caught up in the moment'.

Spectators – people who came just to watch the rioting.

Of course, people moved between these categories as their circumstances and behaviour changed.

We know more about the 4,000 people who were arrested after the rioting. 9 out of 10 of these were already known to the police in some way. 90% of those arrested were male, half were aged between 18 and 24, 26% were aged between 10 and 17.

Analysis of court reports showed that, in general, the arrested people came from the most deprived areas – almost three quarters of those arrested. 42% of the young people arrested were on Free School Meals (used as a standard measure of poverty and deprivation) compared to a national average of 16%. These young people were also likely to have been frequently absent from school and had fewer qualifications than the rest of the population. They were also more likely to be unemployed.

In compiling 'After the Riots', the Panel heard from many people living in these same areas who said that not having a good education or a job was no excuse to do wrong. Of course there were people involved in the riots who were not from deprived areas - some of those arrested came from notably privileged backgrounds. Nevertheless, the figures do seem to establish a link between deprivation and rioting – further reinforced by the fact that 30 of the 66 areas that saw rioting are in the top 25% most deprived areas in England

...and what did not cause the riots?

The riots were not political – at least not in the sense of being directed against one particular party or particular law. There was, however, speculation about a climate of contempt created by the news of huge bonuses to bankers and by MPs being caught fiddling their expenses – an atmosphere which encouraged people to feel they too should grab whatever they could. In addition, some commentators thought that the vandalism which had taken place during anti-cuts and student demonstrations might have provided some inspiration.

They were not race riots - although some ethnic communities banded together to protect the areas they lived in. The attacks were on property, any property, rather than on racial groups. The ethnic background of the rioters roughly matched the area of the riot.

Above all the riots - as they continued - seemed mainly about looting. In particular they were about taking the opportunity to acquire things, especially brands, usually out of reach.

Now what?

Since August the legal system has been dealing with those caught, handing out exceptionally harsh sentences, on average at least 25% longer in prison than for the equivalent crime committed outside the riots. But that does not address the underlying problems.

Analysis shows that the 'typical' rioter was a young man with limited qualifications, from an area of significant deprivation who had already had some contact with the police. If disturbances are to be avoided in the future, it is essential that such young men feel, like the majority, that they have a reason not to riot, that they are included in society and that they too have something to lose when their community is damaged.

On his blog the comedian and actor Russell Brand reflected on his own reasons for being involved in earlier protests as a young man:

"A lack of direction, a sense that I was not invested in the dominant culture, that government existed not to look after the interests of the people it was elected to represent but the big businesses that they were in bed with."

In contrast to the rioters however, Russell Brand

Photo: David Jones/PA Archive/Press Association images

The ineffective first police response meant that many joined the riots simply because they saw that they could.

had positive support and privileges in his life:" I felt that, and I had a mum who loved me, a dad who told me that nothing was beyond my reach, an education, a grant from Essex council (to train as an actor of all things!!!) and several charities that gave me money for maintenance. I shudder to think how disenfranchised I would have felt if I had been deprived of that long list of privileges."

It was part of the remit of The Riots Communities and Victims Panel to make recommendations about what could be done. The Chair of the panel, Darra Singh, stated in his introduction.

'Time and again the same themes came up: a lack of opportunities for young people; perceptions about poor parenting and a lack of shared values; an inability to prevent re-offending; concerns about brands and materialism; and finally issues relating to confidence in policing.'

The panel made a total of 63 recommendations including:

* Government help for 500,000 'forgotten families' who need to 'turn their lives around'.

* Schools should help children to build character so that they can avoid bad choices such as becoming involved in rioting.

* Where schools fail to teach children to read and write they should pay a financial penalty, used to help the pupil 'catch up'.

* Government and local public services should fund a 'Youth Job Promise' scheme to get young people a job and so give them a stake in society.

The panel also commented both on how brands were aggressively marketed to young people and on how young offenders could be supported on their release.

Their 14 recommendations on 'police and the public' were mainly to do with the police regaining the trust and confidence of their local community. In particular they stressed: "Many communities, but particularly those in London, do not feel that 'stop and search' is conducted fairly.'"

It remains to be seen whether any of their recommendations will be followed up - and if they are, whether they will have any effect.

But we have to remember that the majority of people did not riot. People in similar areas of deprivation felt that they had enough connection with society, enough personal resources or enough hope to resist the temptation. It was inspiring to see numbers involved in the clear up and in trying to recompense those affected.

The riots shocked Britain but do not yet seem to have changed it.

Sources: After the Riots, the Final Report of the riots Communities and Victims Panel, Metropolitan Police Service Strategic Review into the Disorder of August 2011 & others

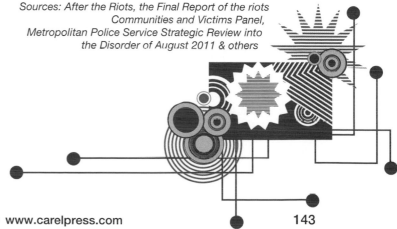

RIOTERS NEED A GOOD THERAPEUTIC TALKING TO

PAUL TAYLOR:

Were you one of the August rioters? If so, the Guardian has a few polite questions to ask you. Yes, in the absence of a public inquiry into last month's riots in London, Manchester and elsewhere, the Guardian and the London School of Economics have launched a study titled Reading The Riots. They will interview not just residents, police and judiciary, but also the rioters.

My guess is that those rioters will have few stunning insights into why they did what they did, no big ideas on how to mend Broken Britain. Many will employ dog-ate-my-homework reasoning – embarrassed and implausible justifications for crimes whose only logical explanation is their own fecklessness. Some may even trot out the oldest excuse in the book: "There's nothing to do around here. We're bored." I have been hearing such reasoning since I was a cub reporter in 1979 talking to the disgruntled residents of the long-demolished Fort Beswick – the ugliest public housing scheme ever perpetrated by Manchester's city fathers.

At first I believed the simple equation, that bored young people inevitably make mischief, ergo, giving them something to do will reduce anti social behaviour. But experience taught me two things. First, the young people who occupied the slum terraces which pre-dated Fort Beswick had even less to amuse them, yet were not so badly-behaved. Second, if you provide an adventure playground or community centre for kids who "have nothing to do round here", those same kids have a nasty habit of destroying it.

When those Guardian investigators go looking for reasons for the riots, they will have to consider the police shooting of Mark Duggan in Tottenham. But the London rioters did not lay siege to their local police station – as they did in the Moss Side riot of 1981. Instead, they battered down the doors of JJB and PC World, or "liberated" themselves a big TV from Currys. And any suggestion that the riots were a response to allegedly insensitive policing of a black community in London seems even more ludicrous when it comes to white youths in Salford battering their way into the local supermarket.

An interesting statistic this week is that, of those aged 18 and over, charged with riot offences, three quarters already had prior convictions. Stealing stuff is what they do anyway; the riots merely presented them with an unmissable opportunity to do it in like-minded company. As for the remaining one in four – those previously-upstanding citizens who helped themselves to a pair of trainers, a packet of chewing gum or a few paltry bottles of water in the melee - we can perhaps explain this as the madness of the crowd.

In a blizzard of self-fulfilling riot prophecies on Twitter, these innocents somehow signed up for the most malign flash mob ever. Since so many of the rioters were already no strangers to the law, Justice Secretary Kenneth Clarke now says that this is proof of a "broken penal system". The logical conclusion from that is that all those rioters given exemplary prison sentences will emerge not rehabilitated but even more hardened criminals.

What do we do about a "broken penal system"? There is an answer, but the hang-em, flog 'em brigade will not like it. The most compelling story of crime and punishment I have ever read was that of Mancunian Mark

They battered down the doors of JJB and PC World, or "liberated" themselves a big TV from Currys. And any suggestion that the riots were a response to allegedly insensitive policing of a black community in London seems ludicrous

Leech, editor of The Prisons Handbook, and now a leading expert on our prisons. His 1993 autobiography A Product Of The System tells how he was abused in the care system and left so angry and brutalised that he became a violent young man, an armed robber and one of the most renowned trouble-makers in the prison population. What changed Leech utterly was a spell at Grendon Underwood in Buckinghamshire, a unique therapeutic prison facility for the rehabilitation of violent recidivists, where staff and inmates were on first-name terms and group therapy was used to give prisoners an understanding of what was at the root of their offending. We have wondered whether rioters lack a moral compass, any sense of right and wrong. If true, perhaps they do not even understand the concept of punishment. The unpalatable truth may be that what those rioters need to mend their ways is not another spell in a prison which to them is merely an academy of crime, but a stretch of sympathetic, soul-searching porridge such as that Leech enjoyed.

Yes, it really may be time to hug a hoodie.

Manchester Evening News, 8 September 2011

Yes, it really may be time to hug a hoodie.

YouTube train eviction: the issue isn't black and white

The ejection of a teenager from a train by a passenger now dubbed the Big Man has split public opinion, says **Dani Garavelli**

SOME ISSUES:

Who is to blame for this situation?

Was the 'Big Man's' action right?

What were the alternatives?

Would you ever intervene in a dispute like this?

What if it was something more important?

See also:

When is it right to take the law into our own hands?
Essential Articles 13, p143

I stood up to muggers
Essential Articles 13, p146

Unacceptable activity
Fact File 2011, p132

www.completeissues.co.uk

IT WAS a scene commuters across the country are familiar with. A teenager hurls abuse at a conductor after being challenged over his ticket, while other passengers shift uneasily in their seats.

On the 9.33pm train from Edinburgh to Perth last Friday, however, not everyone was prepared to wait passively for the authorities to sort the problem out. As 19-year-old student Sam Main engaged in a stand-off and the train sat idle at Linlithgow station, finance manager Alan Pollock decided it was time for action.

Unimpressed by the conductor's attempts to resolve the situation, the 35-year-old stepped in to eject the apparent ticket evader from the carriage, before physically manoeuvring him on to the platform. The student struggled, trying to get back on board, but was eventually bundled off.

Job done, Pollock was greeted with a round of applause from other travellers as the train started moving again.

And that – doubtless – would have been that if IT teacher Ian Helms hadn't filmed the whole incident on his mobile phone.

After it was uploaded on to YouTube, the footage went viral – by this weekend it had racked up two million views. Soon, Pollock had taken on cult status. Now known universally as "the Big Man" – a name that takes its inspiration not only from his girth, but from a Chewin' the Fat sketch in which a tough male Glaswegian sorts out everyone's problems by violent means – he has split public opinion down the middle. Some hail him as the kind of have-a-go-hero Scotland needs. Others see him as a bully whose reaction was disproportionate to the circumstances.

"Given that I commute quite a lot and am often confronted by people behaving in ways that are quite unpleasant to other people, and that most people look at their newspapers and very rarely do they remonstrate with the people concerned, I think what he did was entirely understandable," says sociologist Professor Frank Furedi. Not everyone agreed, especially when more details about the incident emerged.

Many commentators on both sides of the fence predicted that Pollock, however well-intentioned, would soon find himself at the centre of a police inquiry, with Main being seen as "the victim". And so it came to pass. Soon Main – a student from Heriot-Watt University – was being interviewed on TV, sporting a nasty cut to his head and insisting he had indeed bought a ticket. Revealing he had made a complaint against Pollock, he said his injuries had been sustained when he was physically thrown on to the platform.

Asked why he had attempted to reboard the train after his first ejection, he said he was a diabetic and his bag containing insulin was still on board. "This man should be charged and have his day in court," Main's father Lenny said. "He had no right to do what he did."

The incident – which was on one level quite quotidian – has captured the public imagination. Talked about on virtually every chat show, it was the burning issue of the week because it touched on some of the most contentious social and legal issues of our time. The two and a half minutes of footage highlights once again the problem of youth behaviour; the dilemma over whether or not to intervene in the face of such disorder; and the difficulty of striking a balance between taking a stand against antisocial behaviour and committing a crime.

It also raises challenging questions about the filming and subsequent publicising of such incidents; like two other recent outbursts involving passengers spewing racist abuse at fellow travellers on public transport, the event has taken on an added significance as a result of being widely viewed. But does the trend for putting such footage on YouTube provide a valuable insight into human behaviour, or merely allow minor skirmishes to be blown out of all proportion?

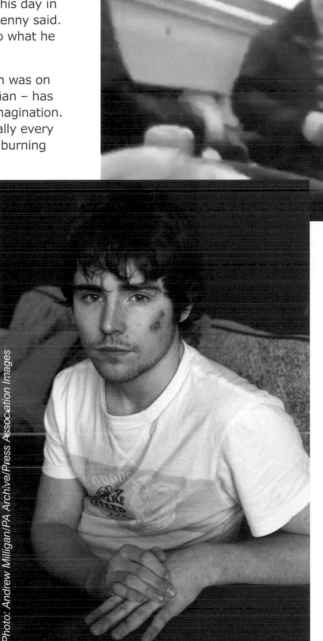

Photo: YouTube

Photo: Andrew Milligan/PA Archive/Press Association Images

Now the Crown Office finds itself between a rock and a hard place: it has to take a decision on whether or not to pursue Pollock, aware the whole country is watching and that, whichever decision it makes, there will be those who vehemently disagree.

If it decides to take no action against "the Big Man" it might be seen to be condoning acts of vigilantism, but if Pollock goes to court (particularly if Main does not) then the message clearly is: "Don't get involved." At a time when the UK government is talking up the benefits of a "Big Society", it seems, the fracas on the train goes to the heart of what it means to be a good citizen.

Although have-a-go-heroes hit the headlines from time to time, the reluctance of most passers-by to get involved in incidents they witness has been established since the Sixties when psychologists coined the term the "bystander effect". This term refers to the tendency of those who see an emergency situation to walk on by because they convince themselves help is not needed or believe that others, who are better qualified, will take the responsibility for providing it. The more people

The more people who witness such an event, the less likelihood there is of anyone intervening

who witness such an event, the less likelihood there is of anyone intervening.

This was thrown into sharp relief during the riots in English cities during the summer, where even the police stood back and allowed young people to throw rocks and loot shops unchallenged.

Recent incidents in which those who have intervened have lost their lives may also discourage people from taking action. In 2005, Richard Whelan was fatally stabbed on the top deck of a London bus after asking a stranger to stop throwing chips at his girlfriend. Just last month, 76-year-old James Simpson was killed as he tried to stop thieves stealing his Land Rover Discovery from outside his Larkhall home. And there has been a spate of cases in which those who have intervened have found themselves in trouble. In 2008, retired police inspector Paul Lawson was arrested after he remonstrated with youths who threatened to kill him and smash up his car. He was released on bail and had to wait several weeks before being told no action as being taken against him.

The following year, businessman Munir Hussain was sentenced to 30 months in prison after attacking a burglar who had raided his home, before the Court of Appeal reduced it to a one-year suspended sentence. In the wake of the Hussain case, David Cameron said he wanted to strengthen the law to allow householders to protect their properties. While at present they are allowed only to use "reasonable force", he said that in future they would only face prosecution for using "grossly disproportionate" force.

According to legal experts, however, the situation on the 9.33pm train, was more complicated than a house burglary or a street mugging, because – although many may sympathise with the passengers' frustration at the delay – it is difficult to see what physical threat was posed by the ticket evader and because, it seems, the authorities had already been alerted.

"The general principle is that criminal behaviour is a matter for the authorities such as the police or the British Transport Police," says solicitor-advocate Gerry Brown, of Livingstone Brown. "Where a civilian does interfere, there has to be moral certainty – in other words, he has to be absolutely certain a crime is being committed and he has to intervene in a proportionate way, taking into account the scale of the crime being committed."

Main, from Falkirk, claims he had bought a ticket (and been given the wrong one) so no ticket evasion took place, but he is clearly heard swearing at the conductor which could potentially constitute a breach of the peace. However, on the footage that appeared on YouTube, he makes no threats of physical violence to the conductors or other passengers.

The majority of people who have viewed the clip appear to believe that – in an ideal world – the conductor would have dealt more effectively with the situation himself.

Recent incidents in which those who have intervened have lost their lives also discourage people from taking action

Last week, the British Transport Police said: "While we welcome the public's support of our zero-tolerance stance on antisocial behaviour, our staff are trained in conflict management and we do not expect members of the public to take matters into their own hands."

It is understood the conductor had a range of options available to him, including asking Main to provide means of ID and, then issuing a ticket irregularity – a ticket form which would have allowed him to be billed later, or requesting assistance from British Transport Police.

However, the footage shows the inspector, who is said to be co-operating with inquiries, repeating: "I'll sit here all night, pal. I'm being paid for this, but they [the passengers] will start moaning." This, for some, seems to sum up society's impotence.

"It's particularly sad the conductor was relatively ineffectual in sorting it out, which you would hope was the conductor's job," says Furedi. "I've seen conductors on trains and they can be very intimidated and not really secure and don't feel they have the authority. They aren't sure if the rest of the train will back them up."

In the footage, it is clear Pollock only intervenes when it becomes obvious Main won't move and, even then, he is heard asking the conductor if he wants help before he acts.

But some have argued that the physical force he uses to man-handle the teenager off the train is excessive. Indeed, one woman on the train expresses concern. "There's no need for that," she says.

"The ticket conductor was being an arse, the teenager was being an arse, but being a cheeky sod doesn't justify violence," says on online commentator.

"You have to ask yourself if he would have been so proactive if the alleged ticket evader had been as big or bigger than him," adds another, drawing attention to the fact that the student was much shorter and more slight in build.

Even the crime-busting group The Guardian Angels, while commending Pollock's public-spiritedness, believes he might be in need of some training when it comes to conflict resolution.

Pollock, a father-of-three, who works in Edinburgh for the blue chip investment management company BlackRock, has refused to talk about his moment of bravado, but his father Jim, a retired accountant, has backed his action, saying: "He's not impulsive, but the situation was getting out of hand."

And Furedi agrees: "If I was him I would organise a support campaign – it's important that when people don't get charged for real crimes and courts tend to ignore real instances of anti-social behaviour, the idea that you would take someone like him to court seems utterly silly."

While the British Transport Police continue their inquiries, both families seem to be marshalling support for their cause. Sam Main's Facebook page is full of supportive comments such as "we are all in your corner, Sam", while the phrase "Team Sam" has appeared on his father Lenny's.

Main's case is that he was advised it would be cheaper to buy two singles for his journey, but he was given two from Polmont to Edinburgh Park as opposed to one going in either direction. He also maintains that – though he had been celebrating with a few drinks after his exams – his diabetes may have affected the way he reacted to the conductor.

Pollock is keeping a low profile, but his father portrays him as a mild-mannered man pushed to the limit. In the end, the Crown Office will

> **Some have argued that the physical force he uses to man-handle the teenager off the train is excessive**

have to decide not only if an offence has been committed by Pollock, but whether, given the circumstances, it would be in the public interest to prosecute.

Unedifying though this has been, some believe it may serve a positive social purpose. "If it is in both the interests of justice and the public interest, the Crown Office might take the view that this is a good case to put before the courts and see if they can get an opinion as to the extent of public involvement in misbehaviour," says Brown.

Others hope it will act as some kind of catalyst, persuading people to take a greater stand against low-level public disorder. "I know a lot of people when they see children misbehaving are scared to intervene [in case they get into trouble] – that's how far things have gone," says Furedi.

"We don't value and affirm people's right to contain the behaviour of youths who are out of control or whose behaviour is potentially harmful to others. I think that if society was more rigorous in relation to this a lot of young kids would behave far better and you wouldn't get all this behaviour on trains and everywhere else."

The Scotsman, 18 December 2011

STOP PRESS:
Following investigation Mr Pollock was charged with assault, but the Procurator Fiscal said it was not in the public interest to prosecute Mr Pollock.

How my rapist walked free

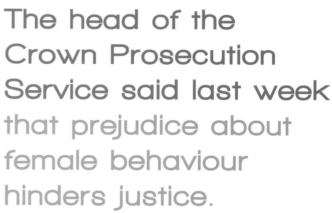

The head of the Crown Prosecution Service said last week that prejudice about female behaviour hinders justice.

Here, a rape victim agrees

The day I met my rapist, a regular in the bar I worked in, I was told he was "a bit sleazy, but harmless". He raped me on a Saturday morning in September. It did not immediately hit me that I'd been raped. I wasn't dragged off the street. It wasn't violent. A group of us went to my flat after a party and the last thing I remember was sitting in my living room with other people. Then I woke up on my bed – with him on top of me.

This is not an account of how I was raped. This is an account of trying to prosecute a rapist. My actions after the event matter because they were examined in excruciating detail by the police and Crown Prosecution Service (CPS) and they are the reason that my rapist is free today.

I did what I now know to be pretty exceptional – I didn't hesitate to call the police. But as I waited for them I started to doubt myself. I had been drunk, I had taken drugs, I have a history of sexual promiscuity and mental illness and my memory was very patchy – a conviction seemed impossible. However, when they arrived the police tried to convince me it could happen.

They took a mouth swab and a urine sample and the next day – after a long significant shower – I went for a full examination, made bearable only by the amazing staff at St Mary's Sexual Assault Referral Centre. There were immediate decisions to make – notably whether to take anti-HIV medication, which has awful side effects. We had to dissect the likelihood of my attacker being HIV-positive. I took the medication and vomited daily for a month, most days violently and repeatedly. After vomiting there is no respite: you have to retake the pills until you can hold them down.

SOME ISSUES:

Do you think the law is failing women who are raped?

How does society's attitudes towards women affect this issue?

What do you think this person should have done?

Can you understand her actions?

See also:
Why I forgave the man who raped me
Essential Articles 14, p136

Insult after injury
Essential articles 12, p149

www.completeissues.co.uk

I quit my job the day after the assault, disgusted and terrified at the idea of seeing him, but talked to a colleague who was with me that night. Realising that I was unconscious, she had cleared all the people out my flat. He must have hidden and returned. I realised these were the actions of a predatory rapist and I felt I had no choice but to try to protect others from him. It was then I decided to prosecute.

At this point the police made one of several inconceivable mistakes. They had said that the swabs and bed sheets would be kept for several years. However, it transpired they had already destroyed all the forensic evidence – and blamed my initial hesitation.

It is easy to vilify the police. Please don't. They made mistakes, but they always treated me with as much respect as possible within the confines of their instructions – for me the villains of the story are the CPS.

The first interview was gruelling and intrusive; however it paled in comparison to the second, some months later. I was grilled like a suspect. I was disillusioned with the process and scared something I said would stop me getting my chance to look him, and a jury, in the eye and say: "This is what this man did. Do not let him do it again." Terrified, I edited my answers – and as a result I never got that chance.

They kept asking me if I had had sexual relations with anyone else there. Over the eight-month period and innumerable questions, I withheld one fragment of information from the police. A piece of information that had no bearing on the rape, or my rapist. I had been told I had gone into my bedroom earlier that evening with a different man, whom I had been kissing. I was so scared I would be judged because of this as promiscuous and unreliable. Of course, in this day and age promiscuity should have absolutely no impact on the perception of rape, but we all know it does. I didn't remember

This is not an account of how I was raped. This is an account of trying to prosecute a rapist. My actions after the event matter because they were examined in excruciating detail by the police and Crown Prosecution Service (CPS) and they are the reason that my rapist is free today.

the incident, it wasn't my testimony, so I convinced myself I didn't need to tell them. Why should it matter? How was something I had done of my own volition relevant to my being raped? But the stifling level of scrutiny I was under made me feel sure it would matter, so I said nothing.

A month later, I got the call. They knew I had lied, which made me an "unreliable witness". The CPS had decided not to prosecute. They said "there was not a realistic prospect of conviction" as the jury wouldn't believe me. Why wasn't I given the opportunity to explain my actions, and convince them that I was raped?

Eight months of hell led to that phone call. I made a rash decision under pressure because of the stereotypes forced upon women ingrained in our legal system. A decision framed from a society obsessed with blaming women for making themselves "vulnerable" to rape, rather than targeting the rapists. One wrong decision led to a rapist walking free. I cannot forgive the CPS for this. I cannot forgive them for putting me in a position where I can't forgive myself. He doesn't even have to stand in a dock and – according to the police and the CPS – that's my fault.

With hindsight, would I encourage another rape victim to go to the police, to face months of interviews, examinations and implicit accusations – not from a jury but from the police and the omnipotent Crown Prosecution Service? I don't know that I could.

The Guardian, 7 February 2012
© *Guardian News & Media Ltd 2012*

THE CHILD SEX ABUSE 'BUSINESS': HOW ONE CHARITY PICKS UP THE PIECES

Barnardo's outreach workers on the systematic exploitation of young people, and why abusers need to be targeted proactively

Alexandra Topping

SOME ISSUES:

How can people avoid being 'groomed' and abused?

Is there more that charities like Barnardo's can do to help?

How can we stop this happening?

Who is to blame?

See also:
Could you tell
Fact File 2012, p58

Fear of racism should no longer be the veil covering up hard truths
Essential Articles 14, p110

Too many of us treat young white women as trash
Essential Articles 14, p112

www.completeissues.co.uk

Sarah is 18 but looks much younger. Her tiny frame is engulfed by a tracksuit top, her hair scraped back, her huge eyes clear of makeup. In the private room of a Barnardo's project, she nervously plays with a heart-shaped cushion.

She was 15, she explains, when she and her 14-year-old cousin met a group of men in a takeaway in a run-down area of their home town. Over a few weeks, the men – who said they were 18 but were in fact in their late 20s – showered them with gifts and attention. Before long – often with their 11-year-old cousin in tow – the girls were going to "parties" around the north of England and further afield where much older men would be waiting.

"They were nice at first," said Sarah, not making eye contact. "Then they got nasty. They started touching me. My cousin went along with it; they said it was a bit of fun. But I don't like people touching me."

Sarah knew what they wanted, but she refused and was punched as a result. "I punched them back," she says. "I'm only little, but I'm tough." Her cousin reacted differently; before long she was having sex with a much older "boyfriend", until one night she was raped by one of his friends.

According to Barnardo's, Sarah's experience is disturbingly common. Tuesday's announcement from the government comes after months of warnings from Barnardo's that grooming and trafficking of children is on the rise and happening in every UK town. The charity said earlier this year that it had dealt with 1,098 children who had been groomed for sex in 2010, a 4% increase on 2009, and they fear it may be the tip of the iceberg.

The Barnardo's centre in the north-east, where the Guardian was recently granted rare access, last year helped 48 sexually exploited children and identified 50 more at risk, as well as running a missing from home service to keep runaways safe. One of 22 Barnardo's centres in the UK, it is homely, with brightly patterned sofas and walls covered in colourful handmade posters. "The Rules", declares one. "Don't meet any-1 on ur own. Be careful who you send pics 2. Never flash your bits on a webcam." The last rule gives an indication of the problems dealt with here: "Trust no-1", it reads.

Holly, 15, who was referred to the centre after running away from home and staying out all night, says she has changed her telephone number since coming here. "I was always getting texts saying we should meet up and stuff. Some of them want photos, some ask for naked photos," she says.

Horrific tales of abuse are commonplace. Recently the centre helped a girl who by the age of 14 had had sex with more than 40 men. Abused by her father, Lucy was targeted by a gang of Kurdish men while living in care. It was only after they had her complete trust that the sexual abuse started. The girl described lying in wait in a room - when she heard them call a certain Kurdish word as they walked up the stairs, she knew to prepare herself for sex. Asked why she kept returning, she said it was clean, they fed her after school and had given her a pink hairdryer. "These men see a vulnerability, a need for affection and they meet it," said centre manager Wendy. "They pretend they care in order to control and abuse."

The centre is dealing with nine cases of suspected trafficking of children, and the suspicion is that around a dozen men are regularly targeting children in this town. "There is a whole business involved. We hear the same names cropping up, but there just isn't enough cross-county work – perpetrators fall through the gaps," said Wendy.

The majority of suspected abusers that the centre encounters are non-UK nationals, including Sri Lankans, Kurds and Afghans, Wendy said. "I'm

IT WAS ONLY AFTER THEY HAD HER COMPLETE TRUST THAT THE SEXUAL ABUSE STARTED

"THESE MEN SEE A VULNERABILITY, A NEED FOR AFFECTION AND THEY MEET IT. THEY PRETEND THEY CARE IN ORDER TO CONTROL AND ABUSE."

not saying it is not different elsewhere, but here one of the models of abuser we see are people with different cultural beliefs that are sometimes not conducive to child safety.

"British-born girls are seen as more liberal, and then [the abusers] see that they can make some money by sharing her with their friends. If there is a cultural thing to discuss then we have to look at that more closely in order to properly protect the child."

The ethnicity of abusers came under the spotlight this year after the ringleaders of a gang of Asian men in Derby were jailed for grooming girls as young as 12 for sex, and a group of nine mainly Asian men were arrested in Rochdale on suspicion of grooming a group of white teenage girls. The former home secretary Jack Straw said there was a "specific problem" in the Pakistani community, and vulnerable white girls were seen as "easy meat" by some Pakistani men.

He was criticised by charities, police and Muslim groups, who said he was wrong to highlight one community, pointing out that the vast majority of convicted sex offenders were white males. The prime minister, David Cameron, has said "cultural sensitivities" should not hinder police action..

Barnardo's have identified different patterns of exploitation: the "inappropriate relationship" with an older men who controls and abuses; the "boyfriend model" where the child is groomed by one man before being passed around his friends; and the most serious and organised sexual exploitation where children are passed through networks, often across the country.

So why isn't more done to tackle suspected groomers? Police work closely with the charity, said Wendy, but with children often unwilling to admit they are in an abusive situation, or give evidence against their abuser, there is little they can do. Perpetrators also cover their tracks, using aliases and moving towns.

"There are people who have been exploiting for years, really dangerous men who think they are untouchable because there have never been any consequences for them," she says. "We need to try a different tactic. We need more surveillance of houses, we need more disruption." But this takes money, and with police making big cuts, extra funding to target groomers seems unlikely.

Which is why Barnardo's workers take to the streets as evening falls, as one puts it: "Children do not get abused between nine and five". They go to areas targeted by abusers and talk to children they believe are at risk of exploitation. Recently they alerted the police to two brothers, aged nine and 10, who were wandering the streets late at night. Later the police said the boys were found living with their mother, who had learning difficulties, and their convicted paedophile father who was supposed to have no contact. The boys had been asking friends if they wanted to come back to their house.

They visit a Barnardo's safe house, before calling in at the local bus station, where they check the men's toilets for phone numbers offering money to boys in return for sex and chat to the security guards to see if they have seen anything suspicious.

At around 10 o'clock, Wendy gets in her own car for a last patrol. She drives past rows of boarded-up houses, pointing out brothels along the way, and pulls up outside a flat above a hairdressers, where girls she has helped have told her they have been sexually abused. Asked how, when faced with their stories, she manages to carry on, she shrugs. "You just do, don't you," she says. "Who else is going to do it if we don't?

"And you see kids come out of it. They grow up, become mothers, have lives – and when you see that, you know you've helped them to get there."

• *Names in this article have been changed for safety reasons*

The Guardian, 17 May 2011
© Guardian News & Media Ltd 2011

Dear victim... it's all your fault

Dear Victim

I dont no Why Iam Writing a letter to you! I have been forced to Write this letter by ISSp. To be honest I'm not bothered or Sorry about the fact that I burgled your house. Basicly it Was your fault anyways. I'm going to run you through the dumb mistakes you made. firstly you didnt drow your curtains Which most people now to do before they go to sleep. Secondly your dumb you live in Stainburns a high risk burglary area and your thick enough to leave your downstairs kitchen Window open. I Wouldnt do that in a million years. But anyways I dont feel Sorry for you and Im not going to Show any Sympath or remorse remories.

yours Sincerly

from

SOME ISSUES:

Would making offenders write to their victims help them reform?

What do you think should happen to this offender?

Was it a good idea for the police to release this letter?

See also:
www.completeissues.co.uk

The Intensive Supervision and Surveillance (ISS) Programme is an alternative to custody for serious or persistent offenders. As part of this scheme a 16-year-old boy had to write a letter to the person whose house he burgled in Leeds.

Putting offenders in contact with their victims in this way is intended to make them understand the effects of their crimes. The letter was released by West Yorkshire police as a warning to people to keep their houses secure.

Source: Various

Religion

Your rules 'end at temple door', says equalities chief

Trevor Phillips, chairman of the Equality and Human Rights Commission, has warned religious groups that they should not expect to be treated differently under the law because of their views

He was speaking as part of a debate organised as part of a research programme into religion and society and seemed to be aiming his remarks at those who had fought legal battles against equal treatment for gay and straight people in the name of their religion.

In the recent past, for example, Catholic adoption agencies wanted to discriminate between gay and straight couples when considering applications. There have also been disputes where Christian bed and breakfast owners have turned away gay couples.

When law and religion conflict, Mr Phillips said, "The law stops at the door of the temple as far as I'm concerned. "Once you start to provide public services that have to be run under public rules, for example child protection, then you have to go with public law... Institutions have to make a decision whether they want to do that or they don't want to do that, but you can't say 'because we decide we're different then we need a different set of laws'."

It was his next example, however, that caused the sharpest reaction: "There's nothing different in principle with a Catholic adoption agency, or indeed Methodist adoption agency, saying the rules in their community are different and therefore the law shouldn't apply to them." He followed this with "Why not then say sharia can apply to different parts of the country? It doesn't work."

You can't say 'because we decide we're different then we need a different set of laws'.

Although sharia courts are used in some parts of the UK Muslim community, they have no legal powers under UK law.

Former bishops called this comparison 'ridiculous' and suggested that he was arguing for a 'totalitarian' view, which did not respect a believer's conscience. Politicians suggested that he was ignoring the fact that the laws of the UK were founded on a Christian culture and suggested that religious belief was being threatened.

However the National Secular Society spokesman, Keith Porteous, defended Mr Phillips' position: "There is no such thing as partial equality and every time an exemption is made, someone else's rights are compromised."

Sources: Various

Strong religious belief is no excuse for intimidation

Joan Smith:

It's been a dreadful week for free speech. A meeting at a prestigious London college had to be abandoned on Monday evening when members of the audience were filmed and threatened by an Islamic extremist. Then the president of a student society at another London college was forced to resign after a Muslim organisation called for a ban on a joky image of the Prophet Mohammed. Finally, on Friday, the author Sir Salman Rushdie cancelled an appearance at India's largest literary festival, saying he feared an assassination attempt after protests by Muslim clerics.

Almost as sinister as this series of events has been the reaction to them. The first has received very little public attention, despite the fact that students who belong to the college's Atheism, Secularism and Humanism Society were unable to go ahead with a perfectly legal discussion of sharia law. They'd come to Queen Mary, University of London to hear Anne Marie Waters speak on behalf of the One Law For All campaign, when an angry young man entered the lecture theatre. He stood at the front and used his mobile phone to film the audience, claiming he knew where they lived and would track them down if a single negative word was said about the Prophet. The organisers informed the police and the meeting cancelled.

The fact that in a democratic country a religious extremist is able to frighten anyone into calling off a meeting is shocking – and so is the lack of a public outcry about this egregious example of intimidation and censorship. Tellingly, what

SOME ISSUES:

What do you think free speech is?

Why is free speech important?

When should our free speech be restricted?

Do you think that religion has the right to restrict on free speech?

See also:
When women and girls are the enemy, p190

Religious beliefs can be tolerated at best
Essential Articles 12, p166

www.completeissues.co.uk

The fact that in a democratic country a religious extremist is able to frighten anyone into calling off a meeting is shocking...

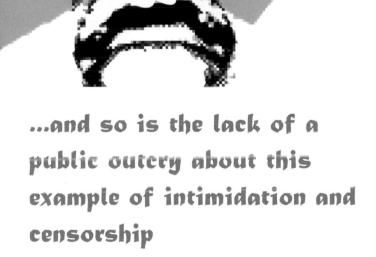

has grabbed media attention is the second incident, when a secularist organisation at University College, London came under attack for publishing an image on its Facebook page of "Jesus and Mo" having a drink together. The Muslim group that wants to ban the image got a sympathetic hearing in the media, despite arguing openly for censorship. Extremist websites, meanwhile, reacted with the fanatical language that so often appears on such sites: "May Allah destroy these creatures worse than dogs," wrote one blogger.

No doubt that kind of inflammatory sentiment was in Rushdie's mind when he decided not to appear at the Jaipur Literary Festival. In a statement read out there, the author of The Satanic Verses said he'd been warned that paid assassins from the Mumbai underworld might be on their way to the event in order to "eliminate" him. While he expressed doubts about the accuracy of the warnings, Rushdie said it would be irresponsible of him to appear in such circumstances.

Why hasn't there been a furore about all these incidents? Why aren't MPs and ministers insisting on the vital role of free speech? None of the people involved was threatening anybody, unlike the three Muslim extremists convicted two days ago of inciting hatred against homosexuals. It's been left to organisations such as the National Secular Society – I'm an honorary associate – to say that a fundamental human right is being eroded in the name of avoiding "offence".

...and so is the lack of a public outcry about this example of intimidation and censorship

Most people in the UK don't condone violence, but a worrying number think we should be careful around individuals with strong religious beliefs. This argument is mistaken, because it suggests that believers aren't as capable of exercising, or under the same obligation to exercise, judgement and restraint as the rest of us.

It's also based on fear, tacitly acknowledging a link between demands for censorship and threats of violence. One often leads to the other, and it isn't just atheists and secularists who should be very worried indeed about that.

The Independent, 22 January 2012

No Heaven?

Why Stephen Hawking's Comment Doesn't Matter

Stephanie Pappas, LiveScience Senior Writer

SOME ISSUES:

Do you believe in life after death?

Why?

What do you think about what Stephen Hawking said?

Could our belief in life after death be a coping strategy?

See also:
www.completeissues.co.uk

Even though famed physicist Stephen Hawking announced he doesn't believe in an afterlife and that heaven is a "fairy story for people afraid of the dark," that doesn't mean we'll stop believing, psychologists say.

The statement by Hawking to the Guardian newspaper reflects the beliefs of plenty of nonreligious people, but will likely get more attention, coming as it does from Hawking, who is famous for his work in theoretical physics. Hawking has already drawn fire from some religious leaders with his assertion in his book "The Grand Design" (Bantam 2010) that the universe did not need God to get started.

"I regard the brain as a computer which will stop working when its components fail," Hawking said in The Guardian. "There is no heaven or afterlife for broken down computers; that is a fairy story for people afraid of the dark."

Fairy story or not, a belief in heaven does seem to come with some benefits. Humans didn't evolve in an environment where an understanding of black holes or the origin of the universe would be helpful, said Daniel Kruger, an evolutionary psychologist at the University of Michigan.

"We're not designed at the level of theoretical physics," Kruger told LiveScience. "What really matters to us is what happens at the human scale, relationships to other people, things we experience in a lifetime."

Rewards and reminders

For that reason, the idea of heaven has a stronger mystique than that of the seven imperceptible dimensions of string theory. On a personal level, Kruger said, the idea of an afterlife offers some hope in a world where, historically, "life has been pretty harsh." Thoughts of heaven may also stave off fears of death, he said.

Studies have shown that a belief in life after death seems to

"The more people believe, the less death anxiety they tend to have,"

play that handholding role, said Nathan Heflick, a doctoral student in psychology at the University of South Florida who has studied belief in the afterlife.

"The more people believe, the less death anxiety they tend to have," Heflick told LiveScience.

Reminding people of death also prompts them to want to believe in the afterlife more, Heflick said, even if they remain sceptical.

Societal glue

On a societal level, religious belief in the afterlife can be a powerful motivator to follow the rules, Kruger said.

"When you have an afterlife that is influenced by the actions that you take now, you basically see a system of rewards and punishments," he said. Those rewards and punishments can keep people in line, or, more charitably, provide a way for humans to codify and pass along moral laws.

A belief in the afterlife may also arise from the perception that we are more than our bodies. In a series of experiments, Heflick and his colleagues subtly reminded people of their bodies — by providing foot massages, for example — while asking them about their thoughts on the afterlife. People undergoing a physical experience reminding them of their bodies were less likely to say they believed in life after death, while those distanced from their bodies showed a slight uptick in belief.

People's perceptions of themselves, then, may influence their belief in what happens after death.

"If you think of your body as a machine, it's kind of hard to believe in life after death," Heflick said. "You're not going to be able to think of yourself as a spirit."

Livescience.com, 16 May 2011

Is there a religion for atheists?

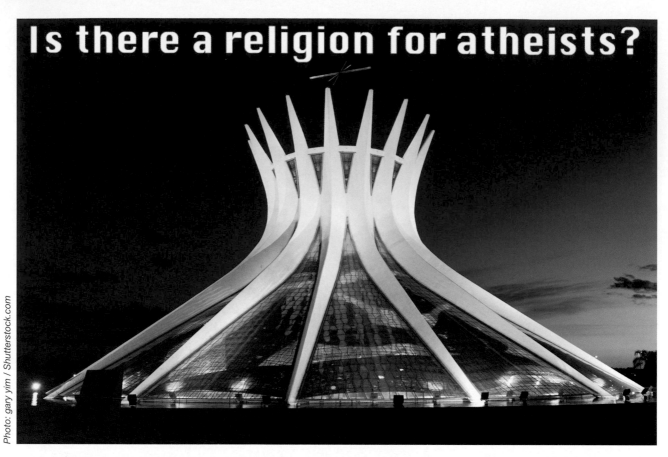

Photo: gary yim / Shutterstock.com

Modern secular culture has no authority with the political or moral clout to impose a single vision.

NELSON JONES

SOME ISSUES:

What do you think about atheism?

Does an atheist temple seems like a good idea?

Why?

What are the benefits of religion?

Can these benefit people who do not believe in any religion?

See also:
www.completeissues.co.uk

Alain de Botton, probably the closest thing Britain has to a celebrity philosopher, has a Big Idea. Religion, he asserts, isn't "true", but its lack of truth is the least interesting thing about it. Instead of indulging in the dogmatic anti-theism associated with the likes of Richard Dawkins or the late Christopher Hitchens, why shouldn't atheists just "enjoy the best bits", as the publicity for his new book Religion For Atheists has it?

Religious celebration

Many of us love Christmas carols, after all. Bach's cantatas are more profound and moving than anything written in the cause of atheism. Think of all those wonderful cathedrals, mosques and temples. Religion's power to transport the human spirit, to offer consolation and hope, to create a sense of belonging and inspire ethical conduct is undeniable even if you don't subscribe to the doctrines of a particular belief system. So let's work out precisely what gives religions their strength, "steal" it, bottle it and create a kind of transcendent secular humanism that will speak to people as deeply as religion does.

Only without all that embarrassing dogma, not to mention the baggage of misogyny, homophobia, parochialism and intolerance with which most bona fide

Religions, like placebos, only work if you believe in them

religions tend to come lumbered.

That seems to be de Botton's message, at any rate. He is struck by the hollowness of much modern culture, the unwillingness of today's education system, for example, to impart wisdom along with information. Secularism, he has said, "is full of holes. We have secularised badly." Among his projects is a "Temple of Perspective", a hollow a 46-metre high monolith in which pious non-believers will be able to contemplate the universe and the insignificant place they occupy within it. He wants to build it in the City of London, which to be fair probably could do with acquiring a sense of perspective.

Religious culture

That religions have been stunningly successful vehicles of human culture is not in doubt, and de Botton offers some genuinely illuminating insights as to why. He notes that religious rituals are powerful because they involve the body as well as the mind, for example, and that religions are "cultures of repetition" grounded in calendars and relatively limited canons of scripture. They are, in a sense, finite universes: finite, because they concentrate on a small number of core teachings which may be elaborated but can never be wholly transcended, but universes because they are self-sustaining logical structures, perfectly adapted for maintaining themselves and neutralising awkward questions.

Secular culture

Modern secular culture is neither finite nor a universe. It is more comprehensive than any religion, but at the same time less complete, because it doesn't even pretend to have all the answers. Which is, of course, why Alain de Botton's idea could never work. We inhabit a culture that has become simply too big, too diverse, too self-

critical. There is too much of it, and it is embraces too many contradictions. There's no single authority with either the political or moral clout to impose a single vision. It would also be necessary somehow to overcome the sceptical distance, the sense of irony, that characterises the secular viewpoint. Put simply, it's hard to imagine anyone, even Alain de Botton, taking the whole thing seriously enough.

Belief

Religions, like placebos, only work if you believe in them. From a sociological perspective, it's true, the inner content of the belief system doesn't seem

to matter. Whatever their theology, the various world religions offer a broadly similar package of rituals, community cohesiveness, moral and ethical teaching, identity and spiritual sustenance. So it might seem that it might be possible to throw out the baby while keeping the bathwater (which, if your interest is in keeping clean rather than looking after a squalling and unpredictable infant, might seem like a good idea).

But from an insider's perspective, the beliefs really are central; the good things that de Botton admires are there to prop up the core beliefs. Even if you regard the doctrines of a particular religion as myths and metaphors that express profound truths of

The good things that de Botton admires are there to prop up the core beliefs

human experience, most of that religion's followers will actually believe them. This is a point too often missed by sympathetic analysts of religion, but which the "dogmatic atheists" ruthlessly (but accurately) home in on. Religions are particular and specific responses to general problems. Without that specificity they would be less dangerous, much less prone to dogmatism, prejudice and group-mindedness. But they would also lose many of those qualities that de Botton recognises and celebrates. People would stop believing in them.

New Statesman, 26 January 2012

Modern secular culture does not even pretend to have the answers

IGNORED AND UNPAID: OUR (FEMALE) SPORTING HEROES

We are world champions in netball but you wouldn't know it

Zoe Williams

A young female rower told me two years ago that the big scandal of the way women were treated in UK sport was best illustrated by netball: it was never covered by the media, even though we were among the best in the world.

As host nation of the Olympics, we could have nominated it as one of our four new events. Instead, we chose women's boxing: no spectator base, no foothold in schools, no realistic chance of it catching on, but you wanted equality, ladies? Here, take a punch in the face.

Two years later, the England women's team has just won the World Netball Series, beating Australia and New Zealand, despite the fact that Australasian leagues are mainly professional, whereas our players have to rule the world while holding down full-time jobs.

Karen Atkinson, captain of the England squad from 2008 to 2011, has won 122 caps. Is she on the shortlist for BBC Sports Personality of the Year (SPOTY)? Do you even know what she looks like? Of course not. All it takes for the patriarchy to triumph is for feminists to not moan loudly enough.

Atkinson, 33, has now retired and coaches the Hertfordshire Mavericks, who are top of the Superleague. I saw them all doing fitness tests in Bisham Abbey on Thursday night.

She said: "Probably the only sport that we're comparably good at is women's rugby, and nobody knows about that either. It's systemic, it's not a surprise.

"The people who are the judges for SPOTY nominations are reporters and they nominate from the sports they cover. If they won't cover female sports, how are they supposed to know about them?"

Many people don't realise that netball is such an exciting sport for spectators, much faster than basketball and with less stopping and starting. You say the word "netball" and everybody gets an image of a load of 10-year-olds, outdoors in the winter, with bright blue legs.

But this isn't the only women's sport that is overlooked by the BBC's list, and by the media generally.

SOME ISSUES:

Why do you think there is not as much TV coverage of women's league games?

Is this sexist?

If we have so many excellent female athletes, then are we missing out by not making more of their achievements?

Shouldn't there be more coverage of such positive role-models?

See also:
Running out of time
Fact File 2012, p144

www.completeissues.co.uk

Chrissie Wellington, four times world champion, has never lost an ironman triathlon, which consists of a 2.4-mile swim, a 112-mile bike ride and a marathon run (raced in that order and without a break); Sarah Stevenson became taekwondo world champion in South Korea this year; we have swimmers and cyclists; we have the best women's cricket team in the world.

Netballer Lindsay Keable, 23, said: "I think it's actually a bit harder when you're in a sport that has a profile male version: because not only do you have to compete on your own terms, then when you win, everybody turns round and says you're not as good as the men."

I can see that point, but looking at the total lack of coverage for all women's sports, it seems to me that they're all equally disregarded. Sasha Corbin, 23, who was part of the triumphant England netball squad, remarked mildly: "When you don't see any women in sport, you do think is that because we're not good enough?"

Keable, incidentally, was selected for the England team but couldn't get the time off work: she's a teacher.

Camilla Buchanan, 27, is captain of the Mavericks and fits in four hours of training a day around a nine-to-five job. She's particularly aware of the, ahem, gender gap, because she has a younger brother who's a professional footballer (Elliott Buchanan, who plays for Newport) and an older brother who was semi-professional.

"I do think we could produce better individual athletes [in netball] if we had more time. But in some respects, I think it makes us better, because we work so hard, we have to fight so hard, that there's no form of complacency.

"When you turn up to a match, you haven't put all that effort in just to go home with nothing. So it gives us an edge."

This is a uniting feature of all the players, a tendency to see the best in every situation. It's possible this is something you need to do in sport in the first place, or maybe they teach it in sports psychology.

Corbin, who has consistently been on the winning team in the Fiat Superleague (she was in Team Bath before the Mavericks), makes this winsome remark, which sort of explains to me why sportswomen don't bang on very much about equality – they

Chrissie Wellington, four times world champion, has never lost an ironman triathlon, which consists of a 2.4-mile swim, a 112-mile bike ride and a marathon run (raced in that order and without a break); Sarah Stevenson became taekwondo world champion in South Korea this year; we have swimmers and cyclists; we have the best women's cricket team in the world.

Photo: Thomas Frey/DPA/Press Association Images

appear to be concentrating on the sport: "It's nice to keep seeing the confetti coming out of the blowing machine."

Nevertheless, it should be chastening for broadcasters to hear Keable's five-year plan. It comprises winning a load of things, culminating in the World Championships of 2015: it all sounds quite likely.

"In four years," she says, "we might have the BBC interested. They could always put us on the red button, so people could turn over."

The Guardian, 2 December 2011
© Guardian News & Media Ltd 2011

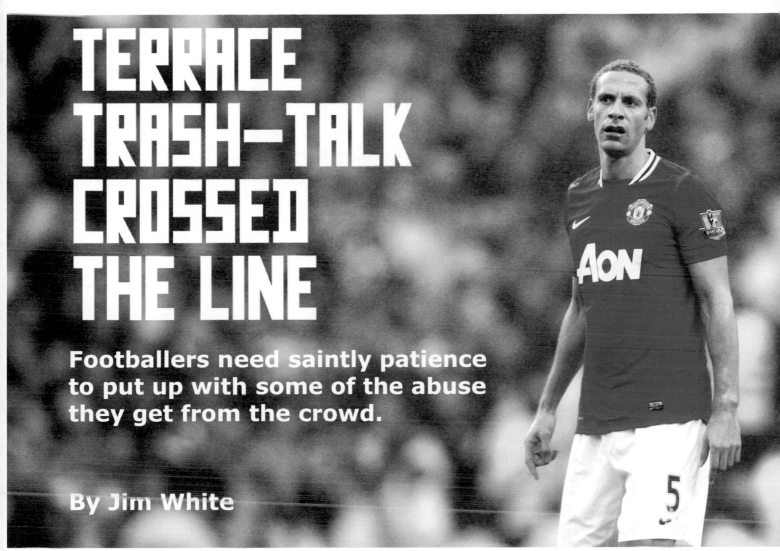

TERRACE TRASH-TALK CROSSED THE LINE

Footballers need saintly patience to put up with some of the abuse they get from the crowd.

By Jim White

Photo: SCOTT HEPPELL/AP/Press Association Image

SOME ISSUES:

What do you think about the abuse people shout at football players?

What do you think is a suitable response to such abuse?

Does the money you get paid affect your right to respond to provocation?

See also:
www.completeissues.co.uk

Without giving too much away about the idiosyncrasies of my first place of paid employment, it has been a while since I have suffered sustained verbal abuse while at work. In the office these days, no one embarks on ritualised public questioning of any of the following: my sexuality, my competence, or the prowess of my partner. When I turn up to do my job, from the desk opposite there is no mockery of the town where I live, belittlement of my financial decision-making or disparaging reference to my tax affairs. But then, I'm not employed in football.

This week, Harry Redknapp, the Tottenham Hotspur manager, became the latest figure in the game to be subject to the growing fashion for public baiting. Throughout his team's Europa League tie in Dublin, Redknapp was taunted about his forthcoming court case on tax issues. Ugly, unrelenting and impossible to ignore, the abuse was not confined to one or two hotheads. Whole sections of the crowd were taking part. And these were – according to Redknapp afterwards – the sort of

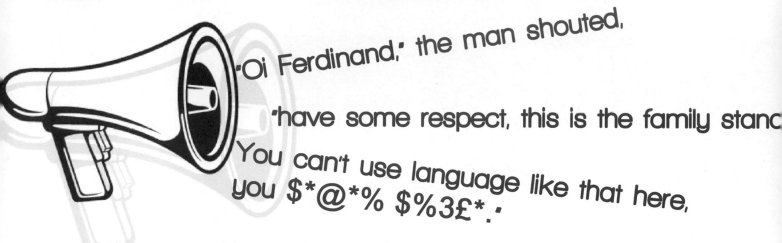

"Oi Ferdinand," the man shouted, "have some respect, this is the family stand. You can't use language like that here, you $*@*% $%3£*."

Irish folk who, in other circumstances, would offer him the most wonderful welcome.

It is one of the oddities of modern times that while legislation has insisted our work life is ever more polite, those who work in football are subject to ever-worsening rudery. Head to a match and you will hear chants of a most pointed nature directed at those involved. They will be routinely dismissed as lazy, venal and useless. And that's just the referee.

There is a school of thought that suggests they deserve it. By accepting the wages of Croesus, the modern player has detached himself from the moral orbit of his followers and has thus invited such critique. It is, however, an argument that does not appear to apply to their pop-singing or movie-acting contemporaries, who are allowed by their audience to conduct business free from public reminder of their fallibility.

And heaven forfend that any of the abused react. Because then the crowd will collectively cry foul. Redknapp, for instance, despite verbals of a kind that would provoke the Dalai Lama, is now the subject of vigorous complaint because he clenched his fist in the direction of the Dublin chanters at the end of play.

Yet the only surprising thing about Redknapp's response is that it is a rarity. Listening to this stuff week in week out, it is amazing that Eric Cantona's unequivocal reaction to a gobby fan back in 1995 did not set a precedent followed every weekend. Instead, most of those who will trot out today will display saintly restraint. The presiding philosophy is: if you ignore it, it will go away.

Except it isn't going away. At Chelsea recently, I was witness to the ultimate in the one-way traffic of abuse. Perhaps in order to keep all the infants in one place, the press box at Stamford Bridge is situated in the family stand. And right in front of us, the visiting Manchester United defender Rio Ferdinand had a feisty disagreement with the linesman, which included some ripe observations, about the direction of a throw-in.

A Chelsea regular was anxious to point out to the player that his industrial language was inappropriate in such a location. "Oi Ferdinand," the man shouted, "have some respect, this is the family stand. You can't use language like that here, you $*@*% $%3£*."

His was an intervention that would have made even my first employer blanch. And what was the reaction of the crowd? Those family types who seconds earlier had been outraged by the footballer's potty mouth cheered their new hero to the echo.

The Daily Telegraph, 16 December 2011
© Telegraph Media Group Ltd 2011

Freddie Flintoff: the hidden pain of sporting stars

Photo: Featureflash / Shutterstock.com

Jim White on
Andrew (Freddie) Flintoff's
documentary about
depression among athletes

SOME ISSUES:

Why do you think sports stars
might feel depressed?

Why do you think it would be hard for
them to talk about their problems?

Does it surprise you that so many stars
suffer from depression?

See also:
A moment of kindness p116

Dark Blues
Essential Articles 13, *p109*

Someone to talk to
Fact File 2012, p60

It's good to talk,
Fact File 2010, p69

www.completeissues.co.uk

Television occasionally comes up with moments that can bring a wobble to the stiffest, tungsten-lined upper lip. And one such came early in Freddie Flintoff: Hidden Side of Sport, the former cricketer's BBC One documentary, about the rising tide of depression among leading sports practitioners. Flintoff is studying a wall-full of pictures with his former England team mate Steve Harmison. Ostensibly they depict scenes of unalloyed joy. Certainly Flintoff can only see happiness in them. He points to two snaps, both of which feature him and Harmison, arms wrapped around one another in the aftermath of Ashes victory. One is taken in 2005, the other in 2009.

"Those are my favourite two pictures of all," says Flintoff, smiling at the sense of ease and satisfaction oozing from the frames. Harmison is less enthused. A man who hauled depression around in his carry-on baggage through a dozen cricket tours, he see things differently.

"I look at that," he says, pointing at the 2009 picture. "And all I see is the end."

Watch that and suddenly you feel ashamed at all those times you shouted at the TV screen when Harmison bowled a rubbish ball: the poor chap was dying inside.

The question Flintoff attempts to address in the documentary is how much sport itself contributes to the sense of depression that afflicts so many like Harmison. He discovers as he canvasses a who's who of the sporting world that even the most apparently impregnable – such as the boxer Ricky Hatton or the hardman footballer Vinnie Jones

While exercise, with its release of positive endorphins into the system, is undoubtedly beneficial, sport at the pinnacle might be seen to create as many problems as it resolves.

– have toyed with thoughts of self-destruction. Is it the unyielding pressure to produce results that unnerves? Or is the prevalence of fear, shame and feelings of pointlessness in so many a sportsman's psyche merely a reflection of the statistic that 10 per cent of us are susceptible to depression? As Flintoff puts it, if that stat is correct, one player in every team in the country could suffer from the condition.

If Flintoff seems an unlikely guide for a documentary of this nature, that is the point. Even he, happy-go-lucky, up-and-at-em Freddie, who seemingly bounded about the place with uncomplicated delight, the Labrador puppy of international cricket, recently admitted he'd succumbed to feelings of desperation, loneliness and inertia during his career. Looking back on it now, you can see it in the pictures of this most photogenic sportsman. At his lowest ebb, as a failed captain of his country, self-medicating on alcohol, there was a haunted, ghostly look in his eyes. At the time we all thought it was the inevitable corollary of too many bad results, not to mention a few too many late nights. So did he. Looking back he now realises there was something more. And how he wishes he had sought help.

But Flintoff also finds that sport has changed in recent years, and is now willing to provide such help. In the past, to admit to mental frailty was to confess to weakness. A carapace of invincibility was part of the sportsman's make-up. To show the slightest crack to colleagues and opponents alike was to falter. As Vinnie Jones puts it, had one of his team mates said he was feeling a bit depressed, he would have got a clip round the ear.

But admissions by figures such as Harmison, the rugby player Jonny Wilkinson and the footballer Stan Collymore, plus the awful death of the German goalkeeper Robert Enke who committed suicide three years ago, have alerted those in control of the need to address mental issues. As Neil Lennon, the manager of Celtic and himself a sufferer of depression, tells Flintoff, these days most coaches are enlightened enough to recognise that the brain is the sportsman's most important muscle. They appreciate the need to treat problems within it as they might any form of physical injury. No-one is clipped round the ear for feeling down these days.

Yet still the question remains: does top level sport depress its participants? While exercise, with its release of positive endorphins into the system, is undoubtedly beneficial, sport at the pinnacle might be seen to create as many problems as it resolves. Because the fact is, sport operates at a different rhythm from normal life. Its frontiers are more clearly defined by the simple, primary diktats of victory or defeat. Its chronology is more condensed, its ephemeral nature emphasised by the speed at which a career is over. Plus it is an entirely self-absorbed pursuit: all that matters is how well you are doing. When self-esteem is so uncompromisingly connected to performance, it can quickly and easily be fractured.

All this is conducted against a backdrop of envy: how we ordinary civilians covet the ability of the successful. In the most intriguing exchange in his programme, Flintoff confronts the former tabloid editor Piers Morgan. He excoriates Morgan for the callous manner in which his profession criticises performance without knowing the real circumstances. Do journalists care about the pain they might cause? And Morgan frankly tells him no – they share with the fans an unyielding jealousy of the great sportsman.

"I would put up with any number of negative tabloid headlines to walk out just once at Lord's," says Morgan.

How happy must be the man who can do that, is the implication. As the writer and ex-table tennis international Matthew Syed tells Flintoff, we fans assume our heroes live in "some sort of emotional nirvana". The truth, as Flintoff discovers in his programme, is at odds with such a shallow assumption. Our heroes, it seems, are as prone to crushing self-doubt as the rest of us.

*The Daily Telegraph,
11 January 2012
© Telegraph Media
Group Ltd 2012*

Watch that and suddenly you feel ashamed at all those times you shouted at the TV screen when Harmison bowled a rubbish ball: the poor chap was dying inside.

Photo: Sergei Bachlakov / Shutterstock.com

Combining the Paralympics and Olympics would be a disaster. Here's why ...

Faced with the choice of the finish of the Olympic marathon or the goalball event for blind athletes, where will sports editors send their reporters?
Peter White

SOME ISSUES:

Do you think that the Olympics and Paralympics should be combined together?

What do you think would be the advantages and disadvantages for the sports involved?

And what about the people?

Who would benefit ?

Is Peter White right about general attitudes to disabled athletes?

See also:

A true sporting hero or a cheat? p174

Stumble at the starting block
Essential Articles 14, p163

www.completeissues.co.uk

Disability politics is strewn with pratfalls, as I know to my cost. One writer's heartwarming story is another's patronising pat on the head. Someone's tale of triumph over adversity is for others just more inappropriate schmaltz. So, if you thought that the Paralympics, that four-yearly festival of disability sport was fireproof, well, think again.

Yes, I know, it's always greeted by whoops of amazement: this groundbreaking discovery that disabled people do play sport, and that some do it very well and even excitingly. It's a sporting equivalent of groundhog day, in which everyone discovers, yet again, wheelchair basketball and Tanni Grey-Thompson – or her latest equivalent – only to forget them all again until the next time.

Nonetheless, by the end of the games, we're all congratulating ourselves on living in a country that gives sport like this such excellent coverage, and declaring that we'll be looking anxiously for the results of games such as "goalball" and Boccia, invented for, respectively, blind and severely disabled people, which two weeks earlier we'd never heard of. So: the Paralympics is fireproof, is it? Not a bit of it: And especially not from disabled people themselves.

The games regularly face two criticisms in particular: first, that they are irrelevant to the everyday concerns of disabled people and that, worse, it often gives the impression everything in the garden is lovely; and second, that staging them as a separate event, far from being a celebration of disability, merely serves to emphasise its separation from the mainstream. The latest salvo to this effect has just come from the disability organisation Scope, which has produced a survey suggesting that two-thirds of the 500 mainly disabled people whose opinions were sought believe that the Paralympics and the Olympics should be combined. (At the moment, and for the past 30 years or so, the Paralympics have taken place a couple of weeks after the Olympics; before that, they often didn't even happen in the same country.)

On the face of it the complaints sound justified and press all the correct liberal buttons. It's integrated, it's inclusive; it's, well, just right!

Wrong! It would be an unmitigated disaster. I shall have coals of fire heaped on my head for saying it, so here are my reasons. First, the Paralympics wouldn't be combined with the Olympics, it would be swamped by it. Smothered. The Olympics is already the largest sporting event in the world (the Paralympics the second largest). It already sprawls all over our television screens and newspapers, threatening to take over the world (and I'm a sports-lover).

Ask the aficionados of judo, curling and hammer-throwing just how much coverage they get, compared with the likes of Usain Bolt and Rebecca Adlington. So can you imagine what, with the best will in the

world, would happen to the Paralympics? It would be plucked from its lone and privileged status as a separate event after the Olympics is safely done and dusted, supported by the bastions of broadcasting diversity and equality, and forced to go slumming it with all the other Olympic events. Faced with the choice of the finish of the Olympic marathon or the final of the goalball event for blind athletes, where are sports editors most likely to send their reporters, and where are TV directors going to train their cameras?

But something far more insidious would happen, which would do even more harm to disability sport than lack of coverage. The reason the Paralympics is the second largest sporting occasion in the world is that, to achieve fairness, like has to compete with like. Therefore, many competitions have multiple versions of each event, to take account of physical differences; the amount of movement in the arms, degree of eyesight loss, etc. I think there are some 14 swimming categories, for example.

If the games were combined, there would be an inevitable compromise. The Paralympics would be asked to cut the number of categories for each event.

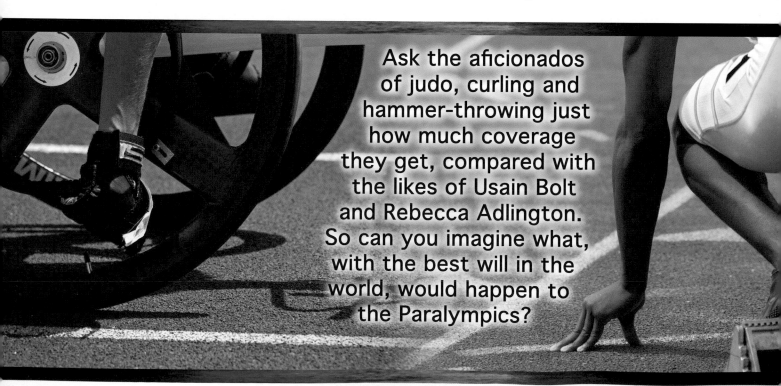

Ask the aficionados of judo, curling and hammer-throwing just how much coverage they get, compared with the likes of Usain Bolt and Rebecca Adlington. So can you imagine what, with the best will in the world, would happen to the Paralympics?

I'm convinced that if it had to fight for coverage with the rest of the Olympics, the Paralympics would lose its coverage and its privileged slot, and its visibility

The range of disability in each event would be wider, thus excluding more severely disabled people, if not from the competition itself, then at least from any realistic chance of success. This is what happened when disability events were included in the Commonwealth Games in Manchester in 2002. The games were highly successful, and indeed those disabled athletes who participated thought it a good experience; but what about those who didn't get the chance, because their category had been broadened to a point which put them out of contention? The ultimate irony, surely; too disabled to be part of the Paralympic games.

Well, you might argue, that's sport. It's about being the best, and there can be only so many winners. The parallel, though, is those mainstream sports that make a distinction between certain body types. After all, a flyweight boxer might as well give up if he has to go into the ring with heavyweights such as the Klitschko brothers.

The truth of the matter is, huge strides have been made over the past 20 years in getting the Paralympics taken seriously. When I went to cover my first games only 15 years ago in Atlanta, there were four of us expected to do the whole of the BBC radio coverage (I managed to fit in a bit of television news as well, although we had to fly a director out from London to get the pieces on screen). The day-to-day TV coverage was all done by an independent company, with less than an hour of highlights each day. (Not long before that, all the coverage the Paralympics got was a Christmas special, the basic theme of which was "isn't it marvellous that they even bother to get out of bed in the morning?")

So the fact that last time, in Beijing, I was one of a full journalistic team from BBC sport, complete with both disabled and non-disabled pundits providing at least six hours of coverage a day, was little short of a miracle. This is now topped by the fact that for the 2012 games, Channel 4 has thought it worth its while to outbid the Beeb to get the gig.

I'm convinced that if it had to fight for coverage with the rest of the Olympics, not only would the Paralympics lose its coverage and its privileged slot, but what visibility it did attract would revert to exactly the kind of patronising attitudes that a fifth of those the Scope survey said they hated.

So, what about that other argument that the games are irrelevant to the daily concerns of disabled people? Well, there are certainly enough concerns at the moment: potential loss of benefits; pressure to find jobs that don't exist; an insidious press campaign, fuelled from goodness knows where, suggesting most disabled people are on the scrounge: these are all very legitimate worries.

What's puzzling to me, though, is the idea that in some way the Paralympics deflect attention from those issues, and that paralympic athletes should be concentrating on solving them, rather than hurtling down the track in a wheelchair.

As far as I know, no one is suggesting Mo Farah and Jessica Ennis should give up the 10,000 metres and the heptathlon to solve the banking crisis, or tackle youth unemployment. No. Leave the Paralympics alone, where most of you will discover it for the first time in 2012, and then discover it for the first time all over again in 2016.

The Guardian, 9 December 2011
© Guardian News & Media Ltd 2011

A TRUE SPORTING HERO, OR A CHEAT?

The controversy continues to rage over Oscar Pistorius.

By Ian Chadband

A momentous event in sporting endeavour, perhaps even in human endeavour, took place in front of 10,000 enthralled spectators at the Daegu Stadium in Korea on August 28th 2011. A man who had his lower legs amputated as a baby ran against some of the best 400-metre sprinters in the World Championships, athletics' greatest event. And beat most of them.

Oscar Pistorius, a 24-year-old from Johannesburg, modestly shrugged that he was just another runner, just the same as thousands of others around the world, just like those hard-working sprinters alongside him who had sacrificed so much to reach their sport's pinnacle.

Except that it did not wash. Korean fans hung over the side of the track just to get close to the man running on the prosthetic limbs, the first double amputee to compete in the championships, because they could recognize this was an extraordinary breakthrough moment in sport. They looked and were amazed. "We love you Oscar!" came the chants, because they could hardly conceive that this figure, balanced seemingly precariously on his carbon-fibre blades, could possibly compete with able-bodied runners on level terms.

But he could. And it was breathtaking to behold. In this job, I have been privileged to witness great sporting feats at close quarters for a quarter of a century and, frankly, the major championship debut of this young South African was as uplifting an occasion as anything I've seen.

OK, Pistorius did not actually win his race. He finished third in his heat, covering one lap in just 45.39 seconds, which booked him a place in the semi-finals. Even he conceded that he was unlikely to go any further in the competition, but when he ran, it felt as if it did not matter; the only thing that did was that we had just watched, awe-struck, as a line between a supposedly able-bodied and a supposedly disabled athlete suddenly became so invisible as to feel quite irrelevant.

That is just as Pistorius would want it. Just another athlete? No, he looked like one in a million. "I don't really feel like a trailblazer or anything like that, to be honest," he told me. "I feel like any other athlete here. Each person works extremely hard to do what they do. I'm not the only athlete here, there are thousands of them. So I don't really feel like a pioneer. Just a runner."

Only he can never be just that. Apart from Usain Bolt, the fastest man in the world, who lost his 100 metres crown yesterday after being disqualified for a false start, Pistorius has been the most

SOME ISSUES:

Does Oscar Pistorius have a disadvantage or an advantage?

Is he a 'trailblazer'?

If the technology allows disabled athletes to beat able-bodied ones, is that a good thing?

See also:
Combining the olympics and paralympics would be a disaster: Here's why...
p171

Stumble at the starting block
Essential Articles 14, p163

www.completeissues.co.uk

Photo: Luca Bruno/AP/Press Association Images

They could hardly conceive that this figure, balanced seemingly precariously on his carbon-fibre blades, could possibly compete with able-bodied runners on level terms.

feted athlete at the competition because in a sense he is also the most important athlete.

A year from today, the Paralympic Games begin in London. Pistorius is desperate to compete there, but it is also his dream to compete in the Olympic Games that take place a month earlier. He will probably end up taking part in both, which one would imagine ought to be a reason for universal delight.

Except that while it is, of course, impossible for anyone not to salute the achievements of a man whose amazing determination has seen him break these barriers, the rumbling undercurrent to his shining success here is that there are many who, frankly, would rather he did not compete against able-bodied athletes at all. They see Pistorius not so much as a hero but a nuisance, an inconvenience, a menace. He has even been called a cheat in his time, but no one would dare do that to his face.

The doubters come in various guises. There are some of the grandees of Paralympic sport, including Britain's greatest, Dame Tanni Grey-Thompson, who feel that should he run the 400m at the Olympics, he will effectively turn the Paralympic event into a "B" race and undermine the movement.

Then there are those able-bodied athletes he runs against who cannot abide the idea of being beaten by a man shooting around on specially designed blades, which they are convinced are providing him with an unfair advantage. As Martyn Rooney, his British friend and rival, put it here: "The ones who complain about Oscar are the ones getting beaten by him."

They are probably also the ones who fancy that, though Pistorius has actually run on the same Cheetah blades for seven years, he must somehow be taking advantage of constant improvements in prosthetic limb technology, which would account for the vast improvement of more than half a second in his time for the 400m this season. Pistorius, though, is an eloquent defender of his own work ethic. It is the man not the machinery, he protests.

This scientific debate is at the heart of the fear that drove athletics' governing body, the International Association of Athletics Federations (IAAF), to first ban Pistorius from their competitions in 2008. The IAAF are

> **One critic maintains that because the blades are so much lighter than legs, Pistorius uses less energy running at the same speed as able-bodied athletes, nor do his blades tire as the lower limbs of an able-bodied athlete do during a race.**

convinced that, although he is still running times which as yet do not make him a medal threat in major events, there will come a time soon when prosthetics technology is so advanced that "disabled" runners will be swifter than the Michael Johnsons of this world. Indeed, Hugh Herr, the scientist who has contributed to Pistorius's achievement, believes that disabled people will soon be smashing world records set by able-bodied sportsmen and women. It was Herr, head of biomechanotronics at the Massachusetts Institute of Technology in Boston, and himself a double amputee, who persuaded the IAAF to reverse its ban, allowing Pistorius to compete alongside able-bodied athletes.

That decision remains controversial, and clouded by a plethora of polarised scientific views, none of which can yet be definitively proved. One critic maintains that because the blades are so much lighter than legs, Pistorius uses less energy running at the same speed as able-bodied athletes, nor do his blades tire as the lower limbs of an able-bodied athlete do during a race. Another professor counters that the blades are a disadvantage, because Pistorius cannot push off and accelerate from the blocks as the able-bodied do, and that his fatigue levels are the same as for those supposedly drowning in lactic acid on the home straight.

In truth, nobody truly knows. What seemed evident yesterday was that Pistorius does run the 400m in a different fashion to most quarter-milers, poor at the start but coming into his own from around the penultimate bend when others are flailing.

Even if some of his rivals harbour private concerns about the future of their event - and LaShawn Merritt, the reigning world champion,

sounded dubious after winning his heat yesterday, shrugging: "I don't know what's going to happen with the technology" - Rooney reckons it was time that everyone embraced Pistorius. "I think it's essential for him to be there. He's a massive thing for athletics, for sport; he's a selling point, a role model for kids with disabilities and such a positive person to be around."

Indeed. How could you not be a fan of Oscar Pistorius? Watching him evaporates cynicism. He will not win Olympic gold but he will win hearts, make spirits soar. The last we saw of him yesterday, he seemed to be pulling off the remarkable trick of beaming and grimacing simultaneously as he conducted a series of post-race interviews which appeared to last about an hour longer than his race.

"I need to get out of here as quick as I can to have an ice bath and get ready for tomorrow," he protested. Not a chance. Just another word, Oscar! The world wanted to celebrate with a proper sporting hero.

> **Another professor counters that the blades are a disadvantage, because Pistorius cannot push off and accelerate from the blocks as the able-bodied do**

The Daily Telegraph, 29 August, 2011
© Telegraph Media Group Ltd 2011

STOP PRESS

Oscar has last chance to make qualifying time in Benin between 27th June and 1st July, 2012

War & conflict

Show some style and fork out for a proper poppy

A paper poppy that constantly needs replacing is so much more beautiful and important than the costly show-off bling ones

Barbara Ellen

SOME ISSUES:

Do you think poppys should be alowed at international sporting events?

Do you think a more expensive poppy is a sign of respect or vanity?

Should retailers be allowed to sell more expensive poppies if they do not give more money to the charity?

Which type of poppy would you wear?

See also:
www.completeissues.co.uk

It's not often that the luminously arrogant Prince William catches the attention for a good reason, so respect to him for being instrumental in overturning Fifa's ban on the England football team wearing poppies for yesterday's friendly against Spain.

Initially Fifa's rationale was that every international team would want to do something similar, and we might end up with questionable politics on kit everywhere. Fair enough, but surely the poppy, of all things, is beyond politics – so potent and elastic a symbol, it can be pro-humanity and anti-war simultaneously.

The new bling style of poppy (snazzy, festooned with crystals, popularised by celebrities) also makes a statement loud and clear. It says: "I'm a self-obsessed airhead, and probably a tightwad with it."

Bling poppies have been selling by the shedload, but while the ones from jewellers Buckley, sold on the Royal British Legion site, give the bulk of their profits to the charity, others such as the £59.95 crystal-studded job by Kleshna, donate only 10%.

Their bling poppy could last for years, while the rest of us keep re-buying. In effect, the blingee is wittingly or unwittingly being a poppy tightwad—remembering the war dead on the cheap. Nice.

"I run a business but genuinely want to give to charity," says the Kleshna owner, seemingly oblivious to obscure business concepts such as loss leaders and positive PR. Elsewhere, people who wear bling poppies talk about the rejuvenation of the poppy concept, giving it a modern, individualistic spin, and what could be wrong with that? Oh dear, where do we start?

First, no one should be messing with the traditional simple paper poppy. It's a design classic, all the more wonderful because it is so badly designed. It has a buttonhole-proof stem (too short, always falling out), and little pins that either stick you, or fall off immediately.

Good. For fundraising purposes, it needs to be badly designed. It means that it must be replaced every year, or even more regularly (I've lost and re-bought four this year).

By contrast, the bling poppy is like a hardy brooch; a robust piece of jewellery that can be recycled year in, year out. It does not get the return traffic of the traditional poppy. Hence for all the initial expense, and despite the fact that wearers pose about like they've made an extra-special effort and care more deeply (and photogenically) than anyone else, the opposite is true.

Their bling poppy could last for years, while the rest of us keep re-buying. In effect, the blingee is wittingly or unwittingly being a poppy tightwad—remembering the war dead on the cheap. Nice.

But, of course, the poppy is being reappropriated, just as its meaning is continually hijacked. Increasingly, there are people fretting about the rights and wrongs of poppy-wearing. What they don't seem to realise is that the poppy has not just been hijacked by the showily pious, but also by these woolly worriers.

They have more in common with the bling poppy-wearers than they like to think. Both are making it all about themselves, placing their feelings, their sensitivities and individualism, at the heart of the issue.

With both groups, it's all: "Me, me, me, how do I feel, what do I think?" When, surely, the whole point of the poppy is to put "self" aside and think of others.

This is why the poppy is so important and beautiful, and a certain type of poppy (paper, easily lost, ridiculously flimsy) will always be more important and beautiful than others.

What you are buying (and feel free to stuff £60 into the tin) is not only a sense of humanity and community, but also patriotism untarnished. Did I say buying? I meant renting. Poppies are supposed to be flimsy and temporary, they're supposed to fall off and get lost, you're supposed to keep buying them, and donating.

Anyone with a more complicated or fashion-forward agenda doesn't deserve to wear one.

The Observer, 13 November 2011
© Guardian News & Media Ltd 2011

Poppies are supposed to be flimsy and temporary, they're supposed to fall off and get lost, you're supposed to keep buying them, and donating.

Which do you think is the best investment? asks **Brian Eno.** A war machine which incurs contempt and hatred everywhere for Britain? Or funding for hospitals, nurses, schools and child-care?

Photo: YouTube

WHAT WE COULD DO WITH THE MONEY WASTED ON THE AFGHANISTAN WAR

Brian Eno - one of the world's most influential musicians and artists, and producer of U2 and Coldplay, among many others - is also a committed activist in the anti-war movement. This is a transcript of the speech he made at Stop the War Coalition's Antiwar Assembly on 8 October 2011.

Many of the speakers today will be addressing the moral issues of the war. I want to talk about the economic facts. So far the war in Afghanistan has cost us £20 or £30 billion.

Billions are hard to grasp, so another way of looking at it is to say that the war is currently costing £12m a day. I'll repeat that: £12 million a day.

What else could we be doing with that amount of money?

Well, how about building some decent schools? For £20 million - that's less than two days of the war - you could build a very modern and large school.

That means about 15 big schools a month. For 20 days of the war you could build a big regional hospital.

And what about the people who work in them, the people who build our future and look after us? How about a pay rise for all our teachers and nurses? An extra £1,000 a year for all 800,000 of them would cost us just 2 months in Afghanistan.

How about child-care? Britain, with the third largest defence budget in the world after America and China, has the highest childcare costs in Europe. British families with young children spend nearly a quarter of their income looking after their children - primarily because we pay so much for childcare. In Germany, by contrast, the figure is 3%. We could become equal with

SOME ISSUES:

Do famous people have any right to use their fame to promote a cause?

Is it fair to say some causes lost money to fund the war?

How would you spend the money raised by taxation?

Is war always wrong?

See also:
Cost of war Fact File
2010, p156
www.completeissues.co.uk

Germany for less than the cost of three months in Afghanistan.

You might have been impressed that in August the government promised £6.5 million to train people in renewable energy technologies - that is until you realise that's about thirteen hours in Afghanistan. Our whole clean-energy research budget was cut dramatically over the last year, and almost crippled as a result. The saving? A few days at war...

And how about culture, one of our country's biggest exports? Well, earlier this year The Arts Council had its budget cut by £100m: that means small theatres, arts labs, etc - the places where future talent is discovered and nurtured - are closing down. The saving? Eight days in Afghanistan.

The BBC World Service had its budget cut by £46m, which meant that it lost about a sixth of its foreign listeners. What did we save by that brilliant piece of international diplomacy? Three days at war. Which do you think is the best investment? A news service whose impartiality is respected all over the world, or a totally ineffective war machine which incurs contempt and hatred for this country?

Even BBC Online, whose total annual budget amounts to 24 minutes in Afghanistan, had its budget cut to pay for an extra 12 seconds of war.

But it's not only the Arts that are being cut back. It's the sciences too. Government funding of science research was reduced by about a billion pounds over the last year. That's a huge loss for British science - and ultimately for our economy - but we shouldn't be too fed up because it'll pay for a whole 11 weeks in Afghanistan.

What about youth centres? In the wake of the recent riots you might think that it would be a good idea to invest in anything that would help young people find their feet. For the cost of the war, you could build at least two a day - and those would be top-of-the-line places. Build a bit more modestly, and you could probably manage five or 10 a day.

Council housing anyone? Very unfashionable at the moment but, as someone who grew up in one, I think I know their value. We have nearly two million people on waiting lists, and we aren't anywhere near keeping up with demand. What would it cost? And how much more would it stimulate our economy to build houses than to fight pointless wars?

We're constantly being told that these are hard times and we have to tighten our belts, but as far as I can see the belts round the biggest bellies aren't tightening at all. As usual, it's the people at the bottom who suffer - both here and in Afghanistan.

stopwar.org.uk, 9 October 2011

For £20 million - that's less than two days of the war - you could build a very modern and large school

Photo: YouTube

'My grief at the loss of my soldier son in Afghanistan...'

Mother's Day:

Helena Tym's 19-year-old son Cyrus Thatcher died in Afghanistan on 2 June 2009. Here, she describes what it's like to prepare for her first Mother's Day without him

HOW to articulate my grief at the loss of my soldier son in Afghanistan? I wear my sadness like a long, dark, damp overcoat that itches uncomfortably and pulls me downwards. It drags along the floor, chilling my bones, hampering my every movement, robbing me of energy and the joy I felt watching my three wonderful sons growing up.

Cyrus, my brave, funny, charming, exasperating boy who was a rifleman in the 2nd Battalion The Rifles was killed on 2 June 2009 while on patrol near Gereshk in Helmand by an IED, an improvised explosive device. There hasn't been an inquest yet so details are sketchy; we think he probably stepped on what was effectively a home-made bomb and was killed outright.

I'm thankful that he didn't suffer, and that knowledge makes it slightly easier somehow to bear the unbearable. Whatever the exact circumstances of his death, the vacuum left at the centre of our lives sometimes makes it hard to pick up the threads of life and carry on.

Our other sons, Zac, aged 22 and Steely, who is 18, still live at home with us in Reading and their world, too, has been irrevocably altered by the loss of their much-loved brother, to whom they were very close. They had an idyllic childhood together as we travelled a lot; they shared mud baths in Turkey, swam with dolphins in the Mediterranean and went scuba diving in the Middle East. They were an inseparable little gang but now that companionship too, has been destroyed.

Steely is at music college, Zac works with his father, Robin, who is a general builder in Reading. Cyrus idolised his father, and when I speak of my bereavement I want to make it plain that I speak for my whole family, and every other army family out there mourning a child.

Cyrus was a typical middle child – desperate to be noticed, with an irreverent sense of humour. You always knew when he was in the room. He had red hair and freckles and a headstrong personality to match, and I can't pretend we didn't occasionally clash. But he was also a sensitive, observant boy who would notice if I

SOME ISSUES:

Would you encourage a friend or family member into this career?

Is there anything which makes the risk and sacrifice worthwhile?

See also:
Not in vain
Essential Articles 13, p175

Moshtarak frontline diary
Essential Articles 13, p177

www.completeissues.co.uk

They had an idyllic childhood together as we travelled a lot; they shared mud baths in Turkey, swam with dolphins in the Mediterranean and went scuba diving in the Middle East

All images used courtesy of Helena Tym

changed my perfume or had my hair cut, and no matter how grown up he acted, he was never too big for a cuddle.

He wasn't naturally academic and had real problems at school, particularly with literacy, and as a result was unsure of himself as a teenager and appeared quite directionless. But that all changed when he joined the army at the age of 17 and was transformed into a confident, happy, disciplined young man, who took a huge pride in what he did.

He felt like he'd finally found his niche and we were so pleased for him, although we weren't an army family and had no other military connections. I remember he was desperate to go to Afghanistan and put his training into practice, but ironically, although I knew he was going into a war zone, I was more worried he might get stabbed on a night out here in Britain, where squaddies are often greeted with hostility and aggression.

After he left for active duty in Afghanistan I was amazed and very touched that he sent us letters; although they were addressed to me, they were meant for everyone, and we pored over them and smiled at the wayward grammar. He wrote the way he spoke, and gave us amusing, vivid accounts of life in the desert and of being so close to the Taliban that he could "count the hairs in their beards".

We'd no reason to think he wouldn't come home to us; with hindsight maybe that was naive. And now, on every special day – a birthday, Christmas, Mother's Day – his absence is a gaping hole in our hearts. Memories come flooding back of that terrible moment when we learned our beautiful boy was dead.

The knock on the door came at 10.30pm on the night he was killed. Robin and I were getting ready for bed, and as I drew the curtains I could see two men in suits coming up the driveway. Given the time of the night and the fact they were in suits we knew there was something wrong.

The men, who were from the military, came in and asked me to take a seat to which I replied "I'm not going to sit while you tell me my son's been killed". When they told us what had happened I cried and then the numbness hit and everything became a long blur as we were swept along by procedures. The army organised the funeral, having consulted us about our wishes. The ceremony took place in Reading Minster; there was a congregation of 500 in the church and another 500 outside.

It might sound strange, but I think Cyrus would have enjoyed it, being the centre of attention, surrounded by friends and comrades and pretty girls. He was buried in the memorial cemetery just up the road from our house; he was the first person to be laid to rest there since the Second World War. I kept my composure until the graveside, when I took the first handful of earth and threw it into his grave. It was then that the cold hard reality of burying my son hit me and I started to cry. Nothing can prepare you for burying your son, it's not the natural order of things and nothing can ever be the same again

Around seven weeks after Cyrus died, we released the letters he'd sent us from the front line, including the final one he'd written to be opened in the event of his death, which was heartbreakingly poignant. The letters were published in the press and we got a huge amount of feedback, but we didn't want anyone to feel sorry for us.

Then, as now, we wanted to put a human face to the Afghan war, and to make the wider public realise that every soldier out fighting in Afghanistan is someone's child, every "casualty" is a devastating loss that ripples outward through families and communities.

Tomorrow is Mothering Sunday, so the media focus will inevitably be on the hundreds of mothers who have lost

When they told us what had happened I cried and then the numbness hit and everything became a long blur as we were swept along by procedures

their children so far in this conflict. But we don't have the monopoly on suffering; the pain isn't ours alone.

Last Mother's Day the boys brought me armfuls of bulbs to plant in the garden. A year on, the tulips and crocuses are poking their heads through the ground, but Cyrus will never see them and that brings tears to my eyes and such a lump to my throat that I can barely swallow.

I cry every day; at hearing a snatch of familiar music, or watching the news, but I can't just sit on the floor rocking backwards and forwards howling, because I still have two children and a partner and I must be strong for them, no matter how hard that might be.

This Mother's Day I will be in Wootton Bassett, where a Bike Run is taking place, organised by Afghan Heroes, the charity set up by the mothers of soldiers killed in the conflict. I have a huge amount of admiration for the work they are doing, and I hope some day I will be able to take a more active role, but right now it's as much as I can do to turn up and be an ambassador for my son, expressing my pride and support for him and all our courageous servicemen and women.

I've been to Wootton Bassett many times since Cyrus died, as often as my work allowed it. I returned to my job, running a day centre for people with head injuries, three weeks after Cyrus's death, but I resigned last month because I couldn't give the role the 100 per cent commitment it demanded and deserved.

On Thursday this week Robin and I joined the crowds as five more soldiers, all riflemen, were brought home. I feel drawn back to the town, partly because there's a real feeling of empathy that's a comfort, partly because it's the least I can do to honour those who have fallen.

Since Cyrus died we have had the most amazing support from the army; I couldn't fault the way we've been kept informed and made to feel part of the army family. No question has gone unanswered, no request for support has been denied. They look after their own – as they should – and I can see why our son wanted to be part of all that.

My son loved the army, he believed in what he did; I'm not sad about the way he died, just the fact he died.

And so tomorrow, on Mothering Sunday, I'll put on my make-up in the morning and hope that my mask stays in place all day. We will go to Wootton Bassett, where I will hold my head up and we will try as a family to lead by example; showing our respect, our solidarity and our gratitude to those who have lost their lives in our name.

The Daily Telegraph, 13 March 2010
© Telegraph Media Group Ltd 2010

To read more about this and to read Cyrus's letters in full see Helena Tym's Book, *Chin Up, Head Down: A Mother's Journey of Madness and Grief,* **Firestep Press.**

CYRUS'S LAST LETTER TO HIS FAMILY:

Cyrus Thatcher was killed on 2 June 2009. This is the letter he wrote to his family, to be delivered if he died:

Hello its me, this is gonna be hard for you to read but I write this knowing every time you thinks shits got to much for you to handle (so don't cry on it MUM!!) you can read this and hopefully it will help you all get through.

For a start SHIT I got hit!! Now Iv got that out the way I can say the things Iv hopefully made clear, or if I havent this should clear it all up for me. My hole life you'v all been there for me through thick and thin bit like a wedding through good and bad. Without you I believe I wouldn't have made it as far as I have. I died doing what I was born to do I was happy and felt great about myself although the army was sadly the ending of me it was also the making of me so please don't feel any hate toward it. One thing I no I never made clear to you all was I make jokes about my life starting in the Army. That's wrong VERY wrong my life began a LONG time before that (Obviously) but you get what I mean. All the times Iv tried to neglect the family get angry when you try teach me right from wrong wot I mean to say is I only realised that you were trying to help when I joined the army and without YOUR help I would have never had the BALLS, the GRIT and the damn right determination to crack on and do it. If I could have a wish in life it would to be able to say Iv gone and done things many would never try to do. And going to Afghan has fulfilled my dream ie my goal. Yes I am young wich as a parent must brake you heart but you must all somehow find the strength that I found to do something no matter how big the challenge. As Im writing this letter I can see you all crying and mornin my death but if I could have one wish in an "after life" it would be to stop your crying and continueing your dreams (as I did) because if I were watching only that would brake my heart. So dry your tears and put on a brave face for the rest of your friends and family who need you.

I want each and everyone of you to forfill a dream and at the end of it look at what you have done (completed) and feel the accomplishment and achievement I did only then will you understand how I felt when I passed away.

[To his brothers:] You are both amazing men and will continue to be throughout your lives you both deserve to be happy and fofill all of your dreams.

Dad – my idol, my friend, my best friend, my teacher, my coach, everything I ever succeeded in my life I owe to you and maybe a little bit of me! You are a great man and the perfect role model and the past two years of being in the army I noticed that and me and you have been on the best level we have ever been. I thank you for nothing because I no all you have given to me is not there to be thanked for its there because you did it cause you love me and that is my most proudest thing I could ever say.

Mum, where do I start with you!! For a start your perfect, your smell, your hugs, the way your life was dedicated to us boys and especially the way you cared each and every step us boys took. I love you, you were the reason I made it as far as I did you were the reason I was loved more than any child I no and that made me feel special.

Your all such great individuals and I hope somehow this letter will help you get through this shit time!! Just remember do NOT mourn my death as hard as this will seem, celebrate a great life that has had its ups and downs. I love you all more than you would ever no and in your own individual ways helped me get through it all. I wish you all the best with your dreams.

Remember chin up head down. With love Cyrus XXXX

Wider world

THE RIGHT TO SAY 'No'

Early marriage is illegal in Bangladesh, but the practice remains widespread. Kiran Flynn reports on the youth groups raising awareness

SOME ISSUES:

What can be done to stop these illegal underage marriages?

Why is it important for young girls and women to get the same standard of education as boys and men?

See also:
Child Brides,
Fact File 2012, p176

www.completeissues.co.uk

Under the watchful stare of her father-in-law, Nargis says she felt "shy" on her wedding day. Away from him, she looks around nervously, whispering "I was frightened. Again and again I felt fear, fear, fear." Nargis was married when she was just 12 years old; her parents made the decision without consulting her. "When I was in school and with my friends, I was very happy," she remembers fondly. Now, Nargis's days consist of cooking, cleaning, and obeying orders.

Nargis is just one of 10 million girls worldwide married every year as children, according to the World Health Organisation. The United Nations identifies children as anyone under 18, and declares the decision to marry cannot be made until that age as children lack the "full maturity and capacity to act". In Bangladesh, early marriage is illegal, yet 66% of girls are married off when they are still considered children in the eyes of the law – the highest rate in south Asia and the fourth highest in the world.

Early marriage abuses a girl's human rights. Boys are affected too, but the effect on girls is more widespread and has greater impact. The practice is at odds with three UN human rights documents that Bangladesh has signed, such as the Convention on the Elimination of all Forms of Discrimination against Women, but its consequences violate many more.

When a girl marries she usually leaves school and is taken to her marital home where she often remains, rarely venturing to towns and sometimes with limited access to her family. Poor maternal health, sexually transmitted infections, infant mortality, violence, abuse, illiteracy, isolation, psychological trauma and suicide are common among young brides. "I want to tell other girls that the age I got married was not good. Not for health, for family, for education, for anything," says Nargis.

"Two years after my marriage, I gave birth to a baby boy." Nargis frowns, looking at the floor. "There were complications after

When a girl marries she usually leaves school and is taken to her marital home where she often remains, rarely venturing to towns and sometimes with limited access to her family.

Photo: Zzvet / Shutterstock.com

Poor maternal health, sexually transmitted infections, infant mortality, violence, abuse, illiteracy, isolation, psychological trauma and suicide are common among young brides.

the birth. I don't know why. He survived for 16 days, but then he died." Nargis was 14 years old.

A teenage girl's child is more likely to be premature and less likely to survive than if the mother is in her 20s, states Unicef. The mother, in turn, is twice as likely to die (five times more likely if under 15). Early marriage hinders Bangladesh's progress towards the internationally agreed Millennium Development Goals, two of which address the need to reduce child mortality and improve maternal health. Nargis was lucky to survive. Four years later she gave birth again – to a healthy son.

"I really want to go back to school," says Nargis sadly. Her education ended after her marriage, which is underreported as a reason for leaving school. Many girls' families believe the primary responsibility of a wife is to the home and children. Without schooling, girls lose the chance to gain skills to build better livelihoods for themselves and their families.

However, child marriage continues and girls' views and needs count for little because of double discrimination: as females, they are disadvantaged by negative attitudes and beliefs about the value of a woman's life; as children, they have reduced status in their household and community because of their youth.

"In Bangladesh, families believe that sons are the ones to take care of the family in the future," explains Runia Mowla, gender specialist in Bangladesh for the charity Plan International. "But if they have a daughter, she just gets married. So, for a poor family, what's the point of investing in her health or education?" When families cannot support their children, marriage can ease the financial burden. Where families value girls less, they are first to go.

Families also think early marriage will avoid the risk of social shame if their unmarried daughters get pregnant, whether through consensual sex or rape. Nargis's family worried that she would receive inappropriate attention from boys if she remained unmarried.

Attempts to enforce laws against child marriage are hampered by a lack of birth registration: without a birth certificate, girls cannot prove they are too young to marry. "We try to prevent, rather than prosecute," says Debashish Nag, government administrator in Nargis's area, Sreepur, "because there is no law to separate a child marriage once it occurs."

Early marriage receives little international coverage because, despite being illegal, tolerance for it comes from all levels of Bangladeshi society: government officials, community elders, fathers, mothers and brothers. However, signatories to the UN's Convention on the Elimination of Discrimination against Women, including Bangladesh, are obliged to prevent child marriage. It is easy to write these girls off as victims of religious, cultural or traditional extremism, but early marriage is just as much a result of poverty, gender inequality, and even increased financial pressure caused by natural disasters or climate change.

Earlier this year, Sheikh Hasina, Bangladesh's female prime minister, made commitments to enforce existing legislation for ending child marriage. Some opponents described this move as anti-Islamic; using the prophet Muhammad, who married a child, Aisha, as an example. Changing traditional belief systems is difficult, but Runia Mowla believes the few people who support child marriage for religious reasons have

> "I want to tell other girls that the age I got married was not good. Not for health, for family, for education, for anything,"

misinterpreted texts, and many Bangladeshi politicians support international efforts to halt the practice.

Education projects raise awareness and encourage collective action at the grassroots. The Bashantek Slum Children's Group, in inner-city Dhaka, meets in a tin shed decorated with posters about health and the impact of child marriage. "Whenever we try to stop a marriage, we visit the family and talk to them about the negative impacts. Then we go to the local elders for help. It is really painful when they don't listen to us, when they don't want to understand," says 17-year-old group member Deepa earnestly. "But when we can stop a marriage we feel proud, and we are happy."

Early marriage happens in the UK too. The Forced Marriage Unit works with diplomatic missions abroad to help UK nationals who are victims. Within the UK, it assists individuals and professionals, such as teachers, to protect these children. Adam Short of Plan UK says it is "leading the way" among donor countries, and hopes that

the government will "step up education efforts in communities to which UK nationals are likely to be taken". Nag emphasises that UK efforts will be most effective in partnership with local NGOs, to ensure cultural sensitivity.

Girls and women show little support for a practice that robs girls of their childhoods and catapults them into womanhood. However, with good public education, proper law enforcement and more attention from the international community, girls like Nargis can be protected in future. "If you read this, tell your friends," shouts an impassioned Jaya, 13, from the Bashantek group. "Tell everybody what is happening to our girls all over the world. If everybody knows, then we can make it change!"

Some names have been changed

The Guardian, 23 November 2011
© Guardian News & Media Ltd 2011
With this article, Kiran Flynn won the 'Best article by an amateur journalist' category in the Guardian International Development Journalist awards.

When women and girls are the enemy

Gender is the new battleground as ultra-orthodox Jews try to impose their conservative values in Israel, writes Ruth Pollard in Jerusalem.

Imagine a world where all photographs of women and girls - on posters, advertising material, buses, billboards and shop windows - gradually disappear from public view; where supermarket lines are segregated and men and women sit in different sections of public transport: men at the front, women at the back.

This is Jerusalem in November 2011.

Israel's ultra-Orthodox, or Haredi, community may be just a large (and growing) minority, but the impact of its deeply conservative values is being felt strongly in the country.

Not content with segregated streets, queues and buses, extremist members of the Haredi have turned their attention to the city of Bet Shemesh, 30 kilometres to the west of Jerusalem.

Here, Jewish girls as young as six, wearing a conservative uniform of skirts below the knee and shirts to the elbow, are being targeted by the Haredi, called "pritzas" (prostitutes) for being "immodestly dressed" as they walk into Orot girls school, a state-funded religious-nationalist school. The Haredi are demanding the girls cover up. And, it doesn't end there. Fresh from their fight last month to segregate an entire street in the ultra-Orthodox Jerusalem neighbourhood of Mea Sharim during the religious celebration of Sukkot - the Haredi have set their sights on billboards and other advertising material that feature images of women.

So far the ultra-Orthodox have managed to ensure a public health campaign to attract organ donors only uses pictures of men, while an insurance company has removed images of girls from its child health promotional material.

Speaking to Israel's Army Radio about his company's organ donor advertisements, Ohad Gibli, deputy director of marketing for the Canaan advertising agency, said: "We have learned that an ad campaign in Jerusalem and Bnei Brak that includes pictures of women will remain up for hours at best, and in other cases, will lead to the vandalisation and torching of buses."

Indeed, as Chief Justice Dorit Beinisch was quoted as saying during a September High Court hearing over the segregation of the Mea Sharim street, gender segregation "began with buses, continued with supermarkets and reached the streets. It's not going away, just the opposite."

SOME ISSUES:

Why do you think people cling to traditional opinions and practices?

What can be done to tackle these issues?

Should religion have such control over society?

See also:
Your rules 'end at temple door' says equalities chief, p157

Strong religious belief is no excuse for intimidation, p158

www.completeissues.co.uk

מסכה ייחודית
בעלת מוטיב בלעדי של
התחדשות, הזנה, לחות ופילינג

Photo: PA/Sebastian Scheiner

An ad campaign in Jerusalem that includes pictures of women will remain up for hours at best

Orot girls school may be the focus of battle between Jews in Bet Shemesh but it is also a reflection of a wider battle across Israel between the ultra-orthodox on one side and the religious nationalist and secular Jews on the other.

Last week Jerusalem Mayor Nir Barkat publicly intervened in the growing dispute over the display of women's images, writing a letter to Police Commander Niso Shaham stating: "We must make sure that those who want to advertise [with] women's images in the city can do so without fear of vandalism and defacement of billboards or buses showing women."

Late 2011, hundreds of demonstrators gathered in Jerusalem, Tel Aviv, Haifa and Beersheba to sing in protest at the Haredi stance against women and an incident at an Israel Defence Forces event, where four ultra-Orthodox male cadets left a function because women were singing.

Describing itself as a "society of scholars", the Haredi community is one of the fastest growing in Israel. A November 2010 report by Haifa University demographers, Arnon Soffer and Evgenia Bystrov, estimates 30 per cent of all Jewish newborns in Israel are Haredi, while government statistics predict that by 2025 the Haredim will have jumped from 9% of the population to 15%.

Tensions are also exacerbated by the fact that, in a country that has compulsory military service for men and women, most Haredi do not serve in the military.

And because of their focus on religious study, most Haredi men do not work, relying instead on social welfare provided by the government, or the income earned by their wives, who also give birth to large numbers of children, often up to eight or nine per family.

Meanwhile, many extreme Haredi do not recognise the authority of the government, the police or the courts, and describe themselves as "anti-Zionist" - they are against anything that is privileged over the Torah.

Jerusalem women are fighting back with a guerrilla campaign of their own - having their photographs taken and hanging them from buildings throughout the city with the slogan "returning women to Jerusalem billboards".

Tamar El Or, a professor of anthropology and sociology at the Hebrew University has lived with Haredi families as part of her research into the community. She says, "Many of these women are modern, Orthodox women who care about the religion and know that it is possible to live a full religious life without these social restrictions, without also stepping outside beliefs or morals," Professor El Or says. "They believe in religious life as well as gender equality."

The rise of the Haredim has been disastrous for the country's economy, according to Gershom Gorenberg, author of The Unmaking of Israel.

dress appropriately, and the battle to guard its residents' morals is hard-fought.

"We beg you with all our hearts, please don't pass through this neighbourhood in immodest dress. Modest dress includes closed blouse, long sleeves, skirts - no pants," one poster reads.

Jewish girls as young as six, wearing a conservative uniform of skirts below the knee and shirts to the elbow, are being targeted by the Haredi, called "pritzas" (prostitutes) for being "immodestly dressed"

Gorenberg writes that Israel's ultra-Orthodox community is becoming ever more dependent on the state and, through it, on other people's labour.

"By exempting the ultra-Orthodox from basic general educational requirements, the democratic state fosters a burgeoning sector of society that neither understands nor values democracy."

It is a subject close to the heart of Jerusalem's deputy mayor, Naomi Tzur, who describes the city as one of the country's poorest, partly because of the growth of the Haredi community.

Yet despite the sustained Haredi campaign to impose their values on others, Tzur is optimistic about returning the city to a place where secular Jews feel comfortable.

"The tide is turning", she says. Previous Jerusalem city councils dominated by the ultra-Orthodox allowed new Haredi neighbourhoods to be built without sufficient infrastructure, such as kindergartens and medical clinics, to support them.

She describes this expansion of ultra-Orthodox institutions into secular neighbourhoods as "wicked" and highlights the need to restore a "demographic balance" to the conflicted city of Jerusalem.

"And by that I do not mean a demographic balance of Jewish, Christian and Muslim ... I mean getting a better balance of families where both parents are working and paying taxes," she says.

In the Haredi neighbourhood of Mea Sharim, a suburb close to Jerusalem's Old City, where ultra-Orthodox Jewish men dress in long black overcoats and large black hats, and where women cover up to ensure as little skin as possible is exposed, it is like taking a step back in time.

Large black and white posters are plastered throughout the neighbourhood urging women to

Shabbat (the Jewish Sabbath) is strictly observed - the streets are closed off with police barriers from Friday afternoon until Saturday evening, and there is a ban on driving and the use of electricity.

Gender segregation is extensive - the supermarkets have men-only and women-only queues, and the ice cream shop has separate entrances. The simple ritual of gathering for ice cream, along with a love of music and books, are three pastimes the extremist Haredi have tried to suppress.

Manny's book shop, a large, ultra-Orthodox book store brimming with texts in Hebrew and English, as well as an excellent selection of Hanukkah candles and other religious artefacts, is one of several businesses in Mea Sharim that has born the brunt of the Haredi fury.

Since it opened in March 2010, a small segment of the ultra-Orthodox community has criticised its customers (some of whom are not dressed modestly enough), its books (some of which are published by secular publishers in English), its signage (too colourful) and its advertising (which focuses on having a good time).

On many occasions Marlene Samuels and her husband Manny have arrived at work to find every single window of their shop smashed, their locks glued, the windows defaced with paint, and excrement strewn throughout the store. Other owners of the bookstore have been threatened and their homes vandalised.

But Marlene she says the group of 60 to 100 men who carry out these acts are on the fringes of the ultra-Orthodox community.

"They are a zealous group of extremists - they are not religious, they do not represent the religious community in Mea Sharim or the Jewish people at all ... this is not Judaism," she says.

Photo: PA/Sebastian Scheiner

"We beg you with all our hearts, please don't pass through this neighbourhood in immodest dress. Modest dress includes closed blouse, long sleeves, skirts - no pants," one poster reads

"They are thugs, hooligans and criminals, and like any criminal they have got to be arrested and put into prison."

Frustrated by the lack of action by police, despite her constant reports and the provision of video evidence, Samuels went to the media.

"The police do not like to come into this area because of the violence they encounter when they do. These thugs throw stones at their cars, they break the car windows, they attack the police when they get out of the cars.

"But eventually the police did come in and make some arrests and things started to quieten down."

"It is such a bad reflection on the religious community because people who are hearing the news are then going to feel negative against the Haredim. But this is a desecration of God's name."

As the symbolic battle over women and the public display of their image continues, a new report from the World Economic Forum indicates women's status in Israel is deteriorating year by year.

On measures such as economic participation, health and education levels and political empowerment, Israel has fallen in the rankings on the Global Gender Gap index for the second year in a row, and now sits at 55 of the 135 countries measured for the report, down from 52 in 2010 and 45 in 2009.

It's hard to see how removing images of women from public life will improve the nation's performance.

Sydney Morning Herald, 21 November, 2011

Emerging economy class

By Justin Rowlatt
BBC News, **Kenya**

Ten years ago, the so-called developed world dominated the global economy but a family holiday in Kenya provides the opportunity to assess how much that balance of power is shifting.

From Our Own Correspondent brings you insights from reporters in extreme locations. What you do not usually hear is a report composed in the comfort of a sun lounger, beside a sparkling pool in a tropical resort.

But I make no apology for admitting that is precisely where this report was conceived. And yes, at times, I enjoyed a long, cool drink as I wrote. Because the palm-fringed, white-sand beach of my Kenyan holiday hotel turned out to provide the perfect vantage point from which to observe one of the biggest stories of our time.

I had expected that the other holidaymakers would be - like us - middle-class Europeans enjoying a special treat. And two-thirds of the guests were just that. What was intriguing was the other third.

At breakfast on the first morning there were two Chinese couples at the table next to ours. They turned out to be from Beijing and were taking a couple of days by the beach as part of an African safari trip.

That did not surprise me unduly because I have reported on the rise of Chinese tourism in Africa for the BBC and I know it is the fastest growing tourist sector on the continent. But there were not just Chinese families at the hotel.

A couple of days later, there was a big wedding. The bride and groom were British, of Indian descent. At least half of the guests had flown in from the sub continent. Add to that the parties of other Indian and Chinese guests, the Russians and the scattering of Kenyan families - escaping from Nairobi for some R and R (rest and recreation) on the beach - and it became apparent that a sizeable minority of the people staying at the hotel were from what economists would call "developing" or "emerging" economies.

Now the top elites even in emerging economies have always had enough money to shell out for a top-class hotel. But the people I was sharing my holiday with were not government ministers or tycoons. They were just ordinary middle-class people like me.

SOME ISSUES:

How do you think things will change once developing countries have more money?

Do you agree that the world is becoming a more equal place?

See also:
www.completeissues.co.uk

Essential Articles 15 • www.carelpress.com

This is not about the West going into decline - what is happening is the rest of the world is just getting richer a whole lot quicker

It began to dawn on me that my Mombasa hotel illustrated, in microcosm, a much larger process - quite possibly the most significant international economic development of all our lifetimes - the great levelling of the world economy. The statistics show just how dramatic the progress of that process is. The International Monetary Fund is forecasting that next year the so-called developing world will out-produce the developed world for the first time.

What a turnaround. As recently as 10 years ago, the developed world still dominated the world economy, producing three-fifths of world GDP. But let's be clear, this is not a product of the financial crisis. The crisis accelerated the process - bringing many developed economies to a standstill - but it did not cause it.

Because this is not about the West going into decline - most developed economies are not shrinking - what is happening is the rest of the world is just getting richer a whole lot quicker. And this vast rebalancing of wealth across the globe should not really come as a surprise.

One day we made the effort to drag ourselves away from the various attractions on offer in the hotel to venture into town, into Mombasa. This great East African metropolis was a cosmopolitan trading hub even while London was a regional backwater. Its ancient trading culture predates the rise of Europe and the West. And you can still see its influence in the mosques and minarets, in the spice markets and in the faces of the so-called Swahili people - the Muslim descendants of marriages between local Africans and Arab traders and settlers.

Indeed, standing in the centre of Mombasa, you realise that the rise of the developing world is really just a return to business as usual. After all, until the 18th Century, India and China were the richest countries on the planet.

The historic anomaly has been the incredible concentration of wealth in Europe and America that followed the industrial revolution. Economists call that chasm that opened up between East and West "the great divergence". Well, looking around the pool of my hotel, I realised that what I was witnessing was nothing less than the growing momentum of a "great convergence" of the world economy.

It will be many, many years before average incomes in developing economies like China and India match those in the West - if they ever do. But what was clear from that sun lounger in a Kenyan holiday hotel was that, for the middle classes at least, the world is rapidly becoming a much more equal place.

BBC From Our Own Correspondent, 5 May 2012

My Mombasa hotel illustrated, in microcosm, a much larger process – quite possibly the most significant international economic development of all our lifetimes – the great levelling of the world economy

Why we're debating 1788 and all that

Describing the 'invasion' of Australia may be a necessary concession to Aboriginal sensibilities, says Oscar Humphries.

SOME ISSUES:

What do you think about the proposal to change 'arrival' to 'invasion'?

Why does this matter?

In what ways might Australia be stronger for being a multicultural nation?

See also:
www.completeissues.co.uk

In January 1788, the first fleet of ships carrying British convicts arrived in Botany Bay after an eight-month journey from Portsmouth. No British ship had been back to Terra Australis since Captain James Cook's discovery 18 years beforehand. Parliament had debated founding a penal colony in Australia on the relatively scant evidence provided by Cook and his officers. This was truly uncharted territory and must have felt even more so, in a way that is nowadays impossible to grasp with a 21st-century mindset. Indeed, up until the Australian High Court's famous 1992 decision in Mabo vs Queensland, which recognised the land title of indigenous peoples, the country was legally deemed to have been terra nullius (no man's land) prior to British settlement.

In Robert Hughes's seminal (and revisionist) account of early Australian history, he describes the ship Sirius sailing past Point Solanda (now part of Sydney). Capt John Hunter watches Aborigines on the shore, flourishing their spears and shouting what, according to Hughes, were the first documented words said by a black man to a white man in Australia: "Warra, Warra!" Go away.

If those Sydney-side Aboriginals had had any premonition of what was in store for them and their neighbouring tribes throughout the country, then they would have shouted this until their voices gave out.

The City of Sydney, as reported this week, has voted 7-2 to remove the words "European arrival" from its official documents. Under pressure from an Aboriginal advisory group, Clover Moore, the lord mayor, accepted the proposed substitute "invasion". Yet just as the term "arrival" has polarised Australia – one "arrives" at a dinner party with a box of chocolates; one doesn't "arrive" in a country with warships and diseases to which there is no native immunity – so, too, will the latter. The term "invasion" is a very strong one and already extremely controversial.

It is very hard to sit on Sydney Harbour and say, "This was all a mistake". Visiting Australia as a tourist, it is unlikely that you will get any sense of the plight, both historical and current, of the Aboriginal people. Tragically, given that their population once numbered a million and now stands at less than half that figure, it is possible that you will not even see an indigenous Australian in the manicured and trendy

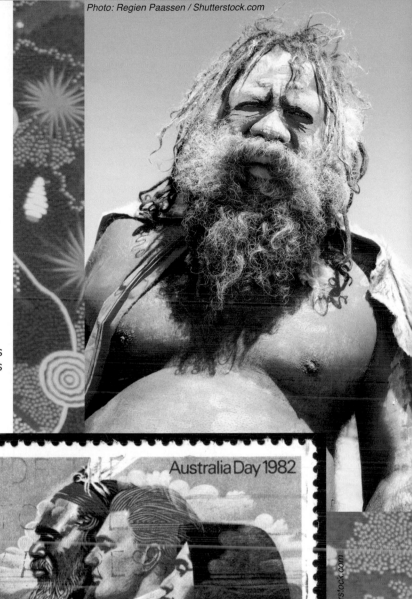

Photo: Regien Paassen / Shutterstock.com

White Australians continue to say "sorry" and, as we have seen this week, make compromises. As long as these compromises and apologies don't cost them too much, they appear to be heartfelt and legitimate

city centre – aside perhaps, from the man in war paint who most days plays the didgeridoo while busking along to a dance-music backing track at Circular Quay, where the ferries depart for the North Shore and Manly Beach.

Should Australia's pride in its economic resilience, extraordinary stage of development, cosmopolitan culture and all-round good luck be clouded with an enduring guilt? How much of this very real pain should we feel, as the descendants of the architects of this colonial adventure here in England, along with those who reaped its benefits in Australia? In other words, can we reconcile the bounty of this prize with the plight of the people who had it first?

More than mere political correctness, the issue – complex, emotive and hugely sensitive – is one of moral culpability. White Australians continue to say "sorry" and, as we have seen this week, make compromises. As long as these compromises and apologies don't cost them too much, they appear to be heartfelt and legitimate. But for Aboriginal Australians, it really is the case that "sorry" isn't good enough.

It would be impossible, given their history, for Australians not to have an uneasy relationship with race, with national identity and with immigration. Australia's murky past is not that distant: until the 1970s a "White Australia" policy was enforced to restrict the inflow of non-white immigrants. Australia's non-indigenous population represents more than 95 per cent of the total, and a quarter of its residents are foreign-born, but still this is not an easy country to emigrate to. Even British people for whose trade or skill Australia has little demand are excluded.

Australia has an island mentality, and to the boat people from such war-torn countries as Sri Lanka and Afghanistan, hoping to start new lives in Australia, it shouts, with less and less ambiguity, "Warra, Warra!" The vast majority of these afflicted peoples do not even make it to the

Australia Day 1982

24c Australia

Photo: rook76 / Shutterstock.com

It would be impossible, given their history, for Australians not to have an uneasy relationship with race, with national identity and with immigration

mainland, being detained on Christmas Island, in the Indian Ocean, for "processing", a word with uncomfortably Orwellian connotations.

Politicians exploit this insularity for their own ends: in the last election, and indeed the last several elections, immigration – especially the issue of boat people – has dominated political discourse. Rather like health care in America, it has split small-L liberal and conservative Australia beyond its traditional

Photo: Glenn Walker /
Shutterstock.com

Australia, despite the residual tensions and occasional conflicts, is multi-cultural, and it is stronger for this reason

The white kids at the party I attended got drunk and groped each other; meanwhile I saw, 300 metres away, a group of Aboriginal teenagers drinking nervously by the river. We wanted to meet them, and began walking their way, only to be told, "Don't go down there – there's darkies by the river." This is a very specific sort of racism, born not perhaps of malice but of ignorance and, I think, as natural to a specific sort of Australian as sunburn and blowflies. Dame Edna summed it up when she said: "I'm not racist; I like all races, especially white people."

Hanson's belief that a truly multi-cultural and cosmopolitan country is not a strong one is misguided. Australia, despite the residual tensions and occasional conflicts, is multi-cultural, and it is stronger for this reason. For if "White Australia" still exists in the hearts of a small but not minuscule minority, there is a new Australian identity made up of varied ethnic groups. They are Greek, Lebanese, Irish, English, Indian, Chinese, Vietnamese and Australian. And Australia is them.

Oscar Humphries is the editor of the art magazine 'Apollo'. He was the launch editor of 'The Spectator Australia'.

party affiliations. Zealous anti-immigration political figures have emerged, such as Pauline Hanson, leader of the One Nation Party who, in her first speech before parliament in 1996, said: "I believe we are in danger of being swamped by Asians – a truly multi-cultural country can never be strong or united."

Hanson was a precursor to such populist Right-wing figures as France's Marine Le Pen, but it is a great compliment to Australia that her initial support and profile waned, and she is now a largely forgotten figure. Or at least, it shows that if some Australians are a little bit racist, then they certainly don't like to be seen as racist.

So, is Australia racist? My own experience, having attended school there until the age of 11, and then lived there during my early twenties, is that underneath the blokey "mateship" of a certain type of Australian male there is a seam of racism. This racism is not only applied to indigenous Australians, but also to, for instance, the Lebanese and Greek immigrants who live there.

The term "wog" is in common use in Australia in a way that would be unacceptable anywhere else – indeed, it has been appropriated, in an act of (some would say misguided) self-empowerment, by the "Mediterranean" communities themselves. There remains a subtle division between white Australians and even their "ethnic" (another unsavoury Australian epithet) friends. They are assimilated, but divided also. It's a very subtle, local dynamic, a hangover from being a country that felt almost entirely "white" from 1788 until the 1950s.

I did a story once for an Australian newspaper on "Bachelor and Spinster" (B&S) balls. These are parties held inland for young people often living hundreds of miles from one another. They come together to drink and get off, and to forget the hardship of an Australian agricultural industry brought virtually to its knees by near-constant drought.

The Daily Telegraph, 29 June 2011
© Telegraph Media Group Ltd 2012

Work

The secret of my success

Hashi Mohamed, 27

Studied: at City Law School

Works: as a pupil barrister at 39 Essex Street

I am a first-generation immigrant. I came here when I was nine. I didn't speak a word of English, and now I'm soon to be a pupil barrister. This does not necessarily mean we're a socially mobile society; I don't want anyone to extrapolate that from my story. I was born in Kenya to Somali parents, and my mum was never formally educated. I was brought up in Nairobi and my father died when I was nine. I came to the UK, without my mother, in June 1993.

I was raised exclusively on state benefits and attended very poor-performing schools in north-west London. I didn't really pay much attention at school – I was moving around different houses and relatives, there were lots of issues – but I scraped through my A-levels. I went to the University of Hertfordshire, starting French from scratch and studying law. My fees were paid for, but I was living off a student loan. When I finished, I wrote an e-mail to the editor of Newsnight – I told him I had no journalism experience; I wanted to explore it. He put me on a project, I got a paid salary, and I worked on several news programmes. I got that job through chutzpah, but also it was the character of that man, Peter Barron, who took a risk with me. You won't often meet people like that.

Meanwhile, I applied to Oxford for a masters and got in, with a scholarship. They offer counselling to people from poorer backgrounds, because it's difficult to adjust. But for me, I thought: 'This is where I was born to be'. Instead of being intimidated by my peers, I was inspired. If I picked up one thing from Oxford, it was sharpened discipline, how to manage my time.

After Oxford, I did the Bar course, without which you can't be a barrister. I got a £10,000 scholarship and took out a loan for £10,000. There are about 2,500 people graduating from these courses each year – and only around 500 pupillages. And before you can get a pupillage, there's a thing called a mini-pupillage. For a year and half, I couldn't get one. Although there's an application process, you really get them through contacts. Of course I think it's unfair. But there's no point trying to pick a fight with a system that has been around for a long time. Now I go into schools, telling kids if they don't stop speaking street slang when it's inappropriate and lift up their trousers, they're not going to get far.

I finished Bar school last May and accepted the pupillage at 39 Essex Street, one of the best chambers in the country.

My story is a combination of people who've believed in me, various e-mails being answered, scholarships that I could never afford, and a discipline that meant I worked very, very hard over many years. That's

SOME ISSUES:

What do you think are the most important things to do to achieve success?

Is it useful to hear about other people's careers?

What do you want to do for your career and how will you go about it?

See also:
For children today, table manners still trump talent
Essential Articles 13, p200

www.completeissues.co.uk

not something that you can expect every child on every estate to replicate. Any government policy that assumes that is a flawed one – and it's quite insulting. There is no easy answer.

Lilly Heine, 27

Studied: Fashion at Central Saint Martins

Works: at Dries Van Noten

My parents are German, and my dad was quite a successful journalist – he was a correspondent for German radio in Washington and then worked in London when I was 10. That was when my interest in fashion started. Both of my parents were extremely supportive and they've always wanted me and my sister to be happy, whatever we wanted to do.

I took sewing lessons from the age of 12, just for fun, though I took it pretty seriously! When I was 13, I worked in my friend's dad's shop, which sold Indian/British designs, textiles and garments. I did an internship at a theatre in Hamburg, in costume design, straight from school, then another one at Oper Frankfurt, after which I realised costume wasn't really for me. I started studying English and French literature at university in Frankfurt but my course was very dry and the people boring.

So I did some drawings and sent them off to Wimbledon School of Art. At 19, I did the foundation course there, which I loved – having tutors who knew what they were talking about and really criticised you. I worked very hard. After that, I did a BA at Chelsea College of Art and Design. That was for three years and every summer I did a long internship. The first year, I did three months at Jonathan Saunders, and in my second year, three months at Alexander McQueen, which was the one that particularly shaped me. I was making prints all day, every day, for 16 hours. And, in the end, I designed prints that actually got used - it was really exciting for me! That was for the spring/summer collection 2008.

The internships were organised through the university, and I took them really seriously. Now if I see interns who are a little bit half-hearted, or going home early – I cannot understand them.

After my third year I went straight on to my MA in fashion at Central Saint Martins. Louise Wilson, the head of that course, looks at what you do and makes you better at designing, but in your own style. It moulded my character and my style and confidence. I wanted to be on the best course; I never did it to earn money, I did it because I wanted to be better than the next person.

I won the Harrods prize at the end of my MA. After that, I did a collection for Topshop – it's like

I was making prints all day, every day, for 16 hours. And, in the end, I designed prints that actually got used – it was really exciting for me! I never did it to earn money, I did it because I wanted to be better than the next person

every designer's dream. Then I did some freelance prints for people like Jimmy Choo and Stella McCartney.

I got to do a lot of great things, but there were also long periods of not having a job and that's pretty frustrating. After nine months, I got a job at Alexander McQueen as assistant print designer – it was thanks to knowing people from having done an internship there. After that, I got a call from Dries Van Noten, and moved to Antwerp to work with him. Now I just want to see what happens.

The Independent, 27 August 2011

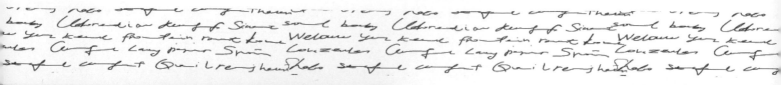

my flatmate had to remove her degree from her cv to get a job

By Rhiannon Bury

An ordinary morning in my flat goes something like this: there's a crash as someone drops a bowl on the kitchen floor, screeches from the shower as the last person in realises there's no hot water left, running feet, four hairdryers on at once, and then the front door bangs, four times.

For the four female graduates in residence, each morning starts with a trip to work. But while two head off to offices, two saunter to the bus stop to go to low-level jobs in the service industry – one in hospitality, and one in retail.

We are the embodiment of data published by the Office for National Statistics this week, which shows in the final three months of last year, a third of people who completed their degree in the last six years was working in a role that was suitable for a school leaver. A decade ago, it was around a quarter.

For the four of us, it has been a bumpy journey to even get this far. The ONS research suggests a fifth of graduates don't have a job at all

Sarah, 24, left a top ten university in 2009 with a 2.1 in English, plus an art foundation degree and a bulging portfolio of illustration work. Frustrated after two years of almost consistent unemployment in her home town in the Midlands, she moved to London in the hope of finding a job in the arts.

Seven months later, she's still looking. There's little to stretch her in her waitressing job at a local café: she had to remove her degree from her CV when she found jobs weren't available because she was seen to be overqualified.

She's got demonstrable experience in arts work and has been paid for freelance drawing commissions in the past, yet each day brings more rejection, or just no response at all.

Jen, who at 23 speaks Italian and Spanish fluently, and passable French, landed a job flogging confectionery in a well-known chocolate shop in the City after a few weeks in London. She's happy – the job is easy and flexible, and because she's polite and intelligent she was promoted within six months. But she's not using any of the skills she got from her languages degree and admits that actually, she need not have done it at all.

SOME ISSUES:

Why do you think it is so difficult for graduates to get work?

What do you plan to do once you leave school?

Will higher education help?

What would you suggest these people do to get a job?

See also:
I'm a graduate get me out of here p204

Class of 2011
Fact File 2012, p186

www.completeissues.co.uk

For her, university was an expensive, if fun, experience, but not one that has got her a job. Yes, she's in work, but apart from the odd conversation with her French colleague, she's not using her hard-earned skills.

Clare and myself, both 24, found that despite each having a 2.1 in a humanities degree from a top university, without a masters degree we would struggle to get a job in journalism. As it stands, Clare is on her third post in 18 months after a shock redundancy and a stint scraping along on freelance work.

I was luckier, landing a job on the back of a work experience placement, but without the financial backing of my middle-class family to fund me through a fourth year of study, it would have been much harder.

The problem isn't even that graduates are being forced to take any job to make ends meet – there are hordes of people who believe a degree is the only way to land a job, when statistics suggest that only slightly fewer people without a degree are currently in work.

Even in a time when the latest government figures put unemployment at a record 2.67 million in the UK – the highest level for 16 years – the difference between graduates in work, and non-graduates in work is only 14 per cent. It's a slim margin, given that graduates who wore their mortar boards in 2009 are at least £9,000 poorer after three years in the library.

For four girls who graduated at the same time, we're in very different places. But, perhaps this is all part of the experience. Sarah's made friends with her colleagues from, at the last count, eight different countries. Jen's got an unrivalled knowledge of cocoa content and, more importantly, brings home an uneatable number of samples. Clare knows how to deal with redundancy and complete her tax return for freelance income. And me, well, I know the value of work experience and doing a huge amount of brown-nosing.

But you don't learn that at university, do you?

for the four female graduates in residence, each morning starts with a trip to work. but while two head off to offices, two saunter to the bus stop to go to low-level jobs in the service industry – one in hospitality, and one in retail.

The Independent, 8 March 2012

'I'M A GRADUATE, GET ME OUT OF HERE!'

Jobless Cait Reilly is taking legal action against being forced to work for nothing in Poundland or lose her jobseeker's allowance. But how typical is her situation?
By Peter Stanford

It's been quite a week for 22-year-old Cait Reilly. After spending 18 months waiting in vain for her phone to ring with the offer of any one of the hundreds of jobs she has applied for since graduating in the summer of 2010 from Birmingham University, these past few days it hasn't stopped. And all because of two weeks on a government unemployment programme in her local Poundland in King's Heath, West Midlands.

A triumph for the scheme presented by ministers as giving 250,000 claimants on jobseekers' allowance a helping hand back into the workforce? Not quite. For Reilly has made headlines because she is mounting a legal challenge to what she says was the "forced labour" of being made to stack shelves for free in the discount retailer, or lose her £53-a-week in dole. "I was told it was mandatory. There were five of us sent there. I was the only graduate. We were doing exactly the same work as the paid staff. It makes no sense. If the Government subsidises high street chains with free labour, they don't have to recruit. It causes unemployment rather than solves it."

What makes the mandatory placement more puzzling, adds Reilly, whose degree was geology, was that going to Poundland meant she had to give up a volunteer post she had at the local Pen Room Museum, part of her plan to gain the experience that would help her along her chosen career path as a curator.

"Right now, I would take any job. I have £18,000 in student debts to pay off and the interest is building all the time. That really worries me. But I have plenty of retail experience already on my CV. I didn't need to go to Poundland. And I was never told I had a choice."

Her adviser at the Job Centre has, she reports, been replaced. The Department of Work and Pensions, which oversees the scheme, has responded to her allegations by insisting that, within reason, such "sector-based work academy" schemes are optional. And Chris Grayling, the employment minister, has in the past robustly defended the programme, pointing out that "half of young people leave benefits after they have completed their placement".

The problem in Reilly's case seems to be that, as a graduate, her career expectations were different from many other claimants. But she is not, in reality, so unusual. Of those who

SOME ISSUES:

What do you think about this scheme?

Do you think people should have to do work experience for free if they are unemployed?

Should graduates or people with specific work experience get different treatment?

See also:
My flatmate had to remove her degree from her cv to get a job
p202

Class of 2011
Fact File 2012, p186

Poor prospects
Essential Articles 14, p194

www.completeissues.co.uk

Photo: @ Martin Pettitt

"RIGHT NOW, I WOULD TAKE ANY JOB. I HAVE £18,000 IN STUDENT DEBTS TO PAY OFF, AND THE INTEREST IS BUILDING ALL THE TIME. THAT REALLY WORRIES ME. ...

...BUT I HAVE PLENTY OF RETAIL EXPERIENCE. I DIDN'T NEED TO GO TO POUNDLAND. AND I WAS NEVER TOLD I HAD A CHOICE."

graduated at the same time as her, in 2010, half were either jobless six months later, or in menial roles. Another survey reports that 38 per cent of graduates have been on the dole after leaving university. And longer-term data from the Higher Education Statistics Agency reveals that 28 per cent of 2006 graduates were not in full-time employment three years later, while, among those who were, only 16 per cent of the men were earning over £20,000, and 29 per cent of the women.

This last figure is particularly significant since, under new tuition fee arrangements, those embarking from this September on degree courses that will cost up to £9,000 a year will only have to start repaying their tuition fees once their income rises above £21,000. The Treasury, it seems, may be about to take a substantial hit.

Reilly remains phlegmatic about her joblessness. "Someone is getting the

posts I am applying for, so I have to believe that one day that person will be me. That's the logic."

Does she regret not tackling something more vocational – law, medicine, engineering – rather than geology?

"I did think about that before I started, but I loved the subject and geology can provide a whole range of careers in civil engineering, mining, oil exploration and property. So it was a practical choice." But of her cohort, she says, only one – "and he got a first" – has got a job that uses his degree.

Defending the hike in tuition fees, the Government argues that undergraduates are speculating to accumulate. By taking out loans to pay for a higher education, they are giving themselves the prospect of better-paid careers than school-leavers that will more than justify that investment. However, the Office for National Statistics reported

last August that a quarter of graduates are earning less than contemporaries who joined the workforce after A-levels. And even with the other three quarters, the graduate pay premium is shrinking. One factor, it seems, is that the rapid expansion in higher education under Labour has seen the percentage of university-educated workers grow since 1993 from 12 to 25 per cent. And it continues to rise.

"I don't regret going to university," says Holly Jerreat, 22, who graduated last summer with a 2:1 in languages from Bath, "but with hindsight I might have done a more vocational course. I chose languages because it was a subject I loved and found intellectually challenging. But here I am, still looking for work."

Jerreat, who has returned home to live with her parents in Kent, has filled in "endless application forms" for graduate posts in marketing, advertising and media, and has come very close several times to landing the job of her dreams, but the competition is stiff and openings few and far between. To pay her way in the interim, she has applied "for every job going in our local Bluewater shopping centre. I write off, send in CVs, go in and ask face-to-face, and then get told I am over-qualified." Currently she is doing a part-time administrative post she got through a family connection. "Basically I do the shredding."

In these hard times for recent graduates, such family connections – much decried by the Deputy Prime Minister, Nick Clegg, as "the exclusive preserve of the sharp-elbowed and the well-connected" – are one way to gain an advantage.

"I spent a year and a half doing various temping jobs," says 25-year-old Howard de Podesta, who graduated in aerospace engineering from Bath, "before getting a job in product design in financial IT off the back of an internship. That is the route many graduates go down now."

People like 24-year-old Kate Ross, who graduated in combined social sciences from Durham in 2009, and then landed a three-month paid internship with a hotel management company with the help of her sister who worked in recruitment. "Having that experience helped me impress my current employer, a property company. Without experience, no one will

touch you, however good your degree or your university. You have somehow to find a way to get that experience."

Unpaid internships, though, especially in London and big cities, depend on being able to rely on family for free accommodation and pocket money. Ross squared the circle by taking a part-time post as a live-in au pair, even though she had no formal training in caring for children. "I was actually better off when I was living for nothing there than when I started work properly and had to pay rent on a flat."

And therein is another problem. Even when graduates find jobs, starting salaries are so low that it makes it very hard to stand on your own.

"It seems to take friends from university around a year to find a 'proper' job," recounts Jerreat, "but they rarely pay more than £18,000. Once you have started paying back your student loans, which kicks in at £15,000 for my age group, and then pay rent, it really doesn't leave anything to live on."

The unpaid internship industry is, says Cait Reilly, pretty much a closed book for her. "I think it probably does skew the market against people like me. I live at home, but my parents can't afford to support me. I have to make a contribution to my living costs. If I had the option of not signing on, I'd take it like a shot. It tars me with the same brush in the eyes of those who see anyone claiming benefits as lazy or scroungers. And yes, I would be prepared to travel

and live somewhere else for work, but it would have to be paid for me to afford to be able to do it."

So has her week of making headlines and taking calls helped her job search? "No," she reports flatly. "Or not yet. Some of my friends think I am mad to go to court, that the legal action will mean that no employer will want anything to do with me, but for me it is an abuse that needs highlighting. The idea that any work experience, however irrelevant and menial, will be beneficial just doesn't add up."

Daily Telegraph, 13 January 2012
© Telegraph Media Group Ltd 2012

STOP PRESS:

Sector-based work academies are collaborations between Jobcentre Plus, businesses and training providers. There should be three elements: Pre-employment training, work experience and a guaranteed interview for a job vacancy. Although taking part is voluntary, once a claimant has agreed to participate, the process must be completed, or the claimant's benefits may subject to sanctions.

> EVEN WHEN GRADUATES FIND JOBS, STARTING SALARIES ARE SO LOW THAT IT MAKES IT VERY HARD TO STAND ON YOUR OWN

Section names are in capitals and in colour. Where the whole or majority of a section is relevant to a topic, the section name is given. Page numbers in black direct you to a specific article.

The page number refers to the whole article rather than the location of the word in the text.

The articles here have been selected because they make a significant reference to, or add to, the topic they are listed under. Alternatively you can search this and past issues along with issues of Fact File and Key Organisations on our Complete Issues online service. Simply type in your topic to instantly call up all the relevant articles.

www.completeissues.co.uk

Index

Published by Carel Press Ltd
4 Hewson St, Carlisle CA2 5AU
Tel +44 (0)1228 538928,
Fax 591816
office@carelpress.co.uk
www.carelpress.co.uk
This collection © 2013
Christine A Shepherd & Chas White

Acknowledgements
Designer: Anne Louise Kershaw
Editorial team: Anne Louise Kershaw, Debbie Maxwell, Christine A Shepherd, Chas White
Subscriptions: Ann Batey (Manager), Brenda Hughes, Anne Maclagan

We wish to thank all those writers, editors, photographers, press agencies and wire services who have given permission to reproduce copyright material. Every effort has been made to trace copyright holders of material but in a few cases this has not been possible. The publishers would be glad to hear from anyone who has not been consulted.

Cover design: Anne Louise Kershaw
Front cover photos: Clockwise from top left – Cyrus Thatcher image courtesy and © Helena Tymm, London Riot Image Lewis Whyld/PA Wire/ Press Association Images

British Library Cataloguing in Publication Data

Essential Articles 15: The articles you need on the issues that matter
1. Social problems – Study and teaching (Secondary) – Great Britain 2. Social sciences – Study and teaching (Secondary) – Great Britain
I. Shepherd, Christine A II. White, C
361.00712 41
ISBN 978-1-905600-30-4

Printed by Finemark, Poland